Leadership for Sustainability

Leadership for Sustainability is dedicated to the memory of Anita Roddick—and she would have loved the overarching theme that we must now move faster with the implementation of today's organisational change agenda and, at the same time, work out how to disrupt our economic and business models to reboot capitalism for the 21st century.

John Elkington, Executive Chairman, Volans; co-founder, Environmental Data Services (ENDS) and SustainAbility

How can we harness the power of leadership to create a more sustainable, inclusive, and just society? *Leadership for Sustainability* opens a fascinating window into this line of inquiry. It tells the stories of an educational experiment, interweaving first-, second- and third-person action research to offer insights for the emerging foundations of a 21st-century university—and it tells these stories from an authentic first-person view. Highly recommended!

Otto Scharmer, author, *Theory U*; Senior Lecturer, Massachusetts Institute of Technology; Founding Chair, Presencing Institute (www.presencing.com)

Leadership for Sustainability offers many important insights into the qualities and processes of leadership. I highly recommend it to anyone interested in learning how to lead sustainability initiatives.

Bob Doppelt, Executive Director, The Resource Innovation Group

In a world pushed to its ecological, social and economic limits, we don't need more words, we need action. This book describes the work of sustainability pioneers, putting into practice their insights and knowledge in ways that are designed to create significant and lasting change. Many of these insights and much of this knowledge was acquired through their time on the MSc for Responsible Business—a brilliant course where the best thinking on action research and learning collides with a cutting-edge understanding of sustainability. This happy fusion of learning and sustainability, creating a new wave of sustainability practitioners, is critical for achieving the transition from our unsustainable world to an equitable and sustainable future.

Dr Sally Uren, Deputy Chief Executive, Forum for the Future

Alumni of a radically different kind of Master's programme make clear: an individual *can*, in fact, make a difference, but the 'village' is helpful in shaping skills and sustaining courage to practice business in a way that creates real sustained value. The villagers are the lucky graduates of the Responsibility and Business Practice programme; Masters' programmes around the globe will learn from its example.

Judith Samuelson, Executive Director, Business and Society Program, The Aspen Institute, USA

These are front-line stories from the battle to save the planet and they are a testament to the quality of this MSc course. Nothing beats reading about the struggles from so many different situations to understand what it's like and, importantly, how immensely rewarding it can be to navigate the challenges of sustainability and make a difference. As one student described the years following the course, 'These have been both the best and the worst years of my life. But at least now I know that I am alive.' How many courses can you point to where the student comes to understand that *how* they are determines the effectiveness of *what* they do. There's no doubt that those who have the courage to take part in this programme, to engage in active research in this messy terrain, learning the skills of the 'tempered radical', will emerge through their foot-soldiering to become the leaders of tomorrow. Start following their stories now.

Tessa Tennant, Innovator in Sustainable Finance

We live in a culture of mass suicide and too many educators either divert attention from this frightening reality or actively abet the madness by, for example, normalising self-interested economics and emphasising intellectual loftiness over pragmatic engagement. Amid this conventional madness Judi, Peter and Gill, along with their colleagues and students, share the fruits of an important and successful experiment with a more responsive, responsible, sane, humanistic and enlivening educational or inquiry process, namely action research. I hope that it will catch on among more educators and graduate students. In embracing the work described, and doing it together, we may escort each other through the insanity of our unsustainable and exploitative ways of living and studying, reinvigorated by our deeper desire for friendship, truth and ways of acting that honour our more enlightened natures and fellow participants on the planet. Action research or death: it's our choice, encouraged by this volume.

Starting with an important exploration of the 'ground upon which we stand', the author–editors give voice to our daily experience of participation with each other and the larger universe. This is a mercifully different account from the domineering Western myth of each of us separate from the other and the rest of nature. This separation myth, so deep in the psyche of Westerners, has given rise to the exploitative ethos which is now killing us. A participative worldview, described and enacted in this volume, enables a new way of being, learning and acting for ourselves and for the world. This new way also demands a transformative orientation to knowledge creation. Indeed, it has already resulted in an enhanced way of living for students, educators and all they touch, including this reader. Chapter after wonderful chapter, told in the intimate first-person narratives that speak so well to other graduate students, we see the fruits of being honest about our interdependence. Instead of withering under admission of our vulnerability we see lives, careers and people revitalised. We may look forward to the next volume.

Hilary Bradbury Huang, PhD, journal editor-in-chief, *Action Research*; Professor, Division of Management, Oregon Health & Science University, USA

Most thinking people now accept that we must make the transition from a society based on fossil fuels to one using alternative technologies—a transition at least as great as the shift from an agrarian to an industrial society. We also know that we must make this transition *fast*. The key question is not *whether* we should make this move but *how*. Frankly, we do not yet know how. In the words of Antonio Machado: 'Walker. There is no path. The path is made by walking.' *Leadership for Sustainability* provides 29 stories of people who along with their organisations are striking out on paths to a more sustainable future—paths they are defining for themselves, inspired and informed by a course they shared in common. They are all graduates of Bath's innovative MSc in Responsibility and Business Practice and their stories remind us that we must all be leaders where we are: 'tempered radicals' taking responsibility for shaping a more sane world where we live mindfully, aware of each other's needs and the needs of the ecology that supports us. The philosophy of the course is presented here too with accounts of its consequences for some of those who were inspired by it. This is a *must-read* for those who hope, and want to translate hope into action.

Dexter Dunphy, Emeritus Professor, Faculty of Business,
University of Technology Sydney

Building a sustainable society and economy is too often presented as a challenge of technology or policy. The preserve of a few technocrats. In practice, sustainability is all about convincing people to change the way they lead their lives. Not in their millions but in their billions. Not through coercion but through inspiration. Not through management but through leadership. This book shows how a diverse range of people are already leading change. Their stories are a very human testimony that change is not just needed but is also possible.

Mike Barry, Head of Sustainable Business, Marks & Spencer

The Master's in Responsibility and Business Practice at Bath was a benchmark for education in corporate responsibility in Europe. It is exciting to hear the impacts that just some of this innovative course's graduates are having in contributing to change for a more environmentally sustainable and socially just world.

Peter Lacy, Managing Director, Accenture Sustainability Services – EALA;
Founding Director, European Academy for Business in Society (2003–2007)

Leadership for Sustainability

An Action Research Approach

Edited by

Judi Marshall, Gill Coleman and **Peter Reason**

Greenleaf
PUBLISHING

© 2011 Greenleaf Publishing Limited

Published by Greenleaf Publishing Limited
Aizlewood's Mill
Nursery Street
Sheffield S3 8GG
UK
www.greenleaf-publishing.com

Printed in Great Britain on acid-free paper by
CPI Antony Rowe, Chippenham and Eastbourne

FSC
www.fsc.org
MIX
Paper from
responsible sources
FSC® C013604

Cover by LaliAbril.com

British Library Cataloguing in Publication Data:
    Leadership for sustainability : an action research
        approach.
        1. Social responsibility of business. 2. Sustainable
        development--Management. 3. Conservation leadership.
        I. Marshall, Judi. II. Coleman, Gill, 1954- III. Reason,
        Peter.
        658.4'083-dc22

ISBN-13: 9781906093594

This book is dedicated to Anita Roddick, who taught us that actions speak louder than words—and excelled at both.

Contents

1

Taking up the challenge

Offering stories from the field

In 1997 we launched the MSc in Responsibility and Business Practice to address issues of sustainability and social justice in business, adopting an action research approach. In our publicity and on open days we specifically invited people who wished to be explorers and pioneers to join us. And they did, in significant numbers, creating a community that, 14 years later, supports and encourages its members to take on the challenges of living courageously in extraordinary times. This book tells the stories of some of those people as they have sought to take what we call 'leadership for sustainability', recognising that both 'leadership' and 'sustainability' are difficult and contested terms. It offers their accounts of action, their learning and reflections, their challenges and doubts. It explores what it means to take up leadership for sustainability from a variety of organisational and social positions, and considers the consequences of different strategies and practices for influencing change.

Our primary purpose here is to make accounts of MSc in Responsibility and Business Practice graduates' activities more widely available. Many of our graduates have been influential in contributing to sustainability ideas and practices, shaping the fields in which they have engaged through their endeavours. Their activities were developed through the practical projects they conducted while on the MSc programme and subsequently, and illustrate and expand notions of leadership for sustainability.

The book will show and reflect on:

- What practices of leadership and change for sustainability based on action research might look like, and a sense of the personal and professional challenges these involve

- How participants draw on reflective practice both strategically to create contexts in which they can be influential and tactically in moment-to-moment choices about how to act

- What kinds of outcome can be expected from this work—the specific and strategic achievements, and the difficulties, challenges and disappointments

At the heart of the book are 29 stories from MSc graduates. These are a small selection of the total range of our graduates' contributions. We therefore refer to this as the 'first' book from the MSc, hoping that there will be other ways to share the work of this special band of people. Alongside the stories are contributions from us as editors, offering background and an overview, analysing and reflecting on these accounts and their relevance to notions of leadership, practice, sustainability and change.

Bringing this collection of stories together we have a range of readers in mind. We see them as activists of some kind, working in all sorts of places. They are managers, consultants and concerned citizens, they are in commercial, non-profit, public and intergovernmental organisations and in civil society who want to contribute to the development of a sustainable world and to sustainable policies and practices. Some readers will also be in education, working with course participants on sustainability and social justice issues, wanting to help people develop their sense of agency and leadership practices. They all see themselves as citizens first who, beyond their organisational roles, want to help develop a more just and sustainable society.

Current global challenges seem daunting. People wonder if individuals can make any contribution. And while our hopes of having a significant impact must be tempered with due humility, we think we should each explore the possibilities within our realm of action and being.

> As change agents and change leaders, we are only one source of influence in a complex changing reality. Nevertheless let us not underestimate the potential transformative power that we represent . . . Change leadership involves owning our own power and using it responsively and responsibly (Dunphy *et al.* 2007: 322).

For us, the MSc has been part of 'owning our own power': we used our positions as senior educators and our access to a leading school of management to design an educational programme that would address these issues as radically as we were able. When we are asked—and when we ask ourselves—'What did you do in response to the crisis of sustainability?' at least part of our answer is to point to the MSc.

This book is not, though, about the MSc as an educational programme (Marshall and Coleman, in preparation). It is about what people who have connected their lives to the MSc have done. However, we have included a description of the programme, how it operated and the debates we had together, as a background and resource and to help the reader connect with the context of the graduates' stories, which draw, some explicitly and some tacitly, on languages and ideas explored on the programme. The course is described in Chapter 2, and key ideas and practices from it are outlined in Chapter 3.

Before proceeding, we should say something about the history of the degree. The original MSc in Responsibility and Business Practice ran at the University of Bath School of Management from 1997 to 2010, with 254 people graduating from 12 intake groups. The course was then discontinued. A direct successor, the MSc in Sustainability and Responsibility, has now been developed at Ashridge Business School, and a close sibling, the MA in Leadership for Sustainability, at Lancaster University School of Management. We will therefore talk about the Bath MSc in the past tense, but the educational work we describe is very much current at Ashridge and Lancaster. And the course graduates have developed into the RBP community, as they call themselves, through exchanges on an email list that includes all year groups, in other virtual spaces, and through occasional meetings. This community has a reach and connectedness far beyond the programme at Bath.

At the centre of the book, we have organised the stories into broad themes that show different approaches to change that graduates are taking. These themes must not be taken as discrete categories, for there are many overlaps, and each story is a unique narrative. Some of the stories are of completed achievements, but most are still in progress and often in continual reinvention as developments take place and sense-making unfolds. Following the stories we close the book with our own reflections, highlighting issues and challenges in seeking to take leadership for sustainability. We do not try to be comprehensive. Firmly categorising the narratives or drawing conclusions would deaden the stories and interfere with the reader's, your, own sense-making. Our intent is more to notice interesting strands and raise questions.

In the followings sections of this chapter we explore the context in which this book is offered, consider some notions of leadership, express our thanks to and appreciation of others involved in this journey with us, and say how the stories came to be written.

Well beyond limits

We are convinced that the ecology of our planet is under extreme stress as a result of human activity. We believe that this is incontrovertible in broad terms, although we appreciate that many details are open to debate. The challenge of climate change often grabs the headlines, but is only part of the sustainability story. Other important issues include loss of biodiversity, mass extinction, pollution, depletion of carbon-based energy sources, pressure on water supplies, and food insecurity. First and foremost these are challenges to the integrity of the planet on which humans, along with all other creatures, are dependent. In addition, as Stern has pointed out in relation to climate change (Stern 2006), and Pavan Sukhdev shows in relation to biodiversity (Sukhdev 2010), the economic costs of environmental degradation are overwhelming and growing. Alongside, and in interaction (Westley and Vredenburg 1996), we have global social injustice: poverty, hunger, political oppression, the impacts of war, the impacts of HIV/AIDS, the persistence of widespread curable diseases and loss of cultural diversity. These are the significant challenges of our times, indications of a world well beyond its ecological limits (Meadows *et al.* 2004; Lovelock 2006; IPCC 2007). Our concerns are for the more-than-human world (Abram 1996) as well as whether the planet can remain a safe operating space for humanity (Rockström *et al.* 2009). We accept the warnings of those who say we have violated safe limits for us all, and that appropriate, significant action is required—urgently.

The challenge, then, is to find ways to address these issues radically, to find ways to live together within the carrying capacity of the planet, with equality and justice for all human communities while allowing vibrant space for other life forms. This is what we mean by 'sustainability'. We are living in interesting and challenging times, times which require something from us. To respond adequately we need to acknowledge the enormity of the challenge, the uncertainties it brings, and discover and develop appropriate strategies and disciplines for living, now.

These stark comments may seem dramatic. That is part of the problem. It is hard to imagine that something so radical might be happening. We can barely conceive it, and we have to reach towards understanding it from current patterns of mind and values, while knowing their flaws and inadequacies. While some politicians and pundits offer plausible but all too easy solutions, the challenge we face is that at individual, community, societal and global levels, humanity simply does not know how to respond to the enormous challenge of living sustainably on the Earth.

As this book will show, one of our answers to these challenges is to adopt action research as a soft discipline for living in challenging times. What that means will become apparent through our own and others' voices. You will consider whether you think it an adequate approach.

How can we frame the challenges?

The complexity and scope of the sustainability challenge makes it tempting to focus down on just one question. In about 2005 the notion of climate change as a shared threat to all creatures on the planet seemed to crystallise in public and political fora for a while, giving some semblance of agreement that climate change is happening, is significant and that human activity contributes. This provided an image to focus attention, energies and potential action. Al Gore's touring lecture, DVD and book *An Inconvenient Truth* (Gore 2006) opened up debate and more general awareness. *The Stern Review* (Stern 2006) outlined the significant economic costs of delaying attention. In the UK, the Government's Chief Scientific Adviser, Sir David King, made bold, clear statements about threats. Reports from the Intergovernmental Panel on Climate Change held authority (IPCC 2007). For a while, it was said that the case was accepted, and now we were into what we should do.

But that sense of certainty was fragile. In the UK, Channel 4 TV screened 'The Great Global Warming Swindle' (8 March 2007), prominently featuring the voices of those who were then called sceptics or deniers. Despite some people's attempts to rebut the programme's claims, public consensus seemed to shatter. It took little, it seemed, to seed doubt and the enormity of what might be involved in taking action was daunting. While there was much optimism that a global agreement would be reached at the COP15 in Copenhagen, in the event little was achieved, and the global financial crisis that followed has pushed climate change down the agenda.

While the climate debate has been cast in terms of global agreement, others offer new models of economy and business to make sense of what we might now do. Some explore, for example, whether capitalism and business are forces for change. The book jacket for Paul Hawken's (1993) *Ecology of Commerce* offers the (potential) conviction that business has a major role to play. 'Not only do businesses today need to be more ecological—the world of commerce is the *only* mechanism powerful enough to save the global environment.' Jonathan Porritt suggests that capitalism seems 'the only overarching system capable of achieving any kind of reconciliation between ecological sustainability on the one hand and the pursuit of prosperity and personal wellbeing on the other' (Porritt 2007: 19). While seeing capitalism as the best model we know, he suggests revisioning it to take account of five capitals—natural, human, social, manufactured and financial—and argues that we are facing a crisis because we are consuming our stocks of natural capital faster than they are being produced.

But can business change sufficiently, or is its dominance part of the problem? This is certainly Korten's view (Korten 1995). He sees the insatiable demands of corporations and the market tyranny as destroying livelihoods and the natural world. Is it even possible that those currently prominent in business could envision a new society in which its own positioning might be radically reconfigured? Leading social and environmental accountancy scholars conclude:

> It looks exceptionally likely that the current form of capitalism is not sustainable—it is, after all, based on private property rights, growth and expansion, competition, maximising consumption of non-essentials, maximising returns to shareholders and directors and so on (Gray and Milne 2004: 73).

And they argue that, since sustainability is a system concept, it would be 'profoundly implausible that an individual company could be sustainable (or responsible) in an unsustainable (or irresponsible) system' (Gray and Milne 2004: 73). These arguments suggest that a new economics is needed (Boyle and Simms 2009), which recognises that human and planetary health and well-being cannot be measured in terms of money. Starting from this premise, new shapes for enterprise and business could be designed to fit into a sustainable world. Robertson's (1989) *Future Wealth* offered interestingly prescient models for a new economic order for the 21st century that would be enabling for people and conserving for the Earth's resources and environment. It needed to be organised as a 'multi-level-one-world system' (Robertson 1989: 12).

In addition to these business and economic-based explorations of the sustainability crisis, in our educational work we draw on a wide variety of literature to explore current patterns of thinking and acting, and alternative possibilities. These include the science of ecology (Harding 2006), feminist critiques of Western society (Plumwood 1993, 2002), spiritual perspectives (Berry 1999) and social theories of power (Hardy 1994; Lukes 2005). And beyond different models, the challenge may well be that our current worldviews frame and limit what is conceivable, and thus limit our choices so that what we can imagine will be 'more of the same' (Watzlawick *et al.* 1980). We need to question the very ground on which we stand. As action researchers, we argue that in order to learn to think differently we also need to engage differently with the world in practice.

These kinds of issue were debated, at length and repeatedly, by participants on the MSc course. A typical group included people from business, NGOs and activist organisations in the room together. They brought hugely different experience and points of view, read widely, listened attentively to visiting speakers, and over the course of the programme developed a lively discussion which in turn informed their choices and their practice. In particular, the wide-ranging explorations helped participants discover a 'place to stand' within the intractability of the issues and the anxiety and ambivalence this generates. Many of these questions can be seen at play in the narratives in this book.

Taking leadership for sustainability

Our core interest is in *taking* leadership for sustainability. What gives people the sense of agency, the resources, the awareness, the approach and the crafts of practice to take action of some kind in the service of a more environmentally sustainable and socially just world? We see such leadership as necessarily going beyond conventional notions, because it needs to be able to step outside and challenge current formulations of society and business, and because sufficiently robust change means questioning the ground we stand on.

And we include in this 'action', ways of being—although we realise this is a some-what clumsy designation. Often, participants on the MSc have found that *how* they are—how they approach an issue, the way in which they behold and respond to other people, their openness to potential outcomes—is as important a contribu-tion as *what* they do. And so, taking our line from Gregory Bateson (1972), we sug-gest that we need to learn to think, act and *be* differently in order to face current challenges. And leadership for sustainability needs to be made of this 'stuff', rather than fashioned within mainstream ideas and practices.

We have used the notion of leadership in our educational practice, but lightly, and with copious qualifications. We are not talking about solo, heroic, charismatic figures—although sometimes this kind of leadership will be appropriate, but per-haps only fleetingly, and those involved will need to be able to set it aside. We are not talking about the role, the position, status—although location and associated powers can be used to good effect. We see leadership as relational practice (Fletcher 1998; Reason *et al.* 2009), in complex, multi-influenced, shifting spaces. And it is fundamentally systemic, contextual, working with current patterns to both align and challenge. There is some appreciation for these notions in mainstream leader-ship literature, for example in interest in distributed and servant leadership. But we are certainly not in a wholly post-heroic era (Fletcher 2003; Calás and Smircich 2004; Grint 2005).

We chose, within the course, not to pin down notions of leadership too closely and not particularly to refer our participants to the mainstream literature and debates on the topic (although some found their way there on their own). Instead, we let the concept of 'leadership' be inclusive and emergent, applying as much to the vigilante consumer demanding to know where products have come from as to the chief executive promoting environmentally aware corporate practices.

In the MSc, our offerings for developing leadership ideas and practices were carried by what we termed the cross-woven threads. These were described in the course brochure, in bold:

> In addition [to workshop topics], the course will explore significant cross-woven threads of learning including: inquiry practices, systemic thinking, power, gender, diversity, leadership, change, the processes of learning in a community of peers, and the skills of being a change agent. These pro-vide a vital 'toolkit' for addressing the course issues, and contribute to the process orientation that is a core feature of the programme's educational approach (MSc in Responsibility and Business Practice course brochure, Issue 7 2006: 3).

These 'threads' were our mapping of leadership for sustainability. We envisaged people seeking to influence change through practices of action research and self-reflective inquiry, adopting systemic thinking and paying attention to issues of power and diversity, acting both with and against the grain of their organisations and communities. The notion of tempered radical (Meyerson and Scully 1995), the inside-outsider working for change, became a key figure in the course community, bringing a sense of working at the edges of orthodoxy and radical change, and appreciating the life dilemmas of doing this (see Chapter 3). From this perspective, change is seen as processual, emergent, with any attempts at directive action needing to be open to continuous ongoing inquiry. Through these cross-woven threads we offered intellectual ideas, frameworks for awareness and ways of developing practice alongside each other. (Chapter 3 describes the key models and resources we used from which individuals then explored more widely and in selective depth according to their learning agendas.)

We also offered health and career warnings to those seeking to join the course. Someone attempting to stimulate radical change may well be experienced as significantly threatening by those with power, and often even by those who are currently disadvantaged. As Donella Meadows (1991) points out, challenging people in their paradigms is painful, and they are likely to react.

Taking this approach, we find much mainstream leadership literature is of limited help, if it assumes that people are located in formal, hierarchic organisations, have the power these confer, and that issues on which they are seeking to 'lead' are sanctioned by current organisational and social norms. Really radical, sufficiently radically, ways of addressing issues of sustainability and social justice go against the grain of current mind-sets, paradigms, worldviews and practices. If change starts to reach towards significant issues, it is likely to invoke resistance and reaction, of some kind. This could be considered some indication of having 'impact'.

Just like the graduates, we too have had to work to find our 'place to stand'. We too have taken a position as tempered radicals, working within the management education system in order to transform it. Aligning ourselves with critical management education, as we show in Chapter 2, we have challenged mainstream thinking and taken for granted assumptions. We were successful for a while in running a programme that was acclaimed inside and outside the university. Our longer-term impact is more difficult to assess. But we follow bell hooks, a radical black feminist, who argues that those who consider themselves different can maintain clarity and power by embracing rather than bemoaning their positioning, by acting from the margins.

> I am located in the margin. I make a definite distinction between that marginality which is imposed by oppressive structures and that marginality one chooses as site of resistance—as location of radical openness and possibility . . . We come to this space through suffering and pain, through struggle . . . We are transformed, individually, collectively as we make radical creative space which affirms and sustains our subjectivity, which gives us a new location from which to articulate our sense of the world (hooks 1990: 153).

From this positioning, what notions of leadership *do* we relate to? We have already mentioned relational practice (Fletcher 1998), and this is explored more fully in Chapter 3.

Our approach does have many similarities to those set out by Doppelt (2010) and Dunphy *et al*. (2007). They share our concerns for systemic thinking. Doppelt bases his continuous 'wheel of change toward sustainability' model (2010: 107) on systemic principles of intervention. Dunphy *et al*. are explicit about adopting an action research approach and 'learning as we go' (2007: 307). Both strongly advise sensitivity to an organisation's general context and to its current position on sustainability. Dunphy *et al*. outline 'Phases in the development of corporate sustainability' (2007: 24-29): rejection, non-responsiveness, compliance, efficiency, strategic proactivity and being a sustaining corporation. The appropriateness of different leadership and change approaches and actions may depend on where an organisation is on this model. (Alexander Ballard Ltd [2008] offer a similar helpful model of stages of organisational responsiveness.) We notice that both Doppelt 2010 and Dunphy *et al*. 2007 are labelled 'guides'. It is significant, we think, and important to what they contribute. But we would not presume such a title. Both can appear quite prescriptive and procedural in their advice about prompting change. While we would not disagree with many of their sentiments and suggestions, we doubt if change for sustainability can often be brought about by directed, intentional action, deliberately followed through. And wonder if 'first order' rather than 'second order' change might be the result (Watzlawick *et al*. 1980).

We resonate more with the image offered by influential systemic thinker Donella Meadows (2002), that we need to learn to dance with systems, and her warning against any interpretation that we can predict or control. But, of course, any advice, however wise, if followed prescriptively, becomes a tyranny.

In our language, we suggest taking leadership for sustainability with an attitude of inquiry (Marshall and Reason 2007), requiring experimentation and agility.

Who are we?

This book has been brought together and edited by three of us, Gill and Judi who had the original idea for the degree, simultaneously but separately, making for an exciting sense of rightness, and Peter who immediately joined in, as we all developed the underlying educational philosophy and actual practice.

The MSc in Responsibility and Business Practice was developed in 1996 in an educational partnership between the University of Bath School of Management and the New Academy of Business (NAB), which was established by Anita Roddick, Founder of the Body Shop International, to bring more ethical understanding into management education. Gill was at NAB, while Judi and Peter were at the University of Bath. In 2005, the New Academy of Business was formally dissolved and reorganised as the networked Association of Sustainability Practitioners (ASP). Many members of the Association are graduates of the MSc.

Judi was Director of Studies from 1996, when the MSc received formal University of Bath Senate approval, until January 2008, when she left the university. Peter then took over this role until he retired in July 2009.

Over the years we have been joined by other tutors, all as visiting fellows to the school of management, creating a rich and varied team. Each intake had two 'core tutors' who stayed with them through the programme, with a host of visiting speakers (see Chapter 2). Others from the staff team took individual sessions. In the list below, all are core tutors, apart from David Murphy. In order of appearance on the degree, they are:

- **David Murphy**, working through the New Academy of Business, who organised topic-based sessions, especially for Workshop 4: Sustainable corporate management and Workshop 6: Corporate citizenship, over many years, often bringing people from diverse perspectives into provocative dialogues

- **Chris Seeley**, who was first a participant then co-tutored MSc4 in 2000, and has continued with the programme ever since

- **David Ballard**, who co-tutored MSc5 in 2001, and worked with three intakes

- **Tim Malnick**, who was first a participant then co-tutored MSc10 in 2006, and has continued with the programme

Each has brought their diverse talents and perspectives, enlarging the scope of the programme, working with commitment, travelling alongside us and the course participants. We cannot do justice here to how grateful we are to have worked with them.

Appreciations

This section is difficult to write. We owe thanks to so many people that it is hard to curtail this list. And yet there are some we especially want to acknowledge here, as we look back on the last 14 years.

We would like especially to thank:

- **Anita Roddick** for her dynamic contribution to establishing and developing the degree, and visiting many of the intake groups along the way. Sadly, she died in September 2007, in the week the degree held a celebration for its 10th anniversary, which she had been going to attend

- **Brian Bayliss**, Director of the School of Management in 1996 (and until 2005) who supported us in setting up and establishing the MSc

- **David Matthew**, Director of the New Academy of Business at the time of initiating the course, for his encouragement and support in the early years

- The course administrators who have worked with us with such commitment and so valiantly, in often challenging organisational and practical circumstances: **Wendy Middlemist**, **Debbie Parish**, **Liz Rowles** and **Christine Bone**

- **Kay Elliott**, the University of Bath School of Management Administrator, who patiently and astutely helped us through the often labyrinthine processes of teaching and quality requirements and room bookings

- **Amanda Brooks**, **Angela Webley** and the School of Management's marketing team who understood our work and helped us portray it to the outside world

- All the **MSc course participants** who joined us in this venture

- The visiting speakers who have worked with us, many repeatedly. We wish particularly to mention: **James Robertson**, a pioneer of new economic thinking, who made significant contributions to the early programmes; **Stephan Harding**, Resident Ecologist at Schumacher College, who has taught and inspired every cohort to understand and appreciate Gaia theory; **Paul Ekins**, whose intellectual stature and strong support were very important for many years; and **Nick Mayhew**, who brought his provocations to almost every year group, prompting a trail of radical questioning

- Our external examiners, **Professors John Burgoyne**, **Bill Torbert**, **Ray Ison** and **Katrina Rogers**, who happily and vigorously took the role of friendly critics, supporting our purposes and practices while continually demanding the highest of standards

We would also like to acknowledge present and future participants on the sister programmes which we are now developing informed by our work on the MSc: the **MSc in Sustainability and Responsibility** (Ashridge Business School); the **MA in Leadership for Sustainability** (Lancaster University Management School); and the **Leading on Sustainability Programme** (Lancaster University Management School in partnership with Business in the Community North West).

Developing the stories

To put together this volume, and aware we had limited space, we invited some people, whose stories we knew in some detail, to contribute. We also told the RBP email list about the proposed book asking for further suggestions, and several people volunteered. We worked very actively with our contributors, fulfilling our promise to be strong editors. We did not have a template for the stories, but rather worked from the outline the authors provided so that each could unfold its own shape. We insisted that each story stayed close to agreed word lengths, so some detail may be missing and some succinctness is therefore, we admit, in our editorial voices.

In the next chapter we tell our story of taking leadership for sustainability through education.

2

Educating for inquiring practice in sustainability

In this chapter we offer a context for the stories from course participants that follow. In order to do this, we are providing a story of our own, setting out our initial intentions and choices, giving a sense of the course experiences to which graduates then refer.

In 1996, the three of us (Judi, Gill and Peter) came together to create a new educational venture. We already knew each other: Judi and Peter were working together in the School of Management at the University of Bath, and some years previously had created the Centre for Action Research in Professional Practice (CARPP) with their colleagues David Sims and Jack Whitehead, offering a taught doctoral programme based on action research. They were also teaching undergraduate courses which raised questions about ecological issues, potential emerging paradigms and the place of business in society. Gill was working with the New Academy of Business, a not-for-profit business education organisation developing courses on social and environmental issues, sponsored by The Body Shop and its founder, Anita Roddick. Before that she had been teaching at Bristol University. Judi and Gill had worked together previously, and Gill was a participant on the CARPP programme.

We all knew that we wanted to respond to a challenge: to create a Master's-level course, accessible to people working in businesses and other organisations, that would address questions of sustainability and social justice in a business context and try to evolve creative responses. We wanted to make these questions central to the programme, rather than tacked on to conventional business-education content, and to demonstrate that there could be an alternative to an MBA approach. We also wanted to begin to grow a network of people who, like us, saw the challenges to business-as-usual as significant, and who wanted the support of others around them to help them both understand more about the nature of the problems and take actions in both their work and their lives, often in the face of incomprehension and resistance.

We felt uninspired by attempts to address sustainability issues by management and business educators at that time, particularly given the considerable expansion of MBA programmes through the 1990s and onwards into a substantial industry in its own right. We shared some of the concerns of those who identify themselves with critical management (French and Grey 1996; Grey *et al.* 1996; Sinclair 1998; Currie and Knights 2003; Grey 2004; Fenwick 2005; Grey and Willmott 2005), that much business education operates within a tacit taken-for-granted set of assumptions as to the goals of profit-oriented enterprise. And we recognise that many of the 'consumers' of this education pay considerable sums of money to learn the skills deemed necessary to operate within these assumptions, so are not seeking to unpick them. One of the results of this seemed to be that, where they were addressed at all, questions of sustainability, social justice and corporate responsibility were being added into MBA programmes as electives. These tended to appear relatively late in the course, after 'basic' business skills had been absorbed, by which time participants had become committed to and adept in a conventional way of assessing the accepted value of business organisations, through maximising profitability and return on investment. The implied message of such an approach was that nothing in the current ways of understanding business activities needed fundamental reform.

The advent of corporate social responsibility as part of a legitimate business operation in the late 1990s offered, we felt, a fragile opening—a possibility for a different kind of discussion, one that could prise open the narrow confines of the language in which business is discussed and admit some consideration of what could be talked about in what terms (Coleman 2002). But our intent was not just to critique mainstream business education. We were—and are—particularly interested in the connection between ideas and practice, and how we might use an educational programme to develop a community of practitioners in a territory that did not yet have any precedents. Most MBA programmes offer practical projects, as do other professional education courses, in which there is already a somewhat well-defined idea of what good practice looks like. We wanted not just to offer opportunities for developing practice, but also to enable our participants to carry out *inquiring* practice which would help them evolve their actions and knowledge in the course of understanding more about the contexts in which they were working. The reasons for this lie in our understanding of 'sustainability'.

Like many others (Bateson 1972; Orr 1994), we believe that modern, Western societies are caught in a conceptual trap that renders our accepted ways of understanding our world unequal to the task that the sustainability challenge offers. Some have termed the currently dominant view the 'Industrial Growth Society' (Macy and Brown 1998). Over four centuries we have refined and developed our ways of understanding the world based on a model of apparently value-free scientific knowing which has enabled us to do many things that have benefited humanity, and yet has failed adequately to make sense of the connection between humans and the planet that we rely on and are part of. Our mode of accepted understanding relies on the separation of mind from body and of person from place. We have created a culture in which it is taken for granted that worthwhile knowledge is held in disembodied minds, and that what is not known in that way is of secondary importance. But, we believe, the idea of sustainable living on a finite planet requires that we loosen our reliance on the rational thinking mode that has led us to treat our 'environment' as something 'other', a resource at our disposal to be mapped, controlled, exploited and consumed. In other words, we believe that the 'problem' of sustainability is partly a problem in the way we think.

> The crisis we face is first and foremost one of mind, perceptions, and values; hence, it is a challenge to those institutions presuming to shape minds, perceptions, and values. It is an educational challenge. More of the same kind of education can only make things worse (Orr 1994: 27).

This poses, of course, some difficult educational challenges. Institutions of higher education in general and business schools in particular are places in which disembodied rational knowledge is generated and disseminated. Creating a Master's degree with the intention to move away from established and embedded ways of knowing in such a context is an exercise in paradox, or perhaps folly. Finding out how to stay inside this setting, with credibility and integrity for ourselves and for the participants who chose to join us, was one of the challenges we set ourselves.

This initiative did not come out of nowhere. For all of us it was the culmination of a longer story, of epistemological explorations, of student-centred learning experiments, and of building and working with feminist awareness. We came together with a history of pedagogical explorations which we wove together for the programme. And developing the MSc was a further experiment in radical management education that we knew would require considerable learning as we went along; we knew broadly what we wanted to do, but not initially how to do it in practice.

The 'obvious' way that we could think to shape the course involved taking seriously Bateson's (1972) notion that *form* is a primary mode of communication, giving the context for meaning in which *content* is interpreted. We believed that delivering a conventional taught course, with content about sustainability, would be to negate the very communication of change that we wished to offer. We envisaged that it might be possible for us, collectively, to act our way into a different response to the challenge of sustainability, guided by other ways of knowing—experience, practice, presentation, emotion, embodiment, intuition—as well as thinking, and that in so doing we might meta-communicate something important about the human relationship with the more-than-human world (Abram 1996; Harding 2006). The course was therefore innovative in both content and educational process (Reynolds 1998).

We expressed this idea in practice by making some specific educational choices:

- To ground the course in the disciplines of action research as a foundation for the course design and pedagogy

- To respect and work with multiple ways of knowing, informed by an 'extended epistemology' (Heron 1996)

- To seek to cultivate an 'attitude of inquiry' in both the format of the course and the way in which we worked with expert and other forms of knowledge

- To try to create an environment of participatory, collaborative learning

- To align our assessment practices with the course aims and approach

Each of these will be discussed more fully below, after a brief description of the shape and format of the course.

The MSc in Responsibility and Business Practice in brief

We chose to create a part-time programme, to make it accessible to people who were in full-time work and to those who were geographically remote; and because we valued the practical learning that comes from working with part-time adult learners who can bring their ongoing work experience into the course space with them. Based on experience we believed this to be a lively and productive way of working, offering participants the possibility of a continuing field of practice with which to engage between workshops, testing back and forth between theory and practice in real situations immediately. We originally envisaged course participants as those charged with sustainability and social responsibility in business organisations (although at that time there were few people whose roles were wholly dedicated to these issues), but in the event were delighted to work with a more diverse group of participants. We wanted also to work with 'activists' wherever they were placed in society. Participants came from a wide range of job areas and organisations, including large and small companies, consultancies, the public sector and non-governmental organisations. Some people already had professional remits that encompassed sustainability or corporate social responsibility. Others wanted to move their professional lives further in these directions. Many saw themselves as change agents in some way and wanted to develop these skills further. They ranged in age from about 25 to about 60. People came from many parts of the world in addition to the UK: from Argentina, Australia, Brazil, Belgium, Canada, Denmark, Finland, France, Germany, Hong Kong, Hungary, Ireland, Kosovo, Lesotho, Lithuania, Malaysia, New Zealand, Nigeria, the Philippines, Poland, Portugal, South Africa, Sri Lanka, Spain, Sweden, Switzerland, Tanzania, Thailand, the Netherlands, the USA and Vietnam. This diversity was experienced by participants and staff alike as a significant strength, a rich resource for collaborative learning.

We designed the course with eight workshops spread over two years, each lasting five days. Each workshop explored a specific content area in some depth, developing critical questioning, with readings and a range of visiting speakers who had perspectives on ideas, critical issues and relevant business practices. Some course participants were also speakers, from their areas of expertise.

1. Globalisation and the new context of business

2. New economics

3. Ecology and sustainable development

4. Sustainable corporate management

5. Humanity and enterprise

6. Corporate citizenship

7. Diversity and difference in a global context

8. Self and world futures

The workshop titles did not change through the 13 years of running the degree, but we created the workshop weeks afresh each time, in collaboration with course participants, living in practice the degree's action research approach.

Each workshop also incorporated a number of themes that stretched across the course and built over time: systemic thinking and complexity, questions of power and gender, theories of change, practices of action research. We called these 'crosswoven threads' (see Chapter 1, page 7), and saw them as providing integration across more compartmentalised workshop content, and as helping participants to develop their understanding and practice for taking leadership of some kind for sustainability.

Using the disciplines and extended epistemology of action research

The course had action research as a fundamental organising principle—with cycles of action and reflection echoed both in the overall degree format and within each workshop. This pattern was communicated experientially to participants. We drew on our background in the theory and practice of action research because we believed it could give both a base of literature and a range of practices and 'tools' which would help participants move between what they learned during workshops and what they did in their work and lives. It was also an intellectual base for the pedagogical approach of the course, which sought to work with participants as co-learners and autonomous creators of their own inquiries, rather than as supplicant students to whom we were imparting received knowledge and ready-made answers. We echoed Paulo Freire's (1970) notion of question-posing rather than 'banking' education, since the topics we were addressing were ones about which there are many deep questions. We wished to indicate that there are no simple solutions to the dilemmas posed by trying to integrate ecology, sustainability and social justice with successful business practice, and to invite participants to become active explorers and pioneers in this field. Our invitation was to be autonomous co-inquirers in a messy terrain. We discuss our understanding of action research more fully in Chapter 3.

Action research offered us a way to take a radical, action-oriented yet also reflective stance within the university. The substantial reputation and experience of CARPP, nationally and internationally, was a significant factor in this. It gave us a story, an explanation for applicants, sponsors, speakers and collaborators as to what was distinctive about the course, in addition to its content. It also gave us a set of disciplines, criteria on which we could base judgements of quality, and which we were used to working with in other CARPP activities.

We were very aware that we were creating this course within one of the most highly rated schools of management in the UK. There is no doubt that this appealed to some of our applicants, too. The title of their course may have made little sense to their employers and colleagues, but the name of the university did. One of our original sponsors, Anita Roddick, described this as a 'Trojan Horse' strategy, and at times this combination amused us. However, it also placed pressures on us, which we discuss further below.

Action research practices, then, provided potential 'containers' from which course participants could address the challenges of course content, and maintain both an appreciative and a critical, questioning approach, including being critical of the programme itself. But we also wanted the course to be a basis from which people developed actions in the world—practical, useful and innovative responses to complex problems about which understanding is contested. The MBA model of business education usually offers the student a set of ideas and digested examples of 'good practice', carrying a strong implication of how this should be done. An action research approach, by contrast, asks the individual to discover something by doing, and reflecting, and in the light of that reflection, doing some more. It brings the kind of knowing that is only generated through action into connection with the kind of knowing that comes through reading, listening and discussing ideas with others. It places responsibility for creating relevant action on the learner-as-action-researcher, with knowing as something in process, continually evolving, ever provisional and to be tested.

Action research also draws on many ways of knowing—extending the rationalist, propositional ways of knowing on which conventional knowledge-generation is based, to include practical, experiential, presentational, emotional, embodied and intuitive ways of discovering and surfacing what an individual or a group 'knows' (see discussions in Chapter 3 on working with many ways of knowing). The implication, then, is that there is more to knowing than is accessible through our rational minds, that other forms of knowing are intrinsically of value—and that ideas may be enriched and deepened through attention to these additional means of coming to know our world.

Cultivating an attitude of inquiry

We have written elsewhere (Marshall and Reason 2007) about our views of the importance of an inquiring attitude in creating good-quality action research. An attitude of inquiry incorporates curiosity, a willingness to explore and articulate purposes, being willing to work with the idea that your own view may not be right or definitive, a willingness to explore oneself as a participant alongside others, and a scanning attention to potentially disconfirming evidence from a wide variety of sources. These are subtle qualities, developed over time and with practice, and not easily 'taught' in the conventional sense. We therefore offered a variety of ways in which they could be developed through the course: by engaging in cycles of action and reflection within and between workshops, through explicit training in inquiry skills and ideas, by working in learning groups, and by working with all aspects of the programme including the invited speakers in an inquiring way.

At the end of the first course workshop, every participant joined a learning group with 4–5 members, which worked together for the whole of the two years. The groups were largely self-organised, and were assigned a tutor, who spent some part of each workshop with them. Their purpose was to offer participants some fellow-travellers on their learning journey, who would know about their work in some detail and hence could both support and challenge. But also they were a way of practising co-learning—having to develop ways to appreciate and learn from, and offer useful support to, people who were not necessarily just like oneself.

Each workshop started and finished with time spent in the learning groups, where participants brought the questions and topics they were currently working with and shared learning papers, giving each other feedback (provided also by the tutors). The groups therefore acted as bridges between the participants' other worlds and the course world, with people helping each other translate intentions into actions and reflect on the consequences, on a regular basis. Every participant undertook a cycle of self-chosen inquiry between each workshop, writing a learning paper to capture, develop and reflect on what they had done. For some participants this gave an opportunity for repeated, iterative cycles around a major topic with which they were concerned. For others, it was an opportunity to work in varied ways with the ideas, theories and practices they encountered at different workshops.

Movements between action, input and reflection were also built into the workshop timetable, so that participants could experience the value of reflection and build their capacities to act as reflective practitioners.

We also sought to bring an attitude of inquiry to how we approached the sessions from external speakers, who made an important, and much valued contribution to the course. Some found talking to the course group so stimulating (and provocative) that they came year after year, almost becoming part of an extended staff team. They included leaders in businesses addressing some aspect of a sustainability strategy or at the leading edge of practice, willing to offer stories from the field. Some were campaigners or activists articulating alternative ways to work for sustainability and presenting a strong challenge to business practice. Others were thinkers, able to stimulate ideas or offer frameworks for understanding some aspect of the territory. And some were all three. In each case, participants were encouraged to take a holistic and inquiring approach to their contact with the visitors, listening to the content, asking opening questions, respecting their practice, critiquing their positions, noticing absences and contradictions in their accounts, and also paying attention to their own reactions as course participants, so developing a capacity for reflexivity. We kept this process of listening and questioning speakers under constant review and we worked with the course groups to see expert knowledge—whether presented in a book or article, via an invited speaker, or from a course tutor—as something to be appreciatively questioned and thoughtfully considered in the light of many sources of evidence, rather than simply accepted.

Creating an environment of participatory, collaborative learning

It will be seen from this discussion that the role of the course tutors has been important in setting the tone and practices of the groups. It was our intent to honour the principles of democracy and collaboration that underpin action research by creating an educational experience in which participants took as much responsibility for their learning as was feasible. Our belief was that to do this required a style and quality of leadership that, on the one hand, set clear boundaries about the nature of the educational experience participants were joining and, at the same time, encouraged self-directed learning, disengaging from, and where necessary confronting, participants when they looked for authoritative answers and inappropriate tutor direction. We also did our best to manage the boundary between the course and the hierarchical nature of the university setting within which we were operating. This involved working with processes that ensured appropriate consistency and academic quality across year groups, which we grounded in an action research approach integrating attention to quality. The learning groups' processes contributed to the participative educational approach, as did the experience and knowledge brought by all participants on the course, from their diverse backgrounds.

The topic for each workshop was set in advance, and course tutors took responsibility for designing the week afresh each time. As each course group progressed we opened this decision space to participants, so that they increasingly influenced how we approached topics and the speakers we invited. The style in the classroom was also one of 'managed' participation, with frequent use of formats to encourage thinking together and wide contact with each other: Open Space (Owen 1997), World Café (Brown and Isaacs 2005), small group discussions, consultancy triads, paired conversations and so on. There was also use of non-traditional means of reflecting back and capturing learning—collages, freefall writing (see Chapter 3), posters, movement, storytelling, role plays, journalling—as ways of tapping in to people's different learning preferences and ways of knowing.

We also encouraged reflection in the moment during course activities, inviting participants to monitor their behaviour and 'learning edges', and experiment with new actions in real time during the workshops. In keeping with this, we too attempted to model reflection in the moment, for example by drawing attention to the choices we were making as we facilitated the course process and by publicly reflecting on our own learning.

During every workshop we scheduled both content and process reviews. Content reviews were times when participants could reflect on what they were learning about the topic, often comparing learning with the critical questions they had jointly mapped at the outset of the week. Process reviews were opportunities to comment and debate the ways we were together: for example, how some participants found it easier to speak out than others, whether we were challenging visiting speakers enough or too much, sometimes whether men were dominating discussions over women, the balance of attention between content and process, whether staff leadership was appropriately open, whether sufficiently rigorous debate was taking place, and so on. These were dilemmas each course group had to live, discuss and experiment with in action. The form of their learning thus mirrored inherent sustainability and social justice issues, such as reaching for equity in diversity, to be engaged with experientially. Some year groups paid a lot of attention to group process, confronting some quite difficult group dynamics; others involved less contentious debate.

Aligning assessment practices with the course aims and approach

The course was a Master's programme, and we saw our educational intentions as highly congruent with Master's-level work, except that we wanted to expand participants' development to include practice. We therefore devised a set of four explicit assessment criteria, which were agreed through the university quality processes.

We encouraged learning groups to use these criteria in their discussions, and we as tutors used them to rigorously assess course work. The criteria were:

- **Ideas**. Evidence that the participant has engaged with ideas of relevance, from the workshops and from other sources

- **Practice**. Evidence that the participant is thinking about and beginning to test the *practice* that follows from the ideas

- **Inquiry**. Evidence that the participant is engaged with a process of inquiry in some way, and has considered and critiqued action research literature and models

- **Reflection**. Evidence that the participant has included some personal reflection on what the inquiry means for them and how this links to their professional and life purpose

These criteria were introduced to participants early in the programme and much discussed. We encouraged them to take responsibility for meeting the criteria and to interpret them, in consultation with their tutors and learning groups, in ways relevant to their own learning.

In the first year of the course participants completed three learning papers, which were submitted at the end of the first year in a portfolio, together with a reflective review of the year. At each workshop they received qualitative feedback from other learning group members and from their tutor, for their learning and development rather than for perfecting coursework, although this was also addressed. There was ongoing discussion about what constituted good-quality work. In the second year each person completed an extended practical inquiry—with periodic feedback from learning group colleagues and tutor as before—which was written up as a 15,000 word report and submitted for assessment at the end of the year, together with a reflective review of the course as a whole. Participants selected their own topics for learning papers and project, in discussion with their learning groups and tutor, with encouragement to work on what was most important, engaging and challenging, for them.

Taking leadership through education

This, then, has not been an 'ordinary' course. We, and our close colleagues who joined the tutor team, have been strongly committed to its aims. We care about the future of the people who have passed through it, and we want to help them to do their work in the world as well as they can. We feel that we are engaged, together with our graduates, in growing new practices that are somehow responding to current sustainability and social justice challenges. We are not neutral about this. Our approach and educational work are how we hope to make a contribution. It is our way of seeking to exercise leadership for sustainability.

Working in this way, within a highly ranked school of management within a major university, has been a privilege and has presented many challenges. We have seen the holding of the innovative, collaborative, purposeful space of the MSc as an act of meta-communication within a higher education system that is increasingly subject to set routines and formulaic, modularised approaches.

We received good support from many colleagues and managers, and at the same time were repeatedly reminded, often in subtle, trivial and unintentional ways, that our course did not 'fit' the regime. We will not elaborate this aspect of our work here. But we do want to acknowledge how practically, politically and relationally tough things were at times—partly to respect a 'truth' and partly because some readers may be encountering similarly contradictory dynamics in their institutions as they put critical management education for sustainability into practice.

We have also, at times, been very challenged by how best to act as tutors, constantly seeking an appropriate balance between control and letting go, active guidance and facilitation, claiming expertise and standing back to enable groups to find their own way. What we have been doing is not teaching, and not facilitation—but trying to act as guides, mentors, provocateurs and enablers; above all creating and holding a space within which participants could learn. It is a practice that we have developed as we have gone along, informed by feedback from our participants and our own reflective practice and team development processes.

We have had to find ways to handle expert knowledge. The range of ideas and theories touched on during the modules is larger than any of us, individually, can legitimately claim to know well—ranging from ecological science, biology, physics, climate science to philosophy, economics, organisational theory, political theory and much more. Our participants often (and increasingly) know more about specific areas of ideas and practice than we do—and yet we still have to find ways to identify appropriate sources of reading and judge the quality of people's written work and accounts of their practice. These kinds of paradoxical power-relations are recognised by us as tutors, and by many of our participants, who often handle them with grace and generosity.

In this venture, then, we were consciously crafting a learning process that invited participants to engage through a series of challenges to their ways of understanding, experiencing and responding to the world around them. We were very aware that this is an emotional as well as an intellectual process, and participants' feedback repeatedly told us so. They often referred to their experience of the course as a 'journey', involving high points and low points. Their descriptions have included 'challenging', 'draining', 'exciting', 'exhilarating', 'inspiring', 'mind-stretching', 'painful', 'stimulating' and 'terrifying', often intermingling a range of potentially contradictory feelings (Marshall and Coleman, in preparation). We will return to this theme in the closing chapter, and it is expressed in graduates' stories.

What is your evidence?

In this chapter we have made many claims about our educational practice on the MSc in Responsibility and Business Practice, and by implication about its effects on course participants and graduates. As our colleague Jack Whitehead would ask, and we repeatedly ask course participants: where is your evidence for your claims?

We do have a vast wealth of evidence available to us. But as this book is about taking leadership for sustainability, rather than a critical appraisal of the course, we will not present it all here. We have reviewed the MSc elsewhere (for references see Chapter 1). Here we shall briefly give a flavour of that 'evidence' drawing on two comprehensive five-year reviews of the degree, part of the quality assurance process at the University of Bath; an email survey of graduates; and the observations of our external examiners who read and commented on a selection of first- and second-year project work annually.

From these sources we conclude that the degree has a profound impact on the lives of the participants, which we can summarise as follows:

- Many graduates reported that their lives were changed, and that they came to see things differently, with more complexity

- Graduates reported that their learning was professional *and* personal; intellectual, practical *and* emotional

- The course was a containing space facilitating change and learning

- Change was both sought and challenging

- The course could be unsettling, especially in the early stages

- Graduates said that doing the degree challenged the way they lived

- For some participants there was a time lag about what to do next in their careers

- Graduates noted the importance of the diverse course group and of the learning approach as factors supporting their learning

- The importance of action research was strengthened as the programme progressed; for most participants it was very welcome professional and personal development

Of the many statements we collected from course participants, the following capture much of both the spirit and content of their feedback:

> Informative, thought provoking and enlightening. Provided moral support while I ventured outside the business mindset, set new parameters for 'success' and stretched my imagination about what was possible (MSc4).

> Extremely challenging and confronting, had not engaged with this sort of material in this way and in this depth before. Also very much personal

transition time, additional challenge. How can I return to my previous way of living having become aware of the issues we uncovered together? (MSc5)

Our external examiners could be characterised as friendly critics: we invited them to the role because we knew they would by sympathetic to our aims while at the same time holding us to the high standards of our (and their) aspirations. Each of our external examiners made critical observations on our practice that led us to develop our teaching and assessment processes.

Bill Torbert identified the importance of personal transformation in the degree, later including a similar comment in his *Harvard Business Review* article with David Rooke (Rooke and Torbert 2005):

> The MSc in Responsibility and Business Practice is a courageous and innovative programme both in the range of topics and materials it covers, but even more so in terms of the dedication to a truly developmental, transformational focus in its teaching methods. As I read [the papers] it seemed clear that in virtually every case, the student has transformed their worldview and daily practice since entering the programme. As I have learned through my own research on learning outcomes, very few programmes really transform anyone, let alone a significant proportion of their participants.

Ray Ison and Katrina Rogers both emphasised the originality and significance of our educational practice, Ray writing that:

> . . . I have found many of the students' projects to be highly innovative and indicative of activity that will have lasting social benefit. In this regard the programme is to be commended for providing a platform for learners to engage in both personal and social transformation . . .

while Katrina wrote that the programme was

> . . . distinctive and sophisticated in its level of theory and practice for an MSc programme. The pedagogical focus on action inquiry is also unusual and provided a learning environment for students to think about their own educational goals in relation to their professional practice. It is an excellent example of a programme that engages participants in life long learning.

All our external examiners congratulated the School of Management at the University of Bath for its willingness to sponsor such an original educational venture.

While we are pleased with this feedback, we are always aware that our efforts are a drop in the ocean when measured against the extent and complexity of the sustainability challenge, as discussed in Chapter 1. This is work in progress.

3
Ideas and practices

In this chapter we offer key ideas and resources which have informed the MSc in Responsibility and Business Practice and have been introduced to the course participants. Many of these ideas are referred to in the graduates' stories in Chapters 4–11. As Chapter 2 has shown, participants also explored much more widely than this, according to their individual learning journeys.

The chapter contains the following sections:

- The theory and practices of action research
- Worldviews
- Systemic thinking and practice
- Power
- Tempered radicals
- Action inquiry and the leadership development framework
- Relational practice
- Questions of gender: connecting personal and political
- Freefall writing as inquiry

In each section we present ideas and practices, and in some we also refer ahead to how these appear in graduates' stories.

■ The theory and practices of action research

Action research was at the heart of the MSc both in theory and in practice. It informed the structure of the programme and the process of each individual workshop; it guided the behaviour of tutors as they modelled educational practice as inquiring behaviour; it was central to the learning process for course participants as they engaged in their worlds to influence change and as they recorded and reflected on their endeavours in their learning papers and projects reports; it has informed many graduates' approaches to taking leadership for sustainability, explicitly or tacitly, as their stories show.

Action research is a rich and diverse family of ideas and practices. It is not simply a methodology. It is an orientation towards research and practice in which engagement, curiosity and questioning are brought to bear on significant issues in the service of a better world. Action researchers are encouraged to adopt an 'attitude of inquiry' (Marshall and Reason 2007, 2008) towards the ideas they espouse and the actions they take—an attitude that is continually curious about self and other. In this way, action research strives to create a close link between knowledge and practice. It sees research and inquiry as too important to be left to academics studying from a distance, and offers ways for people in organisations and society generally to inquire into their own practice, learn from experience and make sense of their actions and their worlds. In this section we describe the general principles we offered to course participants, each of whom then applied these to the challenges and opportunities of their own circumstances in individual, even idiosyncratic, ways.

Dimensions of action research

One way to describe action research is in terms of five interlinked dimensions (Fig. 3.1).

Addressing practical challenges

Action researchers adopt a reflective and inquiring attitude to complex and messy human challenges, asking 'How to . . . ?' questions: 'How can I put sustainability on the agenda in my company?'; 'How can I influence the gender politics in my organisation?'; 'How can I find work that is worthwhile and makes a difference?' These questions bring research into everyday experience and practice, creating forms of knowing which in turn inform that experience and practice. This emphasis on the pragmatic and the particular makes action research complementary to, but very different from, traditional scientific research, which is more concerned

Figure 3.1 **Dimensions of action research**
adapted from Reason and Bradbury 2001

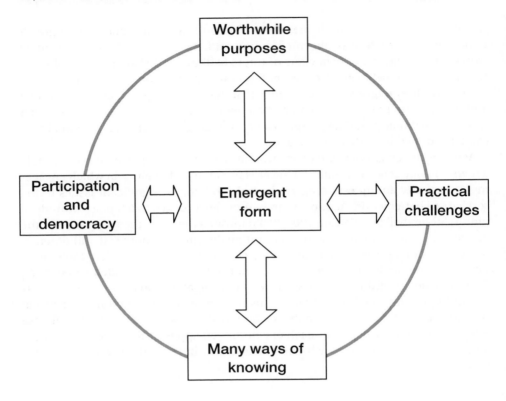

with abstract knowledge, control and rigour (Toulmin and Gustavsen 1996). Action research is about working towards practical outcomes *and* creating new forms of understanding, since action without reflection and understanding is blind, just as theory without action is meaningless.

Worthwhile purposes

Action researchers usually pay attention to issues they care deeply about, and in this sense action research projects are unashamedly value-laden, asking what is most likely to help us build a freer, better society and contribute to the flourishing of human communities and the ecologies of which they are a part. The questions 'What is important here?', 'What do I really care about?' and 'Can I be of service in this situation, and if so how?' need to be continually addressed as part of the inquiry process.

Participation and democracy

Action research is founded in a belief that humans can work and learn together generatively, so helping create spaces for new forms of collaborative exploration is an important aspect of action research practice. In its fullest sense, action research is participative, aiming to engage those involved in the issues to hand as co-researchers and equal partners, rather than treating them as research subjects.

There are several reasons why action researchers emphasise participation. First of all, human beings as social creatures are more likely to create change if they are part of doing so with their fellows. As people engage and begin to think together, they begin to learn together. This may be simply learning to do things better, but very often the learning transforms how they see the whole situation. Through a process of mutual learning, people are able to develop genuinely innovative communities of practice. Participative sense-making, with its 'insider' understandings, is thus both rich and relevant to the challenges of the situation. Most importantly, participative research supports people who thought they were powerless to find they have power to do things. Action research is more than problem-solving; it is, at its best, an educational and liberating process. Finally, from a social justice perspective, people have a right to be involved in creating knowledge, particularly about what concerns them. When it comes to tackling major issues such as climate change, this involves and affects every person on the planet, as well as the other species that live here with us. We cannot ethically leave these critical questions to politicians and scientists.

Many ways of knowing

Western science has developed a very powerful form of inquiry based on rational (often mathematical) thought and empirical evidence. In focusing on the rational, we tend to ignore a wide range of other ways of knowing which include the experiential and intuitive, the aesthetic and presentational, the inter-subjective and relational, the embodied and emotional. For example, we increasingly see the error of basing our theories on the myth of the rational economic man, as classical economics does. Of course these other ways of knowing are open to all the varied perspectives, perceptual selectivities, even distortions, that characterise human knowing, but it is these everyday ways of knowing that guide our actions in all fields of endeavour. Action research seeks to enhance the quality and validity of knowing through a variety of measures (reviewed in Bradbury and Reason 2001; Reason 2006), including individual and collective cycles of action and reflection.

Emergent form

Because action research works with the messiness of everyday life, projects cannot be predefined in any detail. Our world doesn't stand still as we engage with it, so inquiries emerge over time as those involved learn more about the issues to hand, try out new ways of doing things, develop relationships, and gain confidence in their explorations. In the language of complexity theory, action research is 'path dependent': what happens at any point depends in part on the choices that were made earlier. Which means it is really important for those involved to make choices as clearly and explicitly as possible, and to reflect as they go along.

Cycles of action and reflection

Action research, in all its diverse forms, places great emphasis on the integration of action and reflection and it is through such research cycling that the different elements outlined above are knitted together. In these cycles, phases of experimental action are followed systematically by phases of reflection and sense-making; in this way the phenomenal world can be thoroughly explored, ideas and intentions can be checked out in practice, and co-researchers can reach towards more effective and appropriate action in the world. Research cycling brings discipline and system to people's natural learning processes and can ensure that the emergent form of inquiry is informed and knowingly chosen.

Research cycling can be more or less explicit. For example, the practice of co-operative inquiry is described as a collaborative cycling through four ways of knowing (for which see below), while in participatory action research (Fals Borda and Rahman 1991) the emphasis is often placed on the liberating potential of reflection on the life experiences of a community. Research cycles can be longer, as in the contemplation of a phase of life history, or shorter, when action researchers are exploring the effectiveness of a particular pattern of action. Further, some authors make the point that what we are seeking in action research is genuinely aware action that is continually infused with qualities of reflection, so that our choices in the moment are informed by a reflective understanding of what is happening. This collapses the inquiry cycles into moment-to-moment awareness (Torbert [1991, 2004] articulates this most thoroughly).

The MSc was designed so that cycles of inquiry were explicitly embedded in its structure: the reflective workshops punctuated the phases of practical application in work and community. However, for each participant the course as a whole was a major inquiry cycle, made up of smaller, more focused, cycles. We also encouraged reflection in the moment during workshop activities, inviting participants to monitor their actions and to experiment with new actions in real time during the course weeks. In keeping with this, staff attempted to model reflection in the moment by drawing attention to the choices they made as they facilitated the learning process and by publicly reflecting on their own learning. In these different ways we as educators sought to help participants develop a feel for the iterative knowledge-generating process of action research.

Graduates' accounts of their practice in this volume contain many references to action research. They often found that, while the disciplines of action research, such as cycles of action and reflection, are easy to grasp intellectually, processes of 'taking an attitude of inquiry' and of directing one's own learning are subtle, complex and surprisingly novel. As one of our doctoral graduates put it, action research must be learned through practice: it 'cannot be taught, it can only be "caught" ' (Capewell 2008).

Helena Kettleborough provides one of the most thorough accounts of developing an action research practice in an organisation. She writes,

> Ever since I encountered action research, I have wanted to integrate it into my own practice and to offer it to others with whom I work because it has the potential to help us achieve our targets and simultaneously to learn for sustainability in complex times.

She describes how action research experience appealed to her, because it 'fitted with my own earlier learning journey, using participative, empowering and learning methods to improve local government services'. But she also describes how difficult it was to get action research practices adopted in her local government authority because they did not fit readily into the culture. Her story demonstrates well some of the commitment and persistence that is needed to pursue this approach.

First-, second- and third-person forms of inquiry

We have found it useful to differentiate between first-, second- and third-person forms of inquiry in teaching and practice, focusing on individual practice, the face-to-face community or group, and the larger impersonal scale. It is a framework that participants on the MSc have readily adopted.

In many ways action research is best seen as grounded in developing an individual, first-person capacity for the inquiring, reflective, experimental approach that each one of us can bring to our own life and practice. This is living life as a process of inquiry in which little is taken as fixed or certain, an ongoing process of reflecting internally on the nature and appropriateness of our own frames and theories and externally on the adequacy and effectiveness of our actions (Marshall 1999, 2001).

First-person inquiry begins with paying greater attention to everyday practice and how we make sense of our lives, making the familiar less familiar and more open to questioning. A common way of doing this is through a reflective diary or autobiographical writing. Participants in the MSc sometimes wrote their first paper as such a reflective piece. As this kind of attention becomes established, we become more questioning of our actions, our assumptions and the ways we make sense of (and often justify) our behaviour, and we can then draw on systematic ways of reflection. Argyris and Schön (1974) invite us to consider the congruence between our espoused theories (what we say we do) and our theories-in-use (what we do in practice), and to consider whether our actions are really appropriate for what we are attempting to achieve. Torbert (2004) similarly invites us to pay attention to the relationship between our aims and purposes, our conscious strategies, our actual behaviour, and the results we can see in the outside world. For Marshall (2001) the key notion is of engaging between inner and outer arcs of attention, developing awareness of internal sense-making and reaching out to test ideas and practice externally. Jack Whitehead (1989), in his work on living educational theory, emphasises the importance of bringing evidence from experience to support claims to knowing.

After an overview of action research in the first workshop, we introduced ideas and practices of first-person inquiry in the second workshop of the MSc, and invited participants to apply these in their everyday lives. We later offered a variety of exercises and activities to support and develop first-person inquiries using tools such as two column recording, the ladder of inference and the learning pathways grid (Taylor *et al.* 2008).

Second-person inquiry takes place when people work together face to face with others interested in issues of mutual concern, usually in small groups. This can range from the relative informality of mutually inquiring friendship, to more formal disciplines of interpersonal dialogue, and is most fully expressed in explicit methodologies such as co-operative inquiry. Second-person inquiry offers a form within which people can explore important issues together; this can be both challenging and supportive.

A co-operative inquiry group consists of people who share a common concern for developing understanding and practice in a specific personal, professional or social arena (Heron 1996; Heron and Reason 2001). A typical inquiry group will consist of between 6 and 20 people who are both co-researchers and co-subjects. As co-researchers they participate in the thinking that goes into the research—framing the questions to be explored, agreeing on the methods to be employed, making sense of their experiences and drawing conclusions. As co-subjects they participate in the action being studied. The co-researchers engage in cycles of action and reflection: in the action phases they experiment with new forms of personal or professional practice; in the reflection phases they review their experience critically, draw appropriate learning, and develop theoretical perspectives which inform their work in the next action phase. Co-operative inquiry groups thus cycle between and integrate four forms of knowing—experiential, presentational, propositional and practical (see below). We designed the third MSc workshop as three cycles of co-operative inquiry into Gaia and deep ecology so that participants had an experiential as well as an intellectual introduction to this practice (Maughan and Reason 2001; Reason 2007b).

As can be seen, both first- and second-person inquiry take place in relatively contained contexts. A significant challenge for action research practice is to move beyond these relatively small-scale projects to create a wider impact (Gustavsen 2003; Gustavsen *et al.* 2008). Third-person strategies aim to create a wider community of inquiry. For example, this might be a series of inquiry events interconnected in a broader stream, involving people who, for reasons of number and geography, cannot engage face to face. Through this engagement they may come to experience themselves as part of a social movement. While some action research practitioners prioritise working with scale, arguing that first- and second-person inquiry engage too many scarce resources and too much attention with limited impact, we have argued that the more radical transformations of understanding and practice that happen for individuals supported by small groups are an essential foundation of creative large-scale change. However, the challenges of integrating first- and second-person inquiry into third-person scale are tremendous.

The practice of third-person inquiry often involves teams of action researchers working over a long period within an organisation or community. Interventions may take the form of dialogue conferencing events, often including several hundred people and increasingly drawing on digital communication technology,[1] designed to engage representatives of an entire system, whether it be an organisation or a community, in thinking through and planning change (for descriptions see Bunker and Alban 1997). What distinguishes them from other large meetings is that the process is managed to allow all participants an opportunity to engage actively in the planning (Martin 2008). Rather than aim at a single outcome, in dialogue conference (Gustavsen 2001) and whole-system design (Pratt *et al.* 1999), the role of the researchers is to create the conditions for democratic dialogue among participants from which multiple actions can arise.

We encouraged all MSc participants to base their inquiries in first-person reflective practice, believing that this is the ground of all effective inquiry. This is shown in some people's stories. For example, Indrė Kleinaitė describes the experience of the MSc as a 'whole-person transformation', and how she has experimented with 'small disturbances' in a complex system. Kené Umeasiegbu shows how he learned to temper his impetus to indulge in ineffective protest, rather finding ways to draw others into a mutual inquiry. Charles Ainger describes how he learned to take an attitude of inquiry 'by some sort of osmosis' and how that has informed his practice ever since he took the MSc. (He also importantly cautions against the use of over-academic language.)

Other participants' accounts emphasise more the second-person approach. So, while Jane Riddiford refers to her personal learning, her account focuses on her approach to using collaborative inquiry as a vehicle for learning, working with young people to grow food and shift their awareness of their relationship to the planet. Lalith Gunaratne and Mihirini De Zoysa describe how the MSc encouraged them to bring processes of inquiry and democratic dialogue to their work with young people to address the political and ethnic conflicts in Sri Lanka. Ian Roderick describes a process of learning how to lead.

We might say that all MSc participants are engaged in third-person inquiry, since 'we all want to change the world' and are part of the 'Blessed unrest', as Paul Hawken

---

1 'America Speaks', www.americaspeaks.org, accessed 1 January 2011

(2007) calls it, the worldwide movement for a just and sustainable world.[2] All three examples mentioned in the last paragraph might be seen as second-person inquiry with a strong intention to contribute to wider systems change. But some inquiry projects are more explicitly targeted at changing whole systems than others. Jen Morgan's work specifically aims to change attitudes, practices and structures within the finance system. Karen Karp aims to change the way school food is sourced in the whole of New York City. Paula Downey seeks to challenge what she sees as the crazy path that her country has taken. Paul Dickinson and his colleague established the Carbon Disclosure Project to place information about carbon emissions into the finance system and might thus be seen as having institutionalised an activist third-person inquiry. As Donella Meadows has argued, one very effective way of changing a system is 'putting information into a place where it doesn't now reach' (Meadows 1991: 59).

Opening communicative space

Since action research is a collaborative process, based on the principle that people learn and change through interaction, the success or failure of an inquiry venture depends on the conditions that made it possible, which often lie far back in the way the topic was broached, how first impressions were formed, and on the early engagement with participants and co-researchers. We have come to refer to these processes as 'opening communicative space', drawing on Stephen Kemmis's (2001) adaptation of Habermas's work (Gayá Wicks and Reason 2009). To open communicative space, action researchers must have some access to the communities they wish to work with, ability to convene relevant participants, and the position and skills to establish an appropriately legitimate and influential role within that group.

Simon Hicks's account of his work in species conservation starts with the realisation that current practices are inadequate; it follows that much of his work involves creating and sustaining new 'spaces' where different kinds of interaction can take place, including what he describes as 'encouraging unwilling collaborative partners'. Karen Karp tells of the many different attempts to find an opening in 'the system's labyrinthine bureaucratic layers and entrenched hierarchies'. Nick Pyatt is explicit about trying to create conditions for dialogue across differences of perspective and power, and the challenges this entails.

2 Please see the WiserEarth forum as one place to connect up: 'WiserEarth: The social network for sustainability', www.wiserearth.org, accessed 1 January 2011.

Single-, double- and triple-loop learning

As action researchers engage in action and reflection they will discover dissonance and contradiction: they will be challenged by the failure of their actions to bring about the kinds of outcome they were expecting. It is in this dissonance that learning can begin.

A first level of learning is to treat the dissonance as single-loop feedback, to realise that their behaviour may have been inadequate in some way—unskilled, inappropriately timed, clumsy—to bring about the outcomes desired. Single-loop learning is important, because it can lead people to prepare and attend more carefully to what they do, to experiment with different ways of approaching situations. Also, the researcher's willingness to engage in single-loop learning is likely to increase trust with other participants who, in consequence, are likely to be more willing to learn and to listen to others.

But sometimes single-loop learning is insufficient. Double-loop learning draws our attention not only to our behaviour, but also to our theories of practice and our strategies of influence. Double-loop learning invites us to question our understanding of the situation or change the way we approach it. We are still trying to address similar purposes but using a different, maybe more sophisticated, approach.

Triple-loop learning takes us a stage further, to attend not only to our behaviour, or our thinking and strategy, but to our purposes, identity and understanding of the situation as a whole. Triple-loop learning invites us to let go of certainty, regard little as fixed, treat our own purposes with curiosity, and to attend to the interplay between different ways of seeing the situation, different strategies and different behaviour choices. Above all, a person fully engaged in triple-loop learning will be *as* interested in disturbing taken-for-granted perspectives and habitual actions, in engaging as many people as possible in an open learning process and in the opportunities for significant transformation, as they are in the immediate practical outcomes. Of course, very few of us manage to sustain this kind of open attention in the present very consistently. It is this integration of single-, double- and triple-loop learning that makes action research more than problem-solving, but potentially radical, transformational and profoundly relevant for the exploration of issues of justice and sustainability where everything is uncertain and open to different interpretations. The action research approach invites practitioners to consider not only the effectiveness of their actions but also the taken-for-granted assumptions that underlie these; and to seek to engage other actors in this questioning.

While not all of the participants' accounts refer directly to these aspects of learning, such distinctions do nevertheless underpin the whole MSc experience. Roland Widmer refers to the way in which 'critical circumstances' such as 'when the project experiences difficulties' challenge one's 'comfort and patience' and 'prepare . . . the ground for single-, double- and triple-loop learning'. Nick Pyatt encompasses the interplay of practical outcomes and creative novelty when he writes, 'I need the dynamism of challenge that pushes back the boundaries of my imagination so that what we need to do becomes clearer'. Simon Cooper writes, '. . . there was satisfaction to be had in addressing the question that was being asked—but there was often a richer reward from asking new questions, either unspoken or avoided', a shift from single- to double-loop learning. Mark Gater attempts to shift attention in his organisation from single-loop effective attainment of defined goals to a double-loop inquiry into their purposes as a mutual financial organisation. In the process his own learning has to shift towards triple-loop as he relinquishes some of his old identity in the organisation and pays more attention to moment-to-moment learning. And our own account of establishing the MSc in Chapter 2 could be couched as our project to move beyond the single-loop learning of most business education, to double-loop revisions of strategies, and towards a triple-loop 'community of inquiry' with MSc participants and graduates who mutually support ongoing exploration into their/our purposes and practices.

Working with many ways of knowing

Action research, rooted as it is in a participatory and systemic worldview, seeks to integrate action and reflection, thinking and feeling, and so goes beyond learning that is primarily intellectually focused. As we argue below in the section on worldviews, this is a political as well as an epistemological shift.

One language we used on the MSc to value beyond the rational and intellectual and affirm the importance of action and practice, was that of an 'extended epistemology' of experiential, presentational, propositional and practical ways of knowing (Heron 1996; Heron and Reason 2001). How graduates have developed this for themselves is threaded through people's stories and is especially apparent in some accounts that value embodied knowing and build practices on this.

Experiential knowing arises in our everyday lived experience, through our encounter with our 'lifeworld'. It is the foundation of all knowing, yet in many ways tacit and inaccessible to direct conscious awareness. The importance of experiential knowing is illustrated, for example, in the narratives of Jon Alexander and James Barlow.

Presentational knowing grows out of experiential knowing, and provides the first form of expression through the aesthetic imagery of story, drawing, sculpture, movement and dance. As Bruner (2002) puts it, '. . . we come to experience the "real world" in a manner that fits the stories we tell about it'; and, we would argue, in the images of all kinds that we create together. This means that powerful ways of creating change are to portray things in new forms and to tell new kinds of story. Many participants incorporated narrative form, drawing and photography in their learning papers and final project reports on the MSc.

Propositional knowing draws on concepts and ideas and is the link between action and scholarship. Theory can be a way of breaking with the common-sense thinking that prevails in everyday life. The ability to develop alterative theories critical of everyday common sense grows out of in-depth examination of experience and new narratives. The significance of reconceptualising one's work is illustrated by David Bent.

Practical knowing, knowing-in-action, is what action researchers are looking for. Practical knowing is grounded in experience and narrative, is informed by theory and critical thinking, and is expressed through and in what we do. At the heart of practical knowing is an awareness of the quality of the practice in the moment. This is a form of embodied knowing beyond language and conceptual formulation. As tutors we were always thrilled when we saw students experiencing their situation anew, presenting this in imaginative forms, drawing on ideas to make conceptual sense, and integrating all these ways of knowing in new forms of practice.

Another aspect of many ways of knowing appears in the references to spirituality which can be found in many graduate accounts and which seems to open up as the materialist and reductionist worldview loosens its grip. 'Spirituality' is of course a problematic and contested concept referring variously to: the articulation of a sense of purpose beyond the gratification of the ego-self; an holistic, intuitive and connected way of knowing; the self-organising, self-transcending qualities of complex living systems (of which the planet as Gaia is a paradigmatic example); the immanent sacredness of living beings; and for some at least the presence or influence of a transcendental deity. We are grateful to Helena Kettleborough who, in an email, pointed out how important it had been for her to learn a 'cosmological' and 'Gaian' version of action research which incorporated such perspectives at CARPP. As tutors we wish to respect the wide variety of 'spiritual' perspectives that participants embrace, and appreciate the richness of view that these may bring, while not ourselves holding one particular view. We also recognise the contested nature of these perspectives and encourage participants to reflect carefully about what they mean when they use terms such as 'spirituality' and/or ground knowing in their religious commitments. We have strongly challenged both orthodox and non-orthodox appeals to spirituality where we have seen these as poorly articulated and uncritically held. Ian Roderick's reflection on his Christian faith and practices illustrates the significance of careful and sustained reflection on religious and spiritual beliefs.

What we have outlined in this section is a version of action research which has developed through the practice of staff and students at the Centre for Action Research in Professional Practice over some 15 years (see Coleman and Gearty 2007). Many of these ideas were incorporated in a CD which was provided as part of the course materials (Marshall and Reason 2003). Our perspective is strongly rooted in the first-person practices of 'living life as inquiry' (Marshall 1999) and the participatory practice of co-operative inquiry, while reaching out from these to a wider, third-person impact. From this base, course participants were invited to tailor an approach that suited their needs and situation, developing other forms such as participatory action research (Fals Borda and Rahman 1991), appreciative inquiry (Ludema *et al.* 2001), feminist perspectives (Belenky *et al.* 1986), insider organisation development (Coghlan and Brannick 2009) and others.

As we have already pointed out, action research is learned more in practice than in theory. We feel we are most successful as educators when participants have taken the principles we have outlined above and made them their own: adapting them to their own challenges and circumstances, and applying them to more and more aspects of their personal and professional lives. We might say, then, that in its fullest articulation action research is a practice of learning through reflective risk-taking in living.

■ Worldviews

We described our ambition to create an educational programme that would challenge the existing assumptions of business and help participants develop the skills required to contribute to the emergence of a just and sustainable society in Chapter 2. We start from the view that a sustainable society will call for very different foundational assumptions from those currently prevailing. The saying attributed to Einstein that 'We can't solve problems by using the same kind of thinking we used when we created them', while dreadfully clichéd, nevertheless remains apt. We see that much education addressing organisational ethics, 'business in society' and corporate social responsibility does not touch these more fundamental questions, because they are so challenging to 'business as usual' (Giacalone and Thompson 2006).

Our worldview is the fundamental basis of our perceiving, thinking, valuing and acting:

> Every society ever known rests on some largely tacit basic assumptions about who we are, what kind of universe we live in and what is ultimately important to us. Some such set of assumptions can be found to underlie the institutions and mores, patterns of thought and systems of values that characterise society. They are typically not formulated or taught because they don't need to be—they are absorbed by each person born into society as though by osmosis (Harman 1988: 10).

The current global economy has developed in the context of a worldview that has its origins in the European Enlightenment. We have, since the Reformation, the beginning of the era of modern science, and the Industrial Revolution, made enormous strides in our material welfare and our control of our lives. Yet at the same time we can see the costs of this progress in ecological devastation, human and social fragmentation, and spiritual impoverishment. It is questionable whether Western society is undergoing a transition towards a more holistic and ecological worldview, as argued in books such as Willis Harman's quoted above, ambitiously titled *Global Mind Change: The promise of the last years of the twentieth century* (1988). What does seem to us to be certain is that if we fail to make a transition to new ways of thinking, our civilisation will decline and decay as a result of both internal and external ecological pressures (Diamond 2004; Meadows *et al.* 2004; Crook 2009). As Gregory Bateson argued, the most important task facing us is to learn to think in new ways. He was deeply concerned with what he called the epistemological errors built into our ways of thinking (Bateson 1972). So it seems that the challenge of changing our worldview is central to our times.

The notion of a paradigm or worldview as an overarching framework which organises our whole approach to being in the world has become commonplace since Thomas Kuhn published *The Structure of Scientific Revolutions* (1962). Kuhn showed that normal scientific research takes place within a taken-for-granted framework that organises all perception and thinking, which he called a paradigm. However, from time to time the paradigm itself shifts in a revolutionary fashion as a new perspective is deemed to make better sense of the available knowledge. This idea of a paradigm in science can be transferred to the worldview of a whole culture, and the notion that the Western worldview may be in revolutionary transition has been part of intellectual currency for quite a while.

Shifts in worldviews have extremely practical consequences. As Donella Meadows argued, you cannot change a system simply by unilateral action,

> If you want to really restructure a system—the kind of major restructuring that's necessary if we're ever to have a peaceful, just, or sustainable world—that means changing the paradigms that are in our heads.
> Paradigms are the sources of systems. I mean hard, physical systems—they flow out of the deep, socially shared assumptions in our heads, in the culture, in the reigning paradigm (Meadows 1991: 59).

So, as David Orr puts it,

> The disordering of ecological systems and of the great biogeochemical cycles of the earth reflects a prior disorder in the thought, perception, imagination, intellectual priorities, and loyalties inherent in the industrial mind. Ultimately, then, the ecological crisis concerns how we think and the institutions that purport to shape and refine the capacity to think (Orr 1994: 2).

An important change in scientific paradigm can be seen in responses to the work of James Lovelock. When he first proposed the Gaia hypothesis in the 1960s, suggesting that the planet can best be understood as a self-regulating system, with close coupling between the Earth's biosphere, atmosphere, oceans and soil, he was first of all ignored by the scientific establishment and then ridiculed (the story is well told in Lovelock 1979). But although many scientists are reluctant to use the term 'Gaia', the idea that the living and non-living parts of the planet together form a single self-regulating 'biogeochemical' system now, some 40 years later, underpins research into ecological balance, species survival and climate change (Crist and Rinker 2010). This transformation of thinking, from a relatively mechanistic view of planet Earth to that of a living system, although it has not yet worked its way into everyday discourse, may be the most profound transformation that took place in the last years of the 20th century.

As part of the introductory framing of the MSc course, we suggested that worldviews are important, and the first workshop included a presentation and discussion of these issues. We can neither see nor influence worldviews directly, since they are, as the philosopher Ogilvy puts it, made up of the 'models, moods, myths, and metaphors' through which we create our world (Ogilvy 1986: 4). But we can learn to appreciate their influence and to some extent 'see through' it. We do not have to be completely blind to our own perspective. As tutors, we are also critical of what we see as the dominant reductionist and mechanistic worldview in Western society (see below) and suggest that a more systemic and holistic perspective, one that sees humans as participants in life on Earth, part of the community of beings rather than as dominant, could make for a more sustainable future.

We also emphasised in our introduction that worldviews are not only philosophical structures and ways of understanding our world. They are part of the fabric of society, held in place by subtle (and not so subtle) practices of power or 'regimes of truth' so that the interests of the powerful are privileged. This usually means those who are male, white, heterosexual, relatively affluent, able-bodied, literate and living in the global North. And the way that even the most well-meaning of us frame the challenges facing human civilisation will inevitably be influenced by our privileged perspective. Of course, it is difficult to see the metaphorical water one is swimming in, and it is easy for the debate to degenerate into a polarisation of 'old' and 'new', 'good' and 'bad' worldviews. But after this introduction considerations of worldviews were threaded through the MSc course in various forms, invited by a range of speakers and taken up strongly by some participants, and little by others.

Worldviews in the history of the West

The Western worldview can be seen as being formed 300–400 years ago in the period we know as the Enlightenment. The medieval Christian worldview portrayed a world whose purpose was the glorification of a transcendental God. Bacon broke with this, making the link between knowledge and power, and told us to study nature empirically. Galileo told us that nature was open to our gaze if we understood it was written in the language of mathematics. Descartes' *cogito, ergo sum* made a radical separation between human and other modes of being; and Newton formulated an extraordinarily powerful view essentially of the universe as a determinate machine obeying causal laws (see Toulmin 1990; Skolimowski 1994).

This worldview channels our thinking in two important ways. It tells us the world is made of separate things. These objects of nature are composed of inert matter, operating according to causal laws. They have no subjectivity or intelligence, no intrinsic purpose or meaning. And it tells us that mind and physical reality are separate. Humans alone have the capacity for rational thought and action and for understanding and giving meaning to the world. This split between humanity and nature, and the arrogation of all mind to humans, is what Weber meant by the disenchantment of the world.

This disenchantment is exactly what Orr and other eco-philosophers are worrying about. Ecofeminists make a similar critique of 'the western construction of human identity as "outside" nature' (Plumwood 1993: 2), rooted in the dualism of Western thought and the patriarchal assumptions that lead to racism, colonialism and sexism *and* to the domination of nature (see also Griffin 1984; Plant 1989; Merchant 1995; Mathews 2003). The really radical aspect of Gaia theory is not that it shows us how the planet, as a collection of objects, interacts in a curiously self-regulating way, but that it shows us how everything—including humans—participates in the processes of life on Earth. The human mind, certainly in its Western manifestation (Tarnas 1991), has a strange capacity to see itself as autonomous and separate from its context. This allows humans to ask probing questions of the universe. It also dangerously separates us from it. Thomas Berry puts it clearly: unless we understand the Earth not as a collection of objects, but as a 'community of subjects' in which we participate, we are unlikely to be able to make the change in perception needed (Berry 1999). In an interview with one of the editors of this book, he said:

> If we don't have a sense of community, we won't have the psychic energy to carry [necessary changes] through. These ideas . . . will make demands on us. We will only be able to accept the demands if we have a psychic intimacy with the process that rewards us spiritually (Reason 2001: 14).

The challenge of relativism

The main challenge to what Charlene Spretnak calls 'the failed certainties of objectivist modernism' (Spretnak 1997), have been various forms of relativism. The argument here is that what we take for reality is nothing more than a construction of the human mind, supported by various cultural and political forms to create a reality that favours those who hold power. Reality is a human creation embedded in language. All is relative. The extreme relativist position is deconstructive postmodernism, which is suspicious of all overarching theories and 'grand narratives', and asserts that there is no reality behind the 'text', the immediate expression of human understanding we have in front of us. While these perspectives help us immensely in seeing through the myth that is the Western worldview, they do not help us move beyond the problems it has produced. If we were alienated from our experience by the separation of mind and matter introduced by Descartes, we are even more alienated if all we can do is circle round various forms of relativist construction. Any sense of a world in which we are grounded disappears. We lose a sense of the concrete, of existing in a human body as part of the natural, material world.

It is part of the modern human condition to exist in this tension between the objectivity of modernism, where the world exists as an external fact, and a relativist perspective that sees our world as constructed through language. The challenge is to experience the tension as creative rather than debilitating. These perspectives must co-exist: on the one hand our concerns for justice and sustainability must surely mean that the world of Gaia and the suffering of less privileged people are in some sense real, separate from human construing. On the other hand, *how* we construe these is profoundly influenced by our perspectives and interests and our worldview. There is a given cosmos, a primordial reality, but one in which the human mind actively participates. Mind and the given cosmos are engaged in a co-creative dance, so that what emerges as our reality is the fruit of an interaction of the given cosmos and the way mind engages with it (Heron and Reason 1997). 'Worlds and people are what we meet, but the meeting is shaped by our own terms of reference' (Heron 1996: 11).

As Bateson has it, between the extremes of solipsism, in which 'I make it all up', and a purely external reality, in which I cease to exist, there is 'a region where you are partly blown by the winds of reality and partly an artist creating a composite out of inner and outer events' (in Brockman 1977: 245).

Toward a systemic and participatory worldview

In a systemic perspective attention moves from concern about the things that make up the world to an interest in relationships and how they are organised. By shifting focus from things to relationships, we begin to see how living systems are self-organising and self-sustaining, and that many characteristics of living systems are not evident in the separate parts, but *emerge* from their interaction. As Charlton puts it, following Gregory Bateson's systemic perspective: 'The living beings of the world: viruses and bacteria, plants, insects, mammals, the great ecosystems, the seas, the atmosphere, all comprise a single interconnected *mental* system. Radical interconnectedness is inescapable' (Charlton 2003: 116, original emphasis; see also Charlton 2008).

Recognition of the need for systemic thinking is now relatively widespread. But what it means to think, act and live from such a radically interconnected sensibility is elusive. These are issues we have been exploring for some long time, especially through our work in CARPP, and we and our fellow tutors have brought these inquires into the MSc space, to share with participants.

And a systemic perspective also leads us to see that we are not superior beings placed here on Earth by a transcendental god with the right and duty to have dominion over others. Rather, the human species arose from and is integral with all life on Earth. As Thomas Berry puts it:

> The deepest cause of the present devastation is found in a mode of consciousness that has established a radical discontinuity between humans and other modes of being and the bestowal of all rights on the humans. The other-than-human modes of being are seen as having no rights. They have reality and value only through their use by the human. In this context the other than human becomes totally vulnerable to exploitation by the human (Berry 1999: 4).

So, the place of humans in the web of life is as embodied participants, 'living as part of the whole' (Reason 2005). From this perspective we can begin to articulate a participative worldview to re-enchant our world and find new forms of education and inquiry. A participatory perspective will permeate our understanding of what it means to be human, our politics, education, forms of inquiry, sense of meaning and spirituality.

A participatory perspective is not a regression from the objective consciousness of Enlightenment thought to an earlier and more primitive 'participation mystique' or 'original participation' (Barfield 1957) in which human beings are mythically embedded in their world with no differentiation of consciousness. Rather it reaches forward towards an emergent quality of participation that is self-aware and reflexive, in which human experience is highly autonomous and differentiated, and yet recognises its embeddedness in its world. The human mind arises in the evolution of the cosmos, is an expression of the being of the cosmos, is the cosmos rendered self-aware, so that mind, language and symbols are 'no longer imprisoning, contaminating, or alienating barriers that prevent us from a direct, intimate contact with the world . . . [but are] *the very means that enable us to directly participate in the self-disclosure of the world*' (Ferrer 2002: 173, emphasis in original).

The point, very simply, is that we are part of it all, and the moral and practical issue for all humans is to learn to live in a way that does justice to this participation.

Many of the narratives in this volume touch on shifts in worldview that emerged through participation in the Master's programme. Some, such as Roland Widmer and Paula Downey, articulate this in terms of systemic change; others in ecological, Gaian terms, such as Simon Hicks and Jen Morgan; yet others, such as Jane Riddiford, draw on spiritual perspectives that point towards a shift in consciousness. Nearly all participants experienced challenges and tensions that arise from living as it were in 'two worlds', as Mark Gater articulates directly in his contribution. This ability is closely related to triple-loop learning and post-conventional action logics which we describe elsewhere in the volume, the willingness and ability to examine the ground on which one is standing.

■ Systemic thinking and practice

Developing systemic thinking and practice was a vital theme throughout the MSc. It was carried in ideas, and in explorations through practice. With this simple term we refer to an extensive array of ideas that seek to go beyond reductionism and fragmentation, appreciate that everything appears to be interrelated with everything else, and to glimpse wider patterns of connectedness. Flood (2001) provides a helpful review of key strands of thinking and points of difference and debate in the field.

In order to emphasise the importance of systemic thinking right from the start, and to show it is a sensibility and set of practices to be cultivated rather than only a set of ideas to explore, we included a day-long simulation called Fishbanks in the first workshop for each MSc intake. This is based on the World III systems model developed by Meadows *et al.* (2004) which was fundamental to their analysis of the *Limits to Growth*. Fishbanks was introduced to us and run initially by David Ballard. In later years, Carole Bond and Chris Seeley, having trained with David, developed and ran it. Teams own boats, fish in the coastal and deep-sea waters, trade, and respond to environmental inputs from game facilitators. Moves are made in rounds, and after each one team scores and the state of fish stocks are calculated. There is no one pattern to the game. But often the fish stocks are depleted quickly (as they have been worldwide), and when they crash it is a surprise to participants despite relevant data having been available. Competition and suspicion predominate in behaviour; participants with more quantitative skills who calculate fish stock trajectories have trouble being heard; whatever actions are taken are far too late; and thus the tragedy of the commons is enacted by people who are voluntarily and knowingly on a programme about sustainability. It is a salutary experience, giving course participants a lived experience of being 'one source of influence in a complex changing reality' (Dunphy *et al.* 2007: 322), to which they refer back. Debriefing the game reflectively in several rounds is important, surfacing some of the challenges of systemic thinking and practice.

Informing ideas

We have each worked with notions of systemic thinking over many years, influenced by multiple overlapping sources (Bateson 1972; Weick 1979; Watzlawick *et al.* 1980; Capra 1982, 1996; Senge 1990; Senge *et al.* 1994; Flood 1999, 2001; Meadows 2002 and others) for the complex, dynamic senses of the world they offer. We have explored the systemic perspective intellectually and in action (Marshall 2004b). We are particularly drawn to the way in which systems notions place the sense-maker and actor as participant within the situation they are seeking to understand, rather than as a detached observer; any approach we take brings us into relationship, with a perspective, in some way.

We note several of these influences here, to give some flavour of the ideas that MSc course participants have been invited to consider. And, as with all aspects of the programme, people explored much more widely, following their own learning paths. Also, many brought their own interests and expertise in systemic thinking to the programme and developed them in further work. (This is seen, for example, in Ian Roderick's story.) As people wrote learning papers on systemic thinking and complexity science, these explorations were shared more widely, initially with the three or four other members of their learning group for feedback and then with other course participants. This dissemination of learning stimulated wider interest and discussion.

Flood (2001) distinguishes between approaches that assume that real systems exist in the world to be understood and so seek representations of reality, and those that recognise human understanding as always a social construction. The latter invites us to critically reflect on what boundary judgements we make, a key sustainability issue. If we see people as 'individuals', separated from their physical and social environment, we attribute them with inappropriate independence, for example. Bateson (1972) was for ever seeking to draw our attention to relationships and relational patterns, rather than thinking in terms of 'things'. In this sense, there is no clearly demarcated system, such as a person or an organisation. Notions of 'boundaries' are our creation, how we punctuate the world. But the language of 'things' is tempting, and we, too, will use it in places, talking, for example, about 'the finance system' while appreciating the myriad interconnections this short-hand signifies. We prefer to use the notion of systemic patterns, not treating these as fixed or real, but as potential dynamics in which we participate and are therefore co-creators. This raises important epistemological issues which we have considered already in the section on worldviews.

And, in relation to Flood's distinction, as we seek to understand what is happening ecologically now, we do encounter notions of real systems of the planet's carrying capacity that humans are violating: for example, in Rockström *et al.*'s (2009) attempt to map 'a safe operating space for humanity'. What frames of mind can we adopt to understand these, recognising that human knowing is inevitably conditional, and yet not wanting to dismiss important environmental data by taking a radically relativist approach?

In our canon of informing ideas there is, first and foremost, the work of Gregory Bateson (1972), with his attention to relationships rather than things and radical understanding of interconnectivity, including expanding the boundaries of what we might call 'mind' beyond the human into patterns of ecology. He was also clear that we cannot know everything in conscious mind and have to accept incompleteness. Bateson warned fiercely about the ecological damage a limited, linear consciousness, seeing itself as separate from nature and twinned with an advanced technology, would create. And so he offered alternative, systemic patterns of thinking. He also pointed to ways in which we might glimpse a fuller sense of the world, although not completely, through art, poetry and aesthetic experience (Charlton 2008).

Bateson's work informed many others, including Watzlawick *et al.* (1980) who propose that all change is multi-levelled and paradoxical: many apparent outcomes of action will appear 'unintended' and much intended change becomes 'more of the same'. They distinguish significant shifts in systemic patterns and rules (second-order change) from surface change (first-order change)—although these notions are not clear-cut attributions, but issues to puzzle about. For example, is more corporate social responsibility reporting a change of frame on organisational responsibilities or an extension of previous accounting practices untroubled by issues of paradigm? (There is, of course, no clear-cut answer to this question, and much will depend on circumstances.)

Developing this line of thought, Peter Senge and his colleagues, through the Society for Organisational Learning (SOL), identify systems thinking (in his language), as the fifth, significantly integrative, discipline (Senge 1990), setting this alongside personal mastery, mental models, shared vision and team learning to create learning organisations. Every discipline makes the others' practice more effective. Their work includes delineating system archetypes as recurrent patterns. For example, in the Tragedy of the Commons archetype individuals maximise their consumption of a common good, resulting in its destruction. One lesson from their work, and systemic thinking generally, is that often the first proposed solution is a symptom of the problem, so that adopting it will reinforce rather than solve the issues, resulting in increased damage.

Meadows *et al.*'s *Limits to Growth*, originally published in 1972, and the 30 year update in 2004, are key contributory works to any discussions of sustainability. They especially draw attention to how exponential growth of population, capital, resource use and pollution 'can rapidly exceed any fixed limit'; and because of 'delays in feedback from limits, the global economic system is likely to overshoot its sustainable levels' with a speed that is rarely anticipated (Meadows *et al.* 2004: 235).

Flood (2001) and others have developed what they term critical systemic thinking, seeking to incorporate more appreciation of knowledge-power as an aspect of how systemic patterns operate and are held in place. This involves, for example, appreciating how social rules and practices make some approaches to knowing favoured above others (see also the section headed 'Power', pages 51ff.).

Alongside systemic thinking, complexity science, working with notions of patterns (for example, Flood 1999; Harris 2007), has much of relevance to say about thinking and living with radical indeterminacy.

Participants on the MSc were not limited to the ideas set out above. They were encouraged to explore for themselves and many did so, for example focusing learning papers on complexity science (Boulton and Allen 2007) and the implications for their actions as 'change agents'.

Implications for practice

How then can we operate in situations of multiple interactivity? Adopting systemic thinking to inform sense-making and behaviour opens up possibilities. This needs always to be twinned with individual and collective inquiry, as an emergent, lived approach. It involves engaging with uncertainty from curiosity, including reflecting on what is happening, what could happen next, and how we contribute to sustaining current patterns; and at the same time remembering that our understanding is always partial.

Systemic thinking can involve holding in mind ideas of connectedness, systemic dynamics, nested levels, and the potential resilience of patterns; and expecting and respecting emergence and developing processes. It involves paying attention to feedback loops, both balancing and amplifying, and their unfolding consequences. It can entail deliberately seeking to create new feedback loops, putting information where it has not been before to connect up pathways of potential understanding and action (Meadows 1991), protecting these initiatives initially and then letting them take their own course. And it means recognising that inaction can also be a signal in the system; as Bateson reminds us, the tax return we do not send can be treated by others as information.

To think and act we make boundary judgements, but we need to recognise these as our constructions, and treat them as ever-provisional. For example, we may assume from a colleague's challenging comments that they are antagonistic to considering environmental issues in decision-making and start to tone down what we propose. If such attributions can be tested openly, it might lead to quite different interpretations of their perspective and therefore behavioural choices. Even if their antagonism is confirmed, finding ways to refer to this overtly may open up potential for debate.

From a systemic perspective it seems that often aspects of a pattern cannot change unless there is some kind of shift at a more general systemic level, so attempted change is superficial, first order. But sometimes an aspect can be influenced and that prompts change more widely. The tempered radical's attempts at 'small wins' are seeking such wider systemic influence from tactically chosen modest beginnings (see section on 'Tempered radicals', pages 56ff.).

Recognising issues as operating systemically also involves seeing how individual experience is shaped by wider patterns of assumptions and behaviour of which we may be unaware, a radical contextual sensitivity (although context is no more a thing than is system). For example, a corporate social responsibility manager may have difficulty gaining a hearing for his or her proposals at board meetings, and attribute this to their own personal (in)effectiveness. But if these issues are too challenging for colleagues to hear within current mind-sets, the patterns of communication may be more influenced by systemic factors than because of their personal skills. Seeing the dynamics in this way opens up different potential choices of action, such as seeking to promote exploratory dialogue rather than approaching colleagues through advocacy and suggestions.

While we offer these themes for developing sense-making and practice, we must also admit that we find trying to explain systemic thinking as seeking to define something ineffable.

> Systemic thinking . . . is not something that can be explained easily and understood comprehensively. It is not recommended to rush into rationalisation of this sort. Very quickly we will lose touch with the notion of wholeness in a trivialised account of its so-called properties (Flood 1999: 82).

Working systemically, a major dilemma is whether we think that being disturbing, for example offering stark information on climate change and our parts in it, is an effective approach to change. Sometimes it can be just the upheaval that is needed for new patterns of order to emerge. Sometimes perceived confrontation is met with resistance, a hardening of current attitudes and unwillingness to listen and engage. How can we know? How can we work with inquiry with the dynamics that do arise? In our experience, we need an attitude and practices of inquiry to work in the complex territory such unfolding events open up. And there is no one answer to questions of what is effective, especially not when we track events over time. What appeared a 'good' outcome at one point can be reinterpreted as 'bad' at a later time owing to the unfolding play of forces and powers. Operating from systemic thinking and practice thus involves humility and patience, with ourselves as much as with others.

Systemic thinking and practice is, then, certainly not about control. Even writing about systemic thinking and complexity can give a sense that we have the potential to understand fully and therefore a capacity to command and act with certainty. These aspirations seem legacies of another mind-set. Working from systemic thinking implies, for us, recognising that much is unknowable, and taking this as a base for how we operate. In writing this section we have been mindful of these issues, offering ideas and notions of practice, and seeking also to undo edges of certainty that our attempts may imply.

Warning against any interpretation that we can predict or control, influential systemic thinker Donella Meadows (2002) suggests instead the image that we need to learn to dance with systems. She proposes that we: get the beat (of what is already going on); listen to the wisdom of the system; expose our mental models to the open air; stay humble, stay a learner; honour and protect information; locate responsibility in the system; make feedback policies for feedback systems; pay attention to what is important, not just what is quantifiable; go for the good of the whole; expand time horizons; expand thought horizons; expand the boundary of caring; celebrate complexity; and hold fast to the goal of goodness. But, of course, any list, however wise, if followed prescriptively, becomes a tyranny. Drawing on systemic thinking and practice is, rather, a craft adopted with an attitude of inquiry, through which we can seek to learn 'within the unknowable' (Flood 1999: 192). 'Learning our way into a mysterious future calls for continuously revisioning what might be going on, what we are doing and achieving, and the way we are doing it' (Flood 1999: 90).

Systemic thinking on the MSc

As the programme proceeded many of the visiting speakers touched on systemic thinking in various ways, and core tutors introduced models and ideas, opening up discussion of their implications.

For example, we would sometimes present Senge *et al.*'s multi-level model for understanding situations and considering appropriate interventions. This distinguishes events, patterns of events, systemic structure and mental models, each more generic level shaping those nested within it. We can ask whether we are intervening at the appropriate systemic level(s). Condition-setting then becomes vitally important, as change seeking to encourage sustainable practices shows. For example, taxes shape behavioural preferences and can be more or less ecologically helpful, but also have 'perverse' effects of their own. Landfill taxes imposed progressively on local authorities in the UK have encouraged higher recycling rates, but are also an incentive for small businesses to dump rubbish illegally to avoid charges. Being able to influence mental models and systemic structures is therefore very valuable as these help set conditions that can then shape sense-making and action. And these actions too are not means of control, but attempted actions in complex, interactive situations.

■ Power

In many ways it is difficult to write about something as abstract and diffuse as 'power': it is everywhere, and yet encompasses so many forms that the word threatens to become meaningless. But it deserves discussion here, because in all our work with this MSc programme we have been very conscious that we were working with dimensions of power: the definition and creation of 'knowledge' is suffused with power; we have been making an intervention in an educational system that is held together with distinct power relationships; and we are concerned about large-scale changes that challenge current social arrangements and power systems. In this sense, we see what we have been doing as falling broadly within a 'critical' framework (Alvesson and Deetz 2005): that is, one that challenges existing power relationships and seeks more fair, liberating and democratic arrangements.

Not only did this awareness permeate our practice—and form a key part of discussions we had with each other and our colleagues—but it was also built into the fabric of the course. In many respects, we tried to create this MSc course as what Bill Torbert (1991) would call a 'liberating structure': a structure that, with deliberate irony, 'forces people to be free', to transcend it in the process of conforming to it. This sort of power is not logical, it sometimes seems to be counterintuitive, and it is not always comfortable as it moves between various ways of being powerful. Finding ways to do this 'with' participants and not 'on' or 'to' them was part of our ongoing craft and challenge.

We also initiated explicit discussions about the concepts of power, making use of the writings of Steven Lukes (2005), Cynthia Hardy (1994), Stuart Clegg (Hardy and Clegg 1996) and Michel Foucault (1977, 1980) in particular.

Lukes describes three ways of conceptualising or dimensions of power, and more recently added a fourth 'ultra-radical' approach, drawing on Foucault. They are: direct or decision-making power; indirect or non-decision-making power; radical or symbolic power; and the power of the system.

The first dimension: direct or decision-making power

The most obvious and traditional understanding of power is that it is a relationship in which one person or party makes another do something they would not otherwise do (Dahl 1957). There is overt conflict over some desired outcome, and both parties understand the decision-making process. Governments, policy-makers, managers and other 'authorities' regularly exercise power over others in this way. In democratic societies, such power may be seen as legitimate, because it stems from a decision-making process whose terms have been accepted by all involved. In this view, there is no necessary or inevitable exclusion of anyone from exercising such power if they are able to mobilise the relevant resources at the appropriate time. This is a pluralist view, in which power results from an open (and orderly) struggle between competing interests.

The second dimension: indirect power

However, it is often the case that power is not exercised so transparently by one individual or group over another. It can also be done in more subtle ways, by controlling money, rewards, sanctions, the flow of information and so on. Those who hold power can manipulate the system in various ways to their advantage, such as by determining what appears on decision-making agendas and what does not, or by setting terms of engagement or the way in which an issue is debated. This may operate in a top-down fashion, so that minority groups struggle to be heard. In some circumstances it can also be a way for countervailing power to be exercised by less powerful people, who might be able to withhold information or their participation in consultation processes. This so-called 'power of the incumbent' can be seen at play in debates about sustainability and a low-carbon economy, for instance. Well-established businesses are able to find relatively easy access both to policy-makers who can structure new policies and to markets in ways that benefit them, and to establish barriers to entry for new competitors in emerging markets.

The third dimension: radical power

Lukes, together with those of the critical theory tradition (Alvesson and Deetz 2005), see both the above views of power as limited, and overly reliant on the existence of identifiable conflicts of interest as an indicator that power is being exercised. More importantly, they suggest, power-holders are able to prevent such conflict from ever arising, through influencing and structuring what citizens want, what they are aware of and what they see as their alternatives. In some circumstances, the powerful are able to influence consciousness itself, so that people are unable accurately to determine their own interests. Those in positions of power are able to 'manage meaning' (Pettigrew 1979), using symbols, rituals and stories, to create a perceived legitimacy for their actions. A critical approach asks: How is consent and consensus being created and maintained, and in whose interests? Would people choose political or social arrangements that disadvantage them *if* they understood the full implications and were able to envisage alternatives? How is it that much social change seems only to change things at a surface level, while deep inequalities, based on wealth, race, gender, class and so on, persist?

The fourth dimension: the power of the system

But not all forms of power are actively mobilised by dominant groups over others. There are also ways in which systems operate more to the advantage of some people than of others, through the very act of our participation in them. In this view, power is best seen as a capacity that is distributed throughout a social system, in fluid, subtle and complex ways which are not necessarily predictable or deterministic. Foucault (1977, 1980) analyses the ways industrialised societies are pervaded by what he calls 'disciplinary power', overlapping processes exercised unintentionally by social actors, which maintain a certain 'normal' life.

Underpinning such regimes are *discourses*, patterned ways of speaking and acting which determine not just what gets decided, nor what it is safe or important to discuss, but what *can* be discussed without being deemed mad, incomprehensible, or lacking in common sense. This sort of power is not imposed from above, but operates through a self-policing process: Foucault maintains that it is internalised, and becomes part of our most basic understanding of who we are. When we see climate change protestors, for instance, as unrealistic, over-the-top, irrational, we are exercising this sort of normalising power and reinforcing a shared 'regime of truth'. However, Foucault also suggests that such power-systems are dynamic, held together in a pattern of small interrelating actions consisting of compliance, resistance and struggle, and hence are open to change. This way of thinking directs attention to ways in which the everyday, taken-for-granted nature of a particular socio-technical regime is embedded in, and sustained by, the day-to-day practices, habits, assumptions and judgements of individuals in the course of their lives, in relationship with technical infrastructure, social institutions and nature. In this way, power is tightly interwoven in definitions of valid knowledge, including the dominance of rational, propositional ways of knowing discussed in the section on 'Relational practice', below.

These concepts were ones we explored in various places during the course, more explicitly during the second year than the first. We encouraged participants to notice inequalities of power, even (or especially) in apparently 'non-political' arenas. For example, we began to critique the discourses that are expressed in different definitions of sustainability (Dryzek 2005) and to encourage participants to notice how they were used by visiting speakers at different times. Likewise, we drew attention to the relationships of inequality that are expressed in the current configuration of the global marketplace, and encouraged a consideration of what a broader understanding of economic and social benefit might entail.

We tried to help participants take a *reflexive* view of power—seeing themselves as inextricably part of the power systems they noticed—and to make visible our own struggles with these issues as part of our day-to-day practice. We hoped they would be able to see the connections between the extended epistemologies with which we were working on the MSc and the challenge these offered to the current 'regime of truth'. Believing that sustainability challenges cannot be addressed from rational intelligence alone (see Chapter 2 and the discussion of worldviews on pages 39ff.), we invited people into working with multiple ways of knowing. This raises discomfort and disturbance, because we were violating a boundary about accepted ways of knowing. In moving into this contested area, participants found themselves struggling with mainstream judgements and with expected opinions of colleagues, friends and family. We saw these as political as well as personal issues. It is possible to see this disturbance in the stories in this volume. We believe unsettling patterns of expectation to be in the service of participants' learning, and the skills that are developed in working concurrently with multiple ways of knowing to be those that are needed for a more just, sane and sustainable society. But we readily acknowledge that this is demanding work to undertake, as course participants develop its crafts. This is connected to questions about relational practice, which is discussed on page 66ff.

We were also aware that we were an active part of a higher education system that placed us as judges of participants' academic worth, however strongly we reframed this as a process in which they could succeed by taking their own authority over the assessment criteria, with ourselves as mentors and guides to help them. There were occasions when we felt we were acting from a position of liberating power as collaborators with the participants, while participants felt themselves to be on the end of unilateral, disciplinary power (Torbert 1991) as students relating to tutors.

As the accounts that follow show, some graduates are working in overtly 'political' arenas, where conflicts of interest and the suppression of the less powerful by the more powerful—Lukes's third dimension—is evident. Roland Widmer, for instance, describes his work with an environmental NGO to try to counter the power of multinational companies working with governments to build 'mega' dams in the Amazon. Lalith Gunaratne and Mihirini De Zoysa are working with multi-ethnic groups in Sri Lanka in the wake of the country's brutal civil war between the Sinhala majority and Thamil minority. Nick Pyatt is working with small farmers in their negotiations with commercial operators over the establishment of a forest products business in Orissa, India. Kené Umeasiegbu sought to establish a relationship with cocoa-growers in Kenya for the Cadbury Cocoa Partnership. Jo Confino is involved with an innovative long-term development project with a village in rural Uganda. In all of these examples, the accounts show an awareness of dynamics which make it difficult for those who are less powerful to make their points of view heard, and an attention to how large-scale inequalities are played out at the micro level. As Jo (a professional journalist) says, 'the voices of the poor and oppressed are rarely heard directly, and are far more likely to be mediated by professionals, whether from . . . development or journalism'. The stories show how their authors are working to try to increase the capacities of those with less voice to express their views of the world, and struggling with the challenges of that as a practice.

But an appreciation of subtle, systemic power—the fourth dimension—is also evident in the stories in this volume. Helen Goulden, for instance, shows a Foucault-like focus on small acts of resistance to her organisation's denial of its connection to issues of sustainability, always looking for a 'chink or an opportunity to drop something into a conversation'. David Bent is deliberately working with questions of discourse and uses his role with a prominent UK NGO to connect ideas of business strategy and sustainability in business-friendly language. Chris Preist describes an approach to catalyse 'a "subculture" of strategic proactivity' for sustainability within the company he was working for, by creating and joining up small pockets of innovative thinkers. Alison Kennedy, working in publishing, develops an industry-wide group to address sourcing issues through operating largely 'below the parapet'. Mark Gater initiates conversations that deliberately violate implicit rules about what can be talked about in his financial services company. These relatively small acts are expressions of those people's views of themselves as participants in large systems of power which are, in principle, open to influence.

■ Tempered radicals

We introduced the notion of 'tempered radicalism', depicting the inside-outsider promoting change (Meyerson and Scully 1995; Meyerson 2001), quite early in the MSc programme. We find it articulates many of the aspirations and challenges experienced by course participants, and also by ourselves as critical management educators. We very much appreciate the contribution Debra Meyerson and Maureen Scully have made in articulating a concept that so many people recognise. They define tempered radicals as:

> individuals who identify with and are committed to their organisations, and are also committed to a cause, community, or ideology that is fundamentally different from, and possibly at odds with the dominant culture of their organisations. The ambivalent stance of these individuals creates a number of special challenges and opportunities (Meyerson and Scully 1995: 586).

Meyerson and Scully point out that such people are 'radicals' because they challenge the status quo both in their sense of their own identity and through their intentional acts; and at the same time they are 'tempered' in multiple ways.

> These people are tempered in the sense that they seek moderation . . . In the language of physics, they are tempered in that they have become tougher by being alternately heated up and cooled down. They are also tempered because they have a temper: they are angered by the incongruities between their own values and beliefs about social justice and the values and beliefs they see enacted in their organisations (Meyerson and Scully 1995: 586).

Meyerson and Scully argue that people must accept this ambivalence, recognising its advantages. They distinguish it from compromise: 'individuals can remain ambivalent and clear about their attachments and identities' and 'because both parts of a duality are represented, ambivalent responses can be more responsive to equivocal situations than compromise' (1995: 588). At the same time, living with ambivalence is potentially stressful. Tempered radicals can be experienced by others as hypocritical, as they seem to affirm apparently contradictory beliefs and actions, and are thus open to criticism from both (or multiple) sides in any debate. They therefore have to manage the impressions they create for different audiences. This involves significant sensitivity to language. They can experience isolation and pressures to be co-opted, especially by organisational perspectives, as they wish to maintain their position and key relationships to allow them to act for change. There are therefore emotional challenges in taking this approach.

Living this dual existence, the tempered radical faces choices about how to promote change in the direction of ideals such as sustainability, social justice and equality. Meyerson and Scully suggest this can be pursued through 'small wins' and local, spontaneous, authentic action: 'tempered radicals create change in two ways: through incremental, semi-strategic reforms and through spontaneous, sometimes unremarkable, expressions of authenticity' (Meyerson and Scully 1995: 594).

Many of the participants on the MSc programme find themselves relatively isolated in their organisations and communities, believing that radical and far-reaching changes in human behaviour are required if we are to reach a just and sustainable society. The idea of 'small wins' is attractive. Small wins both 'reduce large problems to a manageable size' and also can be experiments that are 'system diagnostic' in some way, and 'uncover resources, information, allies, sources of resistance and additional opportunities for change' (Meyerson and Scully 1995: 589). This approach also involves judging timing and which 'battles to pick'. These characteristics fit well within the attitude of inquiry that is at the foundation of action research, in which the process of inquiry and change is seen as unfolding over time through cycles of experimental action, reflection and learning.

The continual juggling act of aspiring to be a tempered radical involves much craft and effort. It requires a clear sense of purpose, clarity about choices, behavioural skill and flexibility, awareness of the opportunities in the system one is trying to influence as well as of the response of others to one's actions. People seek to stay on the edge between co-option and rejection, constantly making judgements about what is 'too far' or 'not far enough'. This can be a struggle, living with continual uncertainty. Or, perhaps and, it can be experienced as a form of serious play, in which the person works with the shifting politics, possibilities and unfolding systemic patternings, experimenting as they go. The work of building and maintaining a network of relationships is vitally important in this approach as we discuss later in this chapter. But the tempered radical is likely to find few organisational colleagues with whom they can share their full story of aspirations and choices of action. The MSc course space provided colleagues who would understand the inside-outsider's challenges and their dilemmas, with some shared language. Many people sought to maintain such relationships for mutual understanding, coaching and support once they completed the degree. The virtual RBP network continues to fulfil some of these functions.

Of course, there are also traps in the tempered radical position. Because it appears to encompass opposites in an exciting synthesis, it is immediately attractive. Few of us want to be deviant outsiders, and most of those on the MSc would think of themselves as espousing, more or less, radical positions (and of course the ethos of the programme and course community will encourage this). An important question to hold, then, is whether the position and the change we influence are truly radical, or it is a self-description that makes us feel more comfortable about privilege. Is being well tempered an appropriate aim given the challenges we face, or might more outspoken approaches, which could be termed 'hysterical', 'enraged' and strident (Calás and Smircich 2004), be more fitting?

As we discussed these issues on the programme, people debated choices, coming to their own individual resolutions of approach, for that time. Their questions included: whether to be insider, outsider, or inside-outsider; how to be a gentle rather than a battling (and embattled) warrior; in what conditions does disturbing systemic patterns open up possibilities for change and when is it more likely to prompt resistance; and how tempered to be. Throughout the course, we discussed the choices people were making in seeking to pursue a responsible career (Tams and Marshall 2011).

While there were a myriad of opportunities, the language of tempered radicalism offered many course participants an important resource to surface and discuss issues and choices, from micro-actions to major career choices, which they had previously experienced more tacitly. It is appropriate therefore that the notion appears overtly in many stories and covertly in more.

Christel Scholten gives a clear expression of the tempered radical position when she writes:

> An idea I was introduced to during the MSc that I strongly identified with and which supported me was that of tempered radicalism. I knew that my values were different from the dominant culture of business in general and I also knew that, in order to succeed in influencing change towards sustainability, I would need to play by the rules of the game.

Alison Kennedy illustrates the practice of the tempered radical stance. She uses her formal position but works 'below the parapet' to further her action in relation to environmental concerns. She is not acting against the organisation's espoused concerns, but rather is putting energy into developing a more radical position than she suspects would initially be supported. As can be seen, her actions are in the organisation's longer-term strategic interests. Helena Kettleborough's story has similarities. She adopts an action research-based approach to help her organisation achieve its demanding targets. And she believes that propagating action research is in the local authority's long-term interests, contributing to its resources to learn and act in challenging times. She thus pursues this capacity development as an activity strand threaded through her work, flexibly aligning it with other developments and languages to achieve congruence, acceptance and adoption. Chris Preist links the tempered radical idea with Dunphy's framework describing stages of organisational readiness to engage in sustainability issues (Dunphy *et al.* 2007) to articulate clearly for himself where and how he might increase his influence. He speaks the language of the organisation, and builds 'business cases' for a more deeply sustainable position for the company. Notably (see below), he works to build networks of like-minded employees in order to increase influence.

But the tempered radical position is not without emotional tension. Charles Ainger writes about 'Walking the Tightrope', a balancing act between remaining credible in his organisation while taking 'as-radical-as-possible' actions for change, and feeling that the rate of progress is all too slow. And for James Barlow, the tempered radical position sometimes provides 'moments of intense joy', when he feels he and his colleagues 'really are having an . . . effect on one of the world's most powerful institutions', and on the other hand, 'intense . . . anger and frustration when we are not!' Roland Widmer writes of experiencing a strong sense of urgency while avoiding panic and despair. As Helen Sieroda points out, 'questions are uncomfortable, and "right" answers aren't obvious'.

The tempered radical position is one example of a more general question: where do I stand in my work in the world? Thus David Bent and Roland Widmer, for example, chose to work within NGOs, believing that these are organisations that give them the most freedom to influence a wider discourse. Paul Dickinson chose to set up a new venture, the Carbon Disclosure Project, because he saw no other institution addressing the issue of carbon emissions through the financial markets. Kené Umeasiegbu explores the tension between protesting at injustice and engaging within organisations to create change, seeing that, while protesting requires resolve and courage in the face of opposition, so too does engagement: 'Engagement also demands resolve and courage, but this must be combined with collaboration, diligence, focus and optimistic resourcefulness—all sustained over the long term. This makes engagement quite an arduous tactic.'

Mark Gater and his colleagues expand the idea of tempered radical beyond the individual. Inquiring with directors of a UK-based retail financial institution as to what 'sustainable banking' might look like: 'there was a view that we could perhaps be a tempered radical business, supportive of the system in general, but wanting to change some damaging elements of that system from within'. In the end, he wonders if the two worlds can ever meet.

However, for some, the tempered position becomes untenable. Paula Downey illustrates this well in seeing what she describes as the 'madness' as:

> a nation casually trampled its deeper values, proclaimed economic progress an unambiguously good thing, squashed dissent, jeered at those who questioned what we might be losing, and dismissed as a sideshow the social and ecological consequences of turning life into cash.

She chooses to write and speak about the challenges, drawing on a systemic perspective and finding ways to work independently of mainstream clients to tell the truth as she saw it, finding her own voice and 'walking naked into the land of uncertainty'. She shows that the strategy of the '*untempered* radical', while challenging in its own way, can also be a promising path to take.

■ Action inquiry and the leadership development framework

Two interconnected frameworks of ideas and practices we introduced to MSc participants to help facilitate reflective practice were action inquiry and the associated leadership development framework (LDF) developed by our friend and colleague Bill Torbert, with his associates Dal Fischer and David Rooke. Key preoccupations in Bill's work are how we can raise awareness moment-to-moment of the effectiveness, validity and legitimacy of our own behaviour, and thus explore how to act in ways that encourage others to join in mutual inquiry. This set of ideas and practices is called **action inquiry** (Torbert 1991, 2004), and it is thus a form of action research (see pages 27-38) which is grounded in the first-person and moves into second- and third-person engagements (Chandler and Torbert 2003).

Action inquiry starts from the premise that, to be effective, any acting system, whether an individual, a community, an organisation, or indeed a whole society, must seek a quality of attention that explores the congruence between its purposes, its strategies, its actions and outcomes in the world.

> The vision of action inquiry is an attention that spans and integrates the four territories of human experience. This attention is what sees, embraces, and corrects incongruities between mission, strategy, operations and outcomes. It is the source of the 'true natural sanity of awareness of the whole' (Torbert 1991: 219).

In order to do this, people need to generate valid information in these four 'territories' of experience relating to purpose or frame; thinking and feeling; behaviour and practice; and outcomes in the external world. (These four territories can be described in different ways: for example, at an organisational level as mission/strategy/operations/results; at an individual level as awareness/thinking and feeling/acting/perceiving [Torbert 2004: 19].)

The different ways in which people respond to this challenge are expressed in Bill's modelling in a series of increasingly subtle 'action-logics', frameworks of thinking and acting, which articulate human development through childhood and into adulthood. This draws on the extensive work in the field of adult development, notably the work of Loevinger (1976) and Cook-Greuter (1990). The first four action-logics are termed conventional, in that their development is supported by normal education and socialisation and thus can be commonly seen in the developmental pathways of most individuals. The **Opportunist** is focused, often quite ruthlessly, on personal outcomes; the **Diplomat** on adherence to conventionally acceptable behaviour patterns; the **Expert** on the mastery of expertise in a particular skill and discipline. These three come together in the **Achiever**'s concern with effective delivery of success in the system as a whole, an action-logic that therefore integrates concern for thinking, action and outcomes. Most managers in Western organisations can be characterised as Experts or Achievers.

Thus far, the LDF might be seen as another way of articulating different patterns of leadership. However, the later action-logics that follow the Achiever are described as 'post-conventional': they are both relatively rare in our society and, it is argued, increasingly called for to address contemporary challenges. For while Achievers can be highly effective leaders, with a singularity of purpose, focus and drive, they are blind to their own shadow and unable to see the contingency of the frames or purposes within which they operate, unable to reflect on how their worldview influences how they see situations. While excellent in single-loop learning and with some capacity in double-loop learning, Achievers are unable to respond effectively to situations in which radical change of purpose and framing is called for.

As we have explained in Chapter 2, we were clear that attempts to respond to the challenges of justice and sustainability through 'business as usual' would be inadequate. We saw that most management educational programmes operate within taken-for-granted assumptions that we wanted our participants to question. Thus we were interested in ways of encouraging the development of 'post-conventional' action-logics in which the appropriateness of different purposes becomes part of the field of inquiry.

The post-conventional action-logics are subtle and more difficult to describe than the four conventional ones, and the reader is referred to the literature for a fuller understanding.[3] The **Individualist** begins to question the unexamined assumptions of the Achiever, to question not only what he or she believes in, but how one comes to believe that. It is a self-centred stage of openness and at times one of confusion, as hidden social and cultural biases become evident and all perspectives seem relative. Emerging from this turmoil and confusion, the **Strategist** is able to create a new place to stand that actively works the contingencies of framing. Aware that what one sees depends on one's worldview, the Strategist places a high value on the uniqueness and particularity of each situation, embraces paradox and contradiction, and finds a way to operate within rival frames and perspectives. The Strategist encourages mutuality because she or he realises that each perspective shows the situation in a different light that contributes to an understanding of the whole. So for the Strategist, leadership is expressed in an ongoing inquiry, both inner and outer, into the congruence and dissonance of purpose, strategy, action and outcome in each situation they are part of.

Rooke and Torbert (Rooke 1997; Rooke and Torbert 1999) have argued that the level of personal development of the CEO of an organisation can have a critical impact on organisational change efforts. Drawing on this, we would consider that those participants on the MSc who move towards post-conventional action logics over the two years of the programme (and many appear to do so) are more likely to contribute to societal change towards justice and sustainability.

3 See escholarship.bc.edu/william_torbert, accessed 1 January 2011.

Beyond the Strategist, who can still be (just) seen and understood within conventional perspectives on leadership, at the **Alchemist** stage people are committed to transforming themselves and others, and to changing the society and institutions in which they participate. They seek to do this through encouraging and participating in ongoing processes of inquiry, creating events that seek to radically reframe situations in the service of deeper learning, concerned more for the learning and creativity that may emerge than for the achievement of specific outcomes. We may get glimpses in the Alchemist of a transformation from 'being in the right *frame of mind* . . . to having a *reframing spirit*' (Torbert 2004: 189, emphasis in original).

Parallel to these individual action-logics, Torbert describes a set of organisational transformations, the relatively conventional stages of **Investment**, **Incorporation**, **Experiment** and the development of **Systematic Productivity** that mirrors the Achiever action-logic. But again, beyond the conventional, he seeks to articulate the qualities of genuine learning organisations based on collaborative inquiry (Torbert 2004: Chapters 8–10).

The interrelated frameworks in this section assume that action inquiry can be more fully achieved from a post-conventional action logic in the LDF and in the later stage of organisation development characterised as collaborative inquiry, as only then can purposes and framing be brought into active, in the moment, question in the course of action.

A foundational practice for exploring the potential connections of mind-set, assumptions and action is to record problematic and challenging situations in a two-column format, writing what was spoken in the left-hand column, and one's own internal dialogue on the right. This draws attention to the way internal dialogue provides clues to framings of the situation that are usually overlooked. We also used the 'ladder of inference' on the MSc to help people understand how we all create perspectives based on very little firm evidence, and rarely explicitly inquire into that evidence.

We can look at the two-column conversations in terms of the 'four parts of speech' (see Box 3.1)—frame, advocate, illustrate, inquire—which are loosely analogous to the four territories of experience mentioned above. Using this framework helps people see how often they articulate a view from their perspective, but are poor at expressing the frame from which they are speaking, and at inquiring into the views of others. And we used the 'learning pathways grid' as a systematic means of exploring the relationship between the four territories, to help people gain insight into the incongruities of their practice. Finally, we encouraged experimentation both in imagination, through role-play, and in real time, to encourage participants to try new behaviours, and to bring processes of inquiry to everyday life. (These learning processes are well described in Rudolph *et al.* 2001 and Taylor *et al.* 2008.)

For some, these processes of inquiry became quite central to their work on the programme. They used the theory and tools in an ongoing process of self-reflection. Although we do not formally measure changes in action-logic, we did see some significant changes. During the MSc, a number of people identified their adherence to a set of skills and abilities which defined their identity—they realised the extent

Box 3.1 **The four parts of speech**

Torbert and his colleagues suggest that reflective practice experimenting with four key 'parts of speech' can facilitate adult development. They distinguish between:

- **Framing.** Explicitly stating purposes, testing assumptions, reframing
- **Advocating.** Explicitly asserting an opinion, perception, feeling or proposal for action
- **Illustrating.** Giving details which ground and give direction to advocacy
- **Inquiring.** Questioning others, opening any of the above to question, and holding possible actions and interpretations lightly

These are not intended as a linear, prescribed, sequence, but can happen in any order, and much speech has qualities of more than one category. The claim is that advocating and illustrating are predominant forms of speech, but that this leaves much unsaid and untested, and that engaging in more framing and inquiry can enhance the quality of individual and collective action and mutual collaboration.

MSc participants have found the four parts of speech framework helpful. Attempting to be more explicit about framing and working through inquiry rather than assertion, can open more dialogue and mutual learning. Reference to the four parts of speech is found in several people's stories.

to which they were committed to an Expert action-logic—and learned to develop a more encompassing attention. Some others joined the programme firmly within an Achiever action-logic, highly successful while at the same time beginning to see the limitations of this approach in the context of environmental challenges. They often welcomed the articulation of something they were intuitively seeking. Many people through the course of the programme moved towards or into an Individualist action-logic: we saw them recognising the contingency of their earlier commitments, becoming less attached to conventional behaviours, more experimental, more committed to their own learning. However, the Individualist is in many ways a transition stage, and we find it more difficult to help participants move more fully and confidently into the post-conventional action-logics, although we have experimented with different ways of attempting to support this. We suspect that few were acting firmly from a Strategist action-logic by the time they left the programme, although of course the leadership development framework seeks to articulate a lifelong learning process.

As staff, we find using this framework challenging: it puts us on the spot, so to speak. Are we capable of transcending the paradoxes of our role? Are we able, as individuals and as a team, to demonstrate a capacity to inquire across the four territories? Are we able to transform the inevitable conflicts of leading a challenging programme into opportunities for learning and inquiry? Can we exercise transforming power? Can we demonstrate the paradoxical craft of the Alchemist without being simply crafty? Every cohort has given rise to occasions when we are severely tested in this. We are always grateful that we work in staff partnerships, and that we have developed a quality of colleagueship in which we are able to be both 'friends willing to act as enemies' as Torbert puts it (1976: 169), but also 'friends willing to act as friends', as Judi and Peter added (Marshall and Reason 1993: 122).

As an illustration of the process of using action inquiry and LDF approaches to develop insight into action, we offer an account of one participant's learning. M had worked in the public sector for many years at the time he joined the course, expecting to make a major career change to join a family business, a successful niche enterprise making bespoke furniture. As he participated in the early workshops of the course, he became enthused about the possibility of influencing this company to develop a more responsible environmental and social profile. He saw significant opportunities to use environmentally sourced wood, less toxic glue and finishes, to save energy by burning waste; and to pay attention to the company's social role as the major employer in the small community where it operated. He discussed his ideas with his learning group, and went off enthusiastically to see what he could do. He returned to the next workshop bruised and crestfallen, with a written account of his experiences. Although he was sure he had reached agreement with senior people in the firm (and family) and although he thought he had been tactful in making suggestions, his suggestions had been met with resistance and some hostility. He felt he failed to have the influence he wanted, and had actually damaged his position in the company.

As part of that workshop we had already planned to invite participants to write and explore two-column accounts of difficult conversations. We invited M to share his with the whole course group, and then to role-play the situation, with other course members taking the parts of his colleagues. In the role-play, the discussion quickly degenerated, with misunderstandings and hostility clearly growing. So we stopped it, and asked M to step outside and watch someone else take his part. As this second role-play unfolded, observing M we could see the realisation of his contribution to tensions becoming clear on his face. Of course, the other organisation members were relatively set in their ways, and of course they were not too happy about a new family member coming into a senior position with little understanding of the business. Of course they were suspicious of new ideas and had little sympathy with environmental matters. But what M also saw was how he was coming from an Expert action-logic, with a new-found enthusiasm for environmental issues and a strong identification with 'solutions', wanting to make his mark on the company. While he thought he had been polite and tactful he had actually taken little care to understand the perspectives of those he sought to influence, or to seek mutual exploration of the issues. Instead he had advocated ideas that his colleagues felt were in no way connected to their needs and concerns. As he commented after watching the role-play, he had impetuously jumped feet first into a delicate situation. We were able to follow the role-play with a discussion involving the whole group about the learning that could be gleaned, showing that the leadership framework was not a template with which to judge yourself, but an opening to an ongoing inquiry into one's ability to develop awareness in the midst of action.

Many accounts in this volume show the transformations in action-logic of participants during and after the programme. For example, David Bent moves from an Expert position, committed to environmental accounting, to a Strategist concern for helping organisations learn how to respond to the challenges of the environmental crisis. Ian Roderick joins the course having achieved successes in an Expert role and moves through a period of some confusion as he seeks a way to make a new contribution, eventually working on the 'edge' as he describes it, responding to opportunities that appear to be in service of a wider purpose. Mark Gater clearly leaves his comfort zone as a systems specialist in his organisation, goes through a period of significant personal turmoil, and emerges with a commitment to encouraging learning processes, knowing that the outcome will never be clear.

■ Relational practice

An exploration of 'relational practice' underpinned much of the work of the MSc: it was a strong offering from us, as an expression of our view of a participatory world, fundamentally based on relationship. What this may mean was explored at many points during the programme and—in keeping with our action research orientation—we saw it as having a conceptual element, but also being about *how* we *do* relationship, something to be practised, worked at and evolved.

The thinking behind the course draws on the ideas of social constructionism (Shotter 1993; Gergen 1999), that the understanding we have of the world we inhabit is a product of the relationship we have with it and with each other. From this perspective, we live in the midst of a continuous process of co-creation, a moment-to-moment making of our reality, rooted in a relational way of knowing. We think about relational practice in terms of our connections with each other as humans—a fundamental aspect of the sort of leadership for sustainability this course explored—and also as an expression of our connection with the more-than-human world (Abram 1996). Beginning to practice a non-instrumental relationship with our world is a challenging task of trying to work against a current 'regime of truth'; how to do this is a lifelong quest, in which the course induced only the next, necessarily faltering, steps.

To engage in the course learning community, participants on the MSc had to develop relationships with their fellow participants, and we encouraged them to do this reflectively and open to diversity as well as aligning with similar others. This invited them into experimentation from the outset. How people work together and make connections with each other, the capacity to create and sustain relationships, often crossing professional and/or organisational boundaries, seem to be key factors in enabling organisational change and development to take place. This is more subtle than notions of 'good relations' or 'effective leadership'. It is not about people being nice to each other, but about having to do a particular kind of *work*, which Joyce Fletcher (1998) calls 'relational practice'—the act of staying in relationship with others whether there is agreement with them or not. It includes things such as sharing ownership of a task, communicating openly and directly, finding activities that are mutually rewarding and energising, and finding ways to learn deeply together. But it also includes the imaginative leap of finding some way to connect with those who may be strongly different from, or even against, you. It expresses itself in working with diverse stakeholders, mobilising teams, having inclusive dialogues, helping people commit to take action, negotiating roles and priorities, and aligning efforts. It involves finding ways to stay in the game and be a participant even when the dominant view of the nature of that game is very different from your own.

One of the most curious aspects of this demanding relationship-oriented work is the extent to which it takes place *without people noticing or valuing it*. Fletcher

(1998, 1999) points out that relational work is present in all effective enterprise, that it is important for task accomplishment, and yet it 'gets disappeared'—there is a more or less active process through which it becomes hidden and unacknowledged, and turned from a type of work into just 'being nice' or 'getting on well' with someone. The effect of this is to downgrade it from an intentional interactional strategy to a personal style.

But this is about politics, not personality. Fletcher suggests this 'disappearing dynamic' takes place because of the taken-for-granted assumption that work is conducted in a 'public' arena which has become quite separated from the 'private' world of home and family. This is a socially constructed and historically recent division, which assigns some facets of human life to the public/work sphere, and some to the private/home sphere. In the public world, there is a dominant discourse of rationality: it is the place where work is conducted, decisions are made, politics happens. Thinking is predominantly abstract, instrumental and individual. The private/home world is the place where communion and community are dominant, emotions are acceptable, warmth and caring are encouraged. Current dominant discourse emphasises the public world: it carries more status, and is seen as more important as a source of knowledge and action, than the private.

Fletcher draws attention to the gendered nature of this division: men are identified with the 'public' world, and women with the 'private', so that public space attributes have become conflated with stereotyped images of masculinity, and private space ones with stereotypes of femininity, in ways that constrain the behaviour of both men and women. The rational discourse that dominates the work sphere, she says, is not the only way of conceiving of learning, development and growth/improvement. Drawing on the work of psychologist Jean Baker Miller, she sketches an alternative, the idea of growth-in-connection, based on collectivity and interdependence, and offering an expanded model of how work can be effectively carried out.

As Fletcher points out, inviting people to develop relational competence crosses and disturbs these boundaries, engages in the hidden politics.

The ability to develop relational capacity and competence requires certain strengths: empathy, openness to vulnerability, the capacity to experience and express emotion, the ability to participate in another person's development, the expectation that relational interactions will be opportunities for learning and development for all parties involved. But to recognise and name such attributes means bringing the language and meaning of the private/home sphere into the workplace. To most people in contemporary Western societies this seems like a violation, an inappropriate intrusion of 'private' emotions and activities into a professional setting. The result is that this work is rendered invisible, and reconstructed as something other than work and borrowed from the private sphere, such as a personal characteristic of being friendly or helpful. Fletcher's study of female engineers found that people engaging in relational work simply did not have strong, valued language to name what they were doing, even though it played a significant part in the achievement of tasks in the workplace.

Fletcher's critique of the disappearing of relational work suggests that knowledge, language and power are tightly interconnected, so that the separation of 'public' and 'private' sphere attributes, with its gender associations, becomes taken for granted, rooted in common sense, and largely invisible as an active social process. This is an example of the sort of normalisation identified by Foucault (see page 53).

Relational practice, then, is a practical expression of several of the key ideas discussed in the course: systemic thinking, the radical interconnectivity of all the inhabitants of the Earth (Thomas Berry's 'community of subjects'; see page 42), and the emergence of a new, post-heroic form of leadership (Sinclair 1998 and see Chapter 1). It is a recognisable thread in the participants' accounts that follow. Jen Morgan, for instance, discusses the efforts she and her team at WWF put into 'building strong and healthy relationships' as they established their Finance Innovation Lab, incorporating dialogic processes and opportunities for reflection to punctuate members' experience with a different quality of being with each other. Helen Sieroda describes her decision to deliberately pay attention to the relational acts that give meaning to her life, actively countering the disappearance of the 'private', small, local world into the 'public'. Nick Pyatt works at staying in relationship with groups who are conventionally marginalised in negotiations between forest product businesses and farmers in Orissa, India, and in so doing, helps them express their perspective and create outcomes that are better for them.

■ Questions of gender: connecting personal and political

As editors, we have discussed whether, or in what way, we wanted to highlight a gender strand among the themes of this book. It would be easy not to do so—it is often not an overt focus of participants' attention—and at the same time there are many ways in which questions of gender have raised themselves during the course, and it seems appropriate to honour these here.

First, there is the question of who showed up. There has long been concern about the under-representation of women in higher-level business education: a *Business Week* survey of the top 30 business schools worldwide in 2006, for instance, showed women constituting only 30% of MBA admissions (*Business Week* 2006). But our participant profile has been much more evenly balanced, with women even outnumbering men in some year groups. So, we were appealing, somehow, to women applicants—perhaps because the course addressed so-called 'soft' issues, looking at the connections between society and business rather than just business alone: a qualitative rather than a quantitative approach. One of the effects of this participant profile was that women's lives, priorities and concerns were a vibrant and constant part of the experience of year groups (and in one cohort five babies were born to women participants over the two years of the course). Belenky *et al.* (1986) and Goldberger *et al.* (1996) were popular sources for many as they began to explore the idea of 'women's ways of knowing'.

But there was a second aspect of 'who showed up' which was more problematic: we consistently found it difficult to find relevant women visiting speakers. Although we searched for authoritative and experienced contributors, our participants repeatedly noticed and commented on the gender imbalance of those who came to present to them. We have explored conundrums about the gendering of leadership in relation to corporate social responsibility elsewhere (Marshall 2007), and the fact that the male domination of formal leadership roles is reproduced in the sustainability and CSR fields just as much as it is in mainstream business (Coleman 2002). Our experience is that the role of prominent 'expert' is one that is still more frequently filled by men, with masculinity conferring certain kinds of authority and there is a disturbing scarcity of women's voices in these sorts of 'figurehead' position.

Then there was a question of whose voices were heard most in a course learning environment that was based on dialogue and participation in both large and small groups. Despite sometimes being in the numerical minority, male participants were frequently more vocal than female participants in large group settings and when visiting speakers were present. This was noticed and discussed in our ongoing workshop reviews, and became something that people took action about. For both women and men, noticing who speaks and who is silent, practising speaking out, or holding their tongue and listening more, became part of their active inquiries.

This is not a simple issue: we recognise the importance of people with credibility in mainstream worlds—who happen to be mainly men—acting as 'tempered radicals' to transform those worlds (Marshall 2007), and we seek to support and enhance what they are doing. However, we notice that the predominance of men in mainstream power positions means that it is *they* who will then be shaping the future of what sustainability means, how it is practised and what it addresses as priorities. These are vitally important issues. We believe this plays some part in the way sustainability is often conceptualised as a technical and bounded problem, open to expert-led fixes which do not address deeper social and political issues.

Of course, this MSc is part of a context which is 'gendered'—just as it is 'raced' and 'classed'—and we sought to connect the inner and outer worlds, the systemic and the personal, so as to openly draw connections between the dynamics within our course and the global dynamics of the unsustainable world with limited social justice and equality of which we are a part. The concentration of political and economic power in the hands of men worldwide is one of the enduring features of human society, with gender inequalities being cited even by mainstream development practitioners as a hindrance to prosperity (World Bank 2001.)

And more subtly than this, as we discussed more fully on pages 41f., there are connections between our current worldview and the systematic suppression of many aspects of humanity that are now labelled 'feminine': the relational, the emotional, the intuitive, even the spiritual. Eco-feminists (Ortner 1974; Griffin 1984; Merchant 1995) have pointed to modernism's twin subjugation of nature and women, explicitly seeking to connect the impulse to seize and exploit planetary resources with the impulse to subjugate the female and its attendant emotional hinterland (Fletcher 1998, 1999). These are raw themes, sometimes seeming distant from all of our, frankly, privileged lives, and usually wholly disconnected from the disciplines included within 'business studies'. But they are a deeply embedded feature of the problems we are seeking to address when we imagine what it is to live in a just and sustainable way. The absence of debate about these kinds of question within mainstream business education is, we believe, one of the ways in which such inequality is normalised, seeming to be 'nothing to do with' the impact of business operations in the world. And so we supported and welcomed discussion of such issues on the MSc.

The implications of gender for personal identity also showed themselves on the course. As participants struggled with questions about their intentions and values, they found themselves inquiring into some of their gender-bound role assumptions. Some explored issues of difference, including masculinities, with fervour and insight in their learning projects, coming to new realisations of who they were, considering anew social patterns of gendering, and what powers and freedoms they had to operate. They took the opportunity to ask questions of themselves as parents, family and community members, and also as professionals and people with ambition and organisational status. Embracing the multiple ways of knowing they were introduced to on the programme, for example, is politically gendered work—it invites people to engage with relational activity, to value participation, while recognising that the social meaning and personal experience and impact of such work is often different for men and for women.

But if we look for how questions of gender are treated in the participants' stories, we find something implicit rather than explicit. We do not seem to see leadership initiatives rejected because people are women, or men. We cannot readily identify different styles with gender associations. Overall, we have a sense that the MSc invites people to value equally qualities and practices that have previously been labelled 'masculine' and 'feminine'. Living this integration is more commonly espoused for women and men these days (Sinclair 1998), and we see many people through the MSc integrating these qualities.

The stories show them operating in gender-inclusive ways, showing care and concern for others as well as being initiative-takers, adopting these approaches flexibly, not bounded by gender stereotypes in their approaches or behaviour. And we think that acting for change for a sustainable and socially just world may upset the conventional 'credentials' of authority conferred by modernist masculinity, making the change agent somewhat threatening, as Kanter's (1977) early work on the dynamics of tokenism showed. Those in the 'majority' group are under pressure not to align with alternative voices. These are dimensions of the challenge we explore here partly through the image of the tempered radical, aware that they are elements in the demanding, multi-dimensional balancing act lived by many engaged in this work.

■ Freefall writing as inquiry

One of the techniques we have introduced on the course is that of writing as a form of inquiry, particularly 'freefall' writing, in which the writer is encouraged to allow the writing process to take its own emergent form, silencing the critical mind that is forever stopping words finding their way onto paper. We try to help participants move from an approach of first getting their thoughts in order and then writing about them, to using the act of writing itself as way to make sense and discover what they think and feel. As Richardson and St Pierre say, 'writing *is* thinking, writing *is* analysis, writing *is* indeed a seductive and tangled method of discovery' (2005: 962).

We have drawn on the approach to freefall writing of Barbara Turner-Vesselago (1995) who calls it 'writing without a parachute'. Goldberg (1986) offers similar guidance. The basics of Freefall are: keep the hand moving; don't cross out or worry about spelling, punctuation, grammar; don't think—write; show, don't tell—give the sensuous detail, locate yourself in time and place; and go where the energy is, which may be 'fear-ward'. Both authors advocate timed writing exercises as a way to develop a writing voice, and we have found these useful to help overcome the sense that most of us have when we write that we should not, cannot, just write for ourselves, in an uncensored way; the inner voice that says 'I can't say that!' or 'They wouldn't like that back in XYZ organisation!' and maybe 'What would my parents say?!'

We might introduce practices of freefall initially by experimenting with five-minute exercises using simple themes as prompts—borrowing from Turner-Vesselago we often start with 'a sound heard in childhood'—to help people experience the direct potential of the practice and find their voice. We would then suggest other prompts more related to issues the group were exploring at the time—'an image of sustainability for me', perhaps—and increase the time. Even a 15-minute exercise would give scope for exploration. Once people had written we would invite them to read their freefall out, allowing anyone who wanted to to 'pass'. This typically showed the richness of writing people can reach, even in five minutes. Often there were connecting themes across the group. Writing and reading out in several rounds, saving analysis until later in the process, could provide interesting exploration and learning, for people individually and together.

We also often used short, two- or three-minute timed writing pauses as a way to help people process and capture their thoughts and reactions to speaker sessions, discussions or simulations, and in so doing give some validity to their fleeting responses, which are so easily lost or dismissed. Jon Alexander's story, for example, makes reference to just this sort of practice as a continuing part of his way of inquiring into his experience. This writing-as-inquiry enabled participants to return to the material at a later stage, notice recurrent patterns or questions, and make choices about what to develop further or share with others.

Freefall writing has been particularly important in helping participants move beyond the voice that is censored by the dominance of conventional worldviews and taken-for-granted perspectives.

4

Promoting alternative questioning, policies and practices in mainstream organisations

In the next eight chapters we present the 29 graduates' stories in groups, in terms of where they were located and what approach they were taking to act for change. The groupings are not neatly bounded and there are many connections among them, but they provide a minimal ordering device for the stories as the heart of the book.

At the beginning of each chapter we introduce the stories collected in that group, and identify some of the themes and issues we see running through them. In a closing chapter—Reflections—we then look back at all the stories and consider taking leadership for sustainability from their perspective.

After the graduates' names at the head of their stories, we include their intake year numbers, MSc1 and so on. These were important communities of identification for course participants. And here they give some indication of how long it is since the person completed the MSc, as this may be relevant to their story.

This chapter contains eight stories from people who have taken leadership for sustainability in mainstream organisations, six in the business sector and two in local government.

- **Chris Preist**. Catalysing a strategic approach to sustainability in a major IT company

- **Christel Scholten**. On being a change agent for sustainability

- **Helen Goulden**. Imbuing work with ecological values

- **Helena Kettleborough**. Thinking out of the box: introducing action research into neighbourhood practice in the north-west of England

- **James Barlow**. Choose life

- **Karen Karp**. Leadership for change in USA public food procurement: people, products and policy

- **Mark Gater**. Two worlds?

- **Prishani Satyapal**. Putting my learning into practice

In their accounts we see: what informed their actions, how they mobilised organisational support, how they worked through language and communication, what arguments helped enlist senior managers' involvement, the relational work of seeking to influence change, how they deployed inquiry as strategy and practice, their risk-taking and potential vulnerability, some of the emotional dimensions of taking leadership for sustainability, and the unfolding consequences as some organisations paid more attention to sustainability. Given their commitment to business and mainstream organisations as forces for change, people in this chapter can be seen as adopting tempered radical approaches in various forms, helping their organisations engage proactively with the challenges of sustainability. In some cases they met organisational resistance, inertia and patterns of power, to which they then adjusted. Their accounts show how they coped with these challenges. They also reflect on success, impact and scale. One overt message in most of these stories is that leadership for sustainability cannot be undertaken—or claimed—alone and is a collective notion. Given this, graduates seek to make their contribution.

Addenda to the stories

All of the stories in this book will have moved on by the time we submit the manuscript to the publisher. We have not asked people for updates, as this would be a never-ending process. But we would like to make one additional note to stand for this sense of movement.

One of us met with Karen Karp over a pot of tea recently, as she travelled through the UK. She said that writing and finishing her story was cathartic, and also gave her the insight and courage to give it a different ending. Having checked out the possibilities, she met with a new senior manager who has joined the organisation to which she had consulted, asking if they would like to know more about the project she had been involved with. They did, and were duly impressed. The possibilities of this work staying alive in the organisation are now enhanced, and she completed an additional cycle of inquiry about the project and her role in it.

There are likely to be potential additions of this kind to each of the stories in this book.

Catalysing a strategic approach to sustainability in a major IT company

Chris Preist MSc10, 2006–2008

During the time I was studying on the MSc, I was employed in the central research labs of a major IT corporation. I was driven to apply to the course by a desire to fundamentally question the direction of my professional life and the contributions I was making, with a view to reorienting it towards the sustainability crisis. The course exposed me to a variety of different perspectives and attitudes, and out of this I developed a personal 'position'—a set of values and principles that guided my decisions at that time. First, I adopted the belief that significant reform of capitalism is necessary to meet the challenges we face (Porritt 2007). Minor tweaking of business-as-usual is not sufficient, but radical anti-capitalism does not provide practical answers. Second, I chose to focus my energies on climate change, recognising that the various issues are interconnected and other issues should not be neglected, but seeing that the climate crisis is urgent, and failure here will have a very significant impact on other social and environmental issues. Third, I questioned whether it was better to remain within the company I was at, or adopt a more 'external' position such as consultant or NGO activist. I chose the former, albeit tentatively with a view to exploring that position. Hence, the question I chose to explore was: how was the company engaging with sustainability issues, climate change in particular, and what contribution could I make to deepening this engagement?

I was strongly influenced by two ideas the course exposed me to: first, the notion that the stories we tell ourselves collectively, and the emotional engagement that comes with them, influences strongly the way we respond to information and data. A 'story' often has more power than information alone (Mead 1997). Second, I was interested in the perspective that Dunphy's model of organisational engagement with sustainability (Dunphy *et al.* 2007) could give on my company's current and possible future engagement.

By analysing the company's environmental publicity material, corporate social and environmental responsibility report, policies and processes, and networking extensively among staff engaged in producing and implementing these, it was possible to place the company within Dunphy's model. Based on his analysis, I identified that my company was very strongly engaged at the 'eco-efficiency' level: acting to reduce environmental impact of the company was considered a positive thing, to be engaged with seriously and proactively, and could often be carried out hand in hand with cost reduction measures.

It became apparent that this position was solidly entrenched in the company, with formal structures in place to support it, and also an implicit 'story' that was widespread in the corporate culture which went alongside this. The story could be characterised (in my own words) as follows:

> Our company is a good company, which cares for the environment. Where economically possible, we try to make our activities, products and services cause as little environmental impact as possible. Often this is a 'win–win', where environmental improvements also save money, though of course at times business reality means we must make compromises. We do this by having formal structures in our organisation that encourage energy efficiency of our operations and ensure that environmental considerations are factored in during product design and manufacturing. We are willing to work with others in our sector to 'raise the bar' where collective action is needed. However, our sector is not a 'big' impact sector, so environmental issues such as climate change are not likely to have a big impact on us. As a result, our processes, together with more effective marketing of our message and accomplishments, are enough. Environmental issues do not need to be considered as an aspect of business strategy, or within innovation and research.

A question that arose in my mind was: is this enough, both from a planetary perspective and a self-interested corporate perspective? Dunphy *et al.* (2007) speak of the next level of engagement by a company as being 'strategic proactivity', the embedding of the consideration of sustainability issues into strategy and innovation decisions. It felt clear to me that this was appropriate, particularly as climate change was becoming an increasingly 'hot topic' in the media and government policy was likely in the future. How could I use my (relatively junior) position to help move the company to such a position? How could a relatively powerless individual have some impact on the larger system that is the company? The approach I chose to take was twofold: to develop and spread stories (backed up by evidence) which would encourage a corporate move to strategic proactivity; and to network and build relationships with others who were thinking in the same way.

For example, I developed a 'story', drawing inspiration in part from the work of David and Susan Ballard (Ballard 2005; Ballard 2007). It was:

> Our role in corporate research is partly to understand disruptors and how they affect the business. Historically, these have been technological. However, climate change is going to be as great, if not greater, disruptor. It will change the business landscape, meaning that business models that work now may struggle, and new business models will be possible. The changes it will bring will act as both risks and opportunities to business. If we are thinking about long-term investment in innovation, we must take this into account and consider in what ways the business landscape might change.

Note that this story is expressed in terms that are part of mainstream corporate discourse, but the story it tells is (or at least, was at that time) far more radical than the mainstream position. As with many stories in this volume, this echoes the observations of Meyerson (2001) on the activities of 'tempered radicals'.

I met with the, then, international head of the central research labs and presented my story to him. His response to my language was interesting: because I was able to couch it in terms that were 'acceptable' to the corporate culture, he was welcoming and went on to speak in more personal terms about his concerns and hopes about the issue. I found this response gratifying and touching. Partly as a result of this meeting, I was given funding to spend six months exploring these issues further, and was later able to use this story together with further evidence to build a research team focused around IT and climate change.

Networking was also essential to encourage spread of the strategic proactivity perspective. This is something that doesn't come easily to me, and support from the course in this was deeply valuable, both in terms of understanding the importance of this in encouraging real organisational change, and in the practicalities of how to overcome my introversion and engage. There were small pockets of people elsewhere who thought in similar ways, and we worked together to develop and encourage the spread of this perspective. In particular, we worked together with a senior representative of a major NGO which was in a formal relationship with the company. We also worked on specific example business cases to provide supporting evidence to the story, spread external reports supporting our case, and organised an international workshop bringing thinkers from across the company to share ideas. In this way, a 'subculture' of strategic proactivity was catalysed within the company, and began having an influence on thinking at board levels. This is most notable in the public statements of the head of strategy, who now emphasises the potential of the company's technology to transform society to be more sustainable.

The nature of such work is collective, rather than based on individual heroics, and so I cannot claim unique responsibility for the changes that have taken place—merely that I made some contribution to them. It is also worth questioning how deep the change is: will it result in a change only in marketing, or in the business and innovation strategies of the company? Will it survive the cost-cutting and short-term focus that the recession has driven throughout the corporate world? My personal role did not survive, and I lost my job in a major redundancy programme. However, partly because of the 'networking' approach to change, I can leave knowing that the subculture of strategic proactivity remains and, though it may manifest itself differently from how I had envisaged it, it is still an active meme in the company. I can now turn my attention to exploring the role of being a change agent in a different environment . . .

References

Ballard, D. (2007) 'Mostly Missing the Point: Business responses to climate change', in D. Cromwell and M. Levene (eds.), *Surviving Climate Change: The struggle to avert global catastrophe* (London: Pluto Press).

Ballard, S. (2005) *Warm Hearts and Cool Heads: The leadership potential for climate change champions* (Swindon, UK: Alexander Ballard Associates).

Dunphy, D.C., A.B. Griffiths and S.H. Benn (2007) *Organizational Change for Corporate Sustainability* (London: Routledge, 2nd edn).

Mead, G. (1997) 'A Winter's Tale: Myth, story and organisations', *Self & Society* 24.6: 19-22.

Meyerson, D.E. (2001) *Tempered Radicals: How people use difference to inspire change at work* (Boston, MA: Harvard Business School Press).

Porritt, J. (2007) *Capitalism as if the World Matters* (London: Earthscan, rev. edn).

On being a change agent for sustainability

Christel Scholten MSc6, 2002–2004

I was 28 years old when my journey as a change agent for sustainability began within the private sector. Before this, I worked for several years in a non-profit organisation promoting youth leadership and responsibility on a local and global scale and spent some time in Bangladesh working with microcredit. I had travelled to all continents, was young, single and ready to dedicate myself to contributing to shift the system from within the private sector. I found myself in finance in the head office of ABN AMRO in the Netherlands. I felt this would be an excellent place from which I could influence change for sustainability: the greatest potential for change could come from the financial sector as risk policies set could influence entire industries; there were significant opportunities for investment in, and stimulation of, green business; and society was beginning to question where money was coming from and how it was being invested. At around the same time, I began the MSc, which provided me with an intellectual grounding in sustainability, an expanding network of colleagues working for sustainability and a certain level of credibility from which to act in ABN AMRO.

Ideas that were important for me on this journey that I would like to explore in this contribution include change agency and shifting the system and tempered radicalism. I will also touch on my use of different sources of power and the importance of maintaining identity and preserving self.

I consider myself a change agent for sustainability and feel I have been practising this both within and outside formal organisations for years, from my early 20s to today, as a new mother. When I write about sustainability I mean on three dimensions: environmental, social and economic. In an organisational context, I am referring to implementing policies, practices and processes that contribute to reducing environmental impact, enhancing social well-being and enabling economic viability and inclusion.

The reality I faced when I joined ABN AMRO was challenging; sustainability was not yet on the agenda of the leadership and very few isolated initiatives around social and environmental issues existed. I found myself quite alone with few sparring partners and was quite young without much formal power. Using some of the change agency strategies listed below, I gradually connected with the few others in the organisation trying to influence change towards sustainability to build a support network around me, found mentors committed to supporting the cause and to giving a younger person space to experiment and implement change, and began to put sustainability on the agenda whenever and wherever I could to begin shifting the system. A few examples include: bringing external speakers in to raise awareness about sustainability among the top leadership, through my manager; influencing the content (putting sustainability on the agenda) and processes (arranging chairs in a circle and introducing a 'talking piece') at a managing board meeting; and creating a cross-bank change community which drew together employees from all levels in the organisation to explore ways for work to be more consistent with personal values and to create and implement initiatives around sustainability.

During this period, I primarily used informal sources of power, putting sustainability on the agenda whenever I could, asking challenging questions to peers and senior leaders and convening others through initiatives such as the change community. In the change community gatherings we used technologies such as Open Space, World Café and Circle Conversation to give participants space to explore their questions without the hierarchy and bureaucracy of large traditional organisations. We explored important questions and created initiatives that contributed to the sustainability agenda. As a natural response to the internal interest and pressure, sustainability gained a formal place in the organisation. It grew from a bank with few, isolated initiatives in sustainability to an industry leader, setting a new standard for sustainability and banking, culminating in winning the Financial Times Sustainable Bank of the Year award in 2007.

After two years at the head office, I joined Banco Real, ABN AMRO's then Brazilian operation, where I found a completely different environment. The president was very committed to sustainability and to his vision of creating a 'New Bank for a New Society'; more members of the leadership team were engaged; a sustainability department with sufficient resources was in operation; a number of departments had sustainability professionals; and a number of initiatives such as the ethical fund, supplier engagement, social and environmental risk policies, microcredit operations, social and environmental financial products, eco-efficiency, diversity and sustainability reporting were already showing results. Although I moved into a management role, giving me more formal power and responsibility, I quickly realised that I would still need to employ change agency strategies. While formally I had more influence on strategies, plans, projects and allocation of resources, I still needed to create opportunities to put sustainability on the agenda and find ways to engage people in the journey.

One of my key learnings during this period was around the importance of connecting sustainability to the core business. I also became more aware of the larger system and was better able to identify leverage points that would create a greater impact for sustainability. When we began to work with business teams to create business opportunities related to sustainability, they became more engaged and committed, resulting in innovative ideas and practices for more sustainable financial products and services.

A few examples of advances in sustainability I was involved in include the development and implementation of an overall governance model including the setting up of a sustainability board; the setting up and implementation of a methodology to integrate sustainability into the various departments of the organisation; and the design and delivery of numerous training programmes on sustainability for thousands of employees in different departments. Taking advantage of the momentum that had been created in the organisation and realising that we could make a larger contribution to wider society, we set up the *Real* Space for Sustainability Practices, through which courses are offered to clients and suppliers to support them in integrating sustainability into their businesses. The efforts paid off and in 2008, along with numerous other awards, Banco Real was awarded the Financial Times Sustainable Bank of the Year award.

An idea I was introduced to during the MSc that I strongly identified with and which supported me was that of tempered radicalism. I knew that my values were different from the dominant culture of business in general and I also knew that, in order to succeed in influencing change towards sustainability, I would need to play by the rules of the game. By experimenting, and often by making mistakes, I am learning to identify when to push the system and when to step back, when to engage and when to retreat and when to be tempered and when to be radical.

As a change agent for sustainability and especially within a large organisation, I have found that a constant awareness of your values and identity is needed so that you do not lose yourself in the process. It is so easy to do so in the constant drive by business to grow and create shareholder value. I have found it so important to have personal practices that ground me and take me back to my purpose of contributing to creating a more sustainable world. Some of the practices that have supported me along this journey have been meditation, yoga, spiritual retreats, journalling and experiences in nature. I find it important to take time out to be still and to reflect on whether what I am doing is consistent with or in conflict with my purpose. One experience in particular had a deep impact on me. In 2006, I participated in a Sacred Passage with the shaman, John Milton. I spent six days on my own in nature, with no contact with others, no food, no books, nothing to write with and nothing to distract, living within the cycles of nature. It was an intense and profound experience. Among other things that happened on this Sacred Passage, I felt I reconnected to who I am, to my purpose and strengthened my commitment to creating a more sustainable world. Now, when I feel that I am being carried by the busyness of organisational responsibilities and life in general, I create the space to retreat, regrounding myself and reconnecting. I feel this brings strength and grounding to the work I do. Today when I facilitate processes for groups, I try to incorporate this element to support the group and the work.

In 2004, in my final thesis for the MSc, I shared a few tips for young change agents for sustainability, based on what I had learned from my experiments with change agency within a large organisation. Looking at them again now, I feel they continue to be relevant, not only for the young but for change agents of any age.

- Keep in mind that the current economic system is only 400 years old. It was created by humans so it can be changed by us as well

- Know that you are part of a growing movement and group of people who care about sustainability—connect with them

- Be true to your values and beliefs
- Keep your own identity
- Ask open and challenging questions to superiors and peers
- Step forward with confidence
- Be comfortable with uncertainty
- Create support networks internally
- Find the senior-level champions and build good informal relationships with them
- Keep senior executives in the loop. Ask for their advice and input. Respect their wisdom and experience
- Create support networks externally
- Bring the outside world in to support you and to bring in the credibility and expertise that you may lack
- Take care of yourself
- Create spaces for meaningful conversation
- Take action, even if it is from the margins in the beginning
- Help others see a different worldview
- Put sustainability on meeting, workshop and conference agendas
- Connect with other initiatives
- Be tempered. Be radical
- Don't be afraid to lose your job. There are many jobs out there for people like you with courage to stand up for your beliefs
- Keep in mind that you are part of a movement to create the new system. Include and transcend the old system to create the new
- Laugh at the absurdities of the old system
- Find a mentor (inside or outside)
- Make links between sustainability and the strategy and formal goals, systems and processes of the organisation
- Develop your ideas and present them wherever you can
- Don't give up—continue raising questions about sustainability—trust yourself
- Have fun and enjoy the journey

- Share your learning with others

- Spread your passion and commitment

I have recently become a mother and am now being challenged to be a change agent for sustainability in this sphere. I am challenging the system again, using alternatives such as organic food, cloth diapers, chemical-free toys, toiletries and other baby products. My conviction that alternatives are needed in Brazil has led me to set up a sustainable baby business to influence other parents to find more sustainable ways of raising their children.

After an extended maternity leave, I have joined Reos Partners, an international organisation dedicated to supporting and building capacity for innovative collective action in complex social systems. This will give me the opportunity to continue to work for sustainability through various multi-stakeholders projects, shifting from working within one organisation to a wider field of action. My journey as a change agent for sustainability continues.

Imbuing work with ecological values

Helen Goulden MSc8, 2004–2006

I joined the civil service as a contractor in 2001 and until 2007 I leapt from one contract to another, across a number of departments (and back again). Employed initially because I had some knowledge in the field of IT and interactive TV, I began by running a small research and development unit at the Cabinet Office and then delivered cross-departmental national programmes, usually related to innovation and the role of digital technology in our lives.

I was never employed explicitly to work on climate change issues or sustainable development. It seemed to me that it would be more fruitful to imbue the current focus of my work with environmental and ecological values rather than depart that world and essentially lobby it from the outside. I held the view then, as I do now, that I have a responsibility to bring sustainability to the heart of any work I undertake. I have often sought to align my personal beliefs and values with my professional practice. This might be summarised as believing that we humans should live lightly upon the Earth and respect and honour her rhythms and complexity.

In attempting to bring environmental sustainability into the core of my work within government I encountered resistance that manifested in different forms.

In the roles I have undertaken, I have generally begun by trying to expand the work of the team by asking questions about the environmental impact of our operations and the possible environmental (as well as social) outcomes that might result from our work. Resistance to these suggestions and comments came both from colleagues, 'that's not what we're here for', and from my bosses, 'that's not what you're here for'. Memorably, it also once came from a department permanent secretary in the form of 'these issues [of climate change and IT] are not connected'.[1] Resistance also came from the superstructure, from the processes, funding regimes and culture of government departments which, in the main, inhibit cross-departmental or cross-directorate communications to all but the most consummate and resilient of networkers, and compartmentalise work programmes and policy development in such a way as to directly thwart efforts to develop more encompassing, ecological and holistic thinking among civil servants.

In some instances, I have countered resistance by enacting behaviour in ways that have felt uneasy. I was, on at least one occasion, told that 'yes, we must all

---

1 This was a full three years before the Gartner report in 2007 revealed that the environmental impact of ICT was equivalent to global aviation emissions at 2% (www.gartner.com/it/page.jsp?id=503867, accessed 31 December 2010).

consider the environment, but this work is about trying to improve public services'. And on that particular occasion, and on others, I have simply nodded my head, and accepted the comment, and then, when back at the coal-face of project delivery, continued with my own prioritisation of facilitating and creating spaces for dialogue around environmental sustainability. I catch myself for a short second, wondering whether it is OK to deprioritise objectives that I am being paid to pursue and work partly from my own objectives. Is this the sort of behaviour I might find objectionable in someone whose personal values and objectives were at odds with my own?

I often tried to effect subtle, small changes or what might be called gentle action. I attempted to enact what I thought good practice might be: reducing the carbon footprint of my office activities and encouraging others in various ways to do the same; remaining in good humour as far as possible when these encouragements were laughed at—for example, meeting people's gaze with a smile and a twinkle as they called me 'the resident greenie'; and trying to have some sensible answers to questions such as 'do you really think you doing this one little thing will make any difference?'

At one particular time, I was advocating a deep intervention into an emerging cross-departmental policy, trying to shift environmental sustainability towards the centre, rather than the periphery of the policy. I was having little success. Interventions in senior meetings, submissions of papers to various senior colleagues and ministers were not gaining traction. I began to fear that familiar, heart-thumping dilemma of somehow hindering the chances of success through a continual banging of the same drum. Might I just become 'noise'—if I hadn't already—and through my continued actions, I could very well be hampering chances of success.

Acknowledging this made me more mindful, noticing more keenly the actions, reactions and dynamics of the community activity around me. I began to pay more attention to where there was a chink or an opportunity to drop something into a conversation and judged when the best action was to say or do nothing.

At this particular time, achieving so little in my core professional life and feeling very powerless, I found myself getting frustrated about everything I saw about me within the department which spoke of waste of natural resources. I became perhaps unhealthily obsessed with the huge Victorian water cisterns in our toilets. The deluge of water after every flush was almost comical and I became resolute that I would stop the gallons and gallons of perfectly clean water disappearing every hour into the sewage system. I ordered 100 water 'Hippos' from Thames Water and over a period of weeks, placed one in every single toilet (male and female) in the building. The effect of this was twofold: the Cabinet Office is probably still, four years on, unwittingly saving gallons of water a day, which has given me a great deal of Puck-like pleasure; and the thought of the savings on daily flushings gave me some strength as I sat tapping at my computer trying to tackle the bigger things, where success seemed as far away as the moon.

As I said previously, resistance can come in many forms; sometimes from people, sometimes embodied within processes, sometimes in the culture of an organisation and sometimes, sometimes, it's a completely mental construct and only requires a little courage to push a door wide open . . .

Fresh from an MSc workshop in 2007, I began to feel it would be a good thing to totally remove colleagues from their everyday working environment and offer an opportunity for us to connect together more deeply with each other and the work we were undertaking. I decided that we would go to an organic farm and spend a day exploring the relevance of environmental sustainability to digital communications. The idea was to deepen conversations around the environmental impact of increased use in IT, but also to examine the huge potential technology offers in fostering more sustainable patterns of working.

I invited two representatives from ten local authorities and, to my surprise, they all came to a farm in the middle of nowhere and all participated in what turned out to be a deeply rich and rewarding day. I hadn't asked permission to do this; I simply apportioned some of the programme budget to it and set it up. No one sacked me, no one asked any questions, which gave me the liberating but unsettling impression that one could do quite a number of things within this behemoth of an organisation without anyone batting an eyelid; if they noticed at all.

This workshop brought together a group of people that ultimately went on to form a long-term consortium and with the help of €7 million of EU funding have continued their work in the field of 'Green IT'. I don't claim responsibility for this, of course. But am pleased to have offered them some space for collaboration to emerge and grow.

But everything I do seems very, very small. I can't help but feel humbled by some of the great things, the bold initiatives and drive and passion which I see in those working to tackle climate change. Certainly there are many alumni of the MSc in Responsibility and Business Practice who I feel are achieving far greater and more meaningful impact than I. But I think through inquiry and gaining a deeper understanding of complexity and systems thinking, I've come to appreciate and not to belittle the contributions I can make and believe more that the impact of my actions might be felt in different places and different times. And that I may never know the importance, or inconsequence, of any intervention I might make.

One of the keenest learnings from working within government, and this may be true of many large national and complex organisations, is that sometimes resistance to change is real. This might be direct resistance from colleagues, it might be through silent acquiescence to the status quo, it might be resistance within the fabric of the infrastructure and culture of the organisation; all of which are powerful forces with which to contend on a daily basis.

But sometimes, perhaps more often than I had imagined, either through extending the idea of what was within my grasp to change (such as mischievous guerrilla action) or pushing a door only to find it wide open (workshopping with the techies), resistance can be a mental construct, a perception which limits the imagination and ultimately the manifestation of change.

Thinking out of the box: introducing action research into neighbourhood practice in the north-west of England

Helena Kettleborough MSc4, 2000–2002

Telling my story

I am a senior local government manager in the north-west of England delivering services in learning support for neighbourhood development and community empowerment. Ever since I encountered action research, I have wanted to integrate it into my own practice and to offer it to others with whom I work because it has the potential to help us achieve our targets and simultaneously to learn for sustainability in complex times.

This has been a long-term interest, pursued in the small spaces left in an already busy life. It has required much persistence, because action research is seen as innovative and removed from delivery, and it is challenging to release the time and commitment it requires. I have drawn on support from the Responsibility and Business Practice (RBP) and Centre for Action Research in Professional Practice (CARPP) communities to help me in this work. I have needed to learn and adjust continually along the way, and lived the highs and lows.

In this story I describe my journey to bring action research ideas to front-line workers, community activists, managers and leaders in neighbourhoods in the region to help us deliver organisational goals.

I discovered action research in March 2000 when I started the MSc in Responsibility and Business Practice, not having realised its importance as the underlying learning methodology of the course beforehand. It was important that I was not only taught the theory, but I *experienced* action research through the conduct of the programme. Action research fitted with my own earlier learning journey, using participative, empowering and learning methods to improve local government services.

It excited me because it:

- Linked research and action and hence was about making a difference

- Was embedded in a solid history of practice and theory

- Gave a structured way into a range of new ideas[2]

- Provided practices to widen people's behaviour and worldviews

- Encouraged people to change themselves, rather than imposing change from outside

I felt action research offered a way to address some of the myriad challenges facing the public sector which result from social (ageing, youth disaffection), environmental (climate change) and, particularly recently, economic (the recession, worklessness, poverty) factors. They require co-creating solutions with our communities, driving efficiencies through connecting services and delivering more for less. As a result the public sector is continuously looking to transform services and innovate, and I felt that action research offered the means for long-term learning, leading to embedded change.

Bringing the message of action research

Reflecting on my journey, a number of factors were critical:

- Sourcing support from experienced practitioners, both in the learning materials required and facing the challenges of delivery

- Shifting/tailoring language so that action research became understandable rather than academic

- Finding sympathetic practitioners to support initiatives in various services

- Delivering high-quality action research practice

- Responding and learning through feedback

- Keeping going . . .

I illustrate these through my story.

The National Strategy for Neighbourhood Renewal (2002) had sought to lessen the gap between the most deprived neighbourhoods and the rest of England and introduce 'floor targets' to drive improvement. Two facets were the introduction of neighbourhood (rather than town hall) management and neighbourhood wardens. A Regional Resource Centre to support quality and learning for those involved was added to my portfolio of responsibilities in 2004, giving me scope to introduce action research into my work.

My approach to developing action research over the past six years was multi-faceted. I started with my own practice, developing my skills and confidence, seeking to make myself a more effective leader. I continued to seek support in action research methods through various activities at CARPP, including joining the PhD

---

2 I particularly valued being introduced to the ideas of Thomas Berry, exploring our place within the universe (see Berry 1988, 1999; Swimme and Berry 1992).

programme. I reached out to other action learning/research practitioners in the north-west. I also sought to embed action research in all our programmes, initially through training. To achieve this, I had to find low-cost ways and modify the language and timescales of action research to be more widely appealing: for example by focusing on appreciative and reflective practice.

I worked with Chris Seeley and Gill Coleman from RBP to develop potential initiatives. I had to be highly tenacious, applying for funds and then applying again, modifying proposals, advertising training repeatedly, until eventually funding and opportunities could be brought together.

Language proved to be a key issue. I received feedback that the academic language I used in an early paper for internal colleagues was not understandable. Therefore in advertising the first courses on action research, we used the words **reflective** and **appreciative practice**. I explained the courses to colleagues in person, talking about wanting to help people reflect on what they were doing, in order to learn from their work. I used **action inquiry** rather than action research, as it felt more approachable.

One key moment came in 2006 when, after an initially unsuccessful recruitment, we cut a proposed appreciative practice course down to one day. To my delight this time we attracted enough participants to run the course. My action research project was live!

Based on this success, we cut our four-day reflective practice course down to one day as well, but by this time we were unable to offer the course free. RENEW North West stepped in and funded a session as an innovative learning method.[3] The course then ran a second time, but only because we approached contacts individually to achieve the 12 participants we needed. It was a demanding day for the facilitator to run. I was exhausted but exhilarated at the end. By then, I was experiencing some momentum. In the same month, I co-facilitated two half-day appreciative practice sessions for front-line health workers. I enjoyed facilitating and felt more confident at it. People shared their stories of improving health inequalities using community involvement and of the differences they had made.

Developing my leadership: personal reflections

What has it taken?

- **Determination**. An amazing amount of sheer determination was needed to get action research going. The concepts were not common, the language was not out there, resources were scarce and the form of training needed to be established. Also, I needed confidence that what I was doing was valuable and needed

---

3 RENEW North West, the Regional Centre of Excellence 2006–2009, to improve skills and interdisciplinary working among regeneration professionals.

- **Senior management support**. My line manager supported my participation in activities at CARPP and my learning approach

- **Personal inspiration** from reading sources on our current challenges and on new ways forward

- **Finding new language**. The language of action research runs counter to that of local government. It can be seen as intangible and irrelevant to targets, performance management and measurable outputs, and yet the practices deliver directly against organisational goals. In 2007, unexpected help came when my authority paid for an accredited coaching course for Heads of Service, including me, as part of a leadership development programme. The language of coaching is aligned to that of action research and appreciative practice. Participants were initially uncertain of the value of coaching but the group experience was moving. There were moments of quality reflection which participants noted, and which reminded me of action research meetings at Bath! My line manager saw the connections to my action research work. This success helped affirm the culture for action research

- **Gaining confidence in my skills**. As I practised action research and taught it, I could affirm its processes to others

- **Peer support**. The faith and active support of a few key manager practitioners in the region has been central to my ability to keep going

Creating wider ownership: thinking out of the box

One key activity brought our action research initiatives together in an especially accessible form. Again, I worked with supportive colleagues, tailored my work to local conditions, and lived the practice.

In 2008, the Resource Centre expanded to support improvement in neighbourhood delivery and community empowerment throughout the north-west as part of the Regional Improvement and Efficiency Partnership in the public sector. The Partnership advocated transformational learning to address challenges facing the sector. We were commissioned to establish communities of interest to change practice in:

- Community development/empowerment

- Neighbourhood working

- Knowledge, skills and learning

To initiate the latter community of interest we offered an interlinked series of workshops, introducing different ways of thinking in order to improve practice. Themes were chosen from action research methodology which seemed to offer most value to neighbourhood and community empowerment practitioners. The workshops seemed high-risk as the approaches presented were not immediately identifiable as useful in current local government language and required participants to be open to challenge. From my public sector experience, I knew the ideas were relevant but it was not possible to ascertain in advance whether the workshops would be successful. All the one-day workshops were therefore framed as explorations.

Table 4.1 **Thinking out of the box workshops 2009**

Title of workshop	Venue	Topic
Working systemically in a complex world	Stockport	Complexity, change and participation in neighbourhoods
Partnerships towards innovative action	Preston	Innovative ways of dealing with complex challenges using Theory U (Scharmer 2007)
Appreciative practice	Manchester	Can organisations that try to appreciate what is best in themselves discover more of what is good?
Knowledge in neighbourhoods	Birkenhead	Many ways of knowing
Reflective practice	Kendal	Theories and practices
Alternative communication in neighbourhoods	Warrington	Listening more attentively to self
Leadership and sustainable neighbourhoods	Manchester	Creating sustainable communities using systems and futures techniques

The workshops were well supported both in numbers and spread of attendees. The evaluation report demonstrated high levels of satisfaction and a number of participants came to more than one workshop.

The value of the workshops came out clearly in participants' feedback at the review event held in October 2009 in three main areas:

- **Being offered the chance for new learning**. Participants felt strongly that it was powerful knowledge and that it was useful to be exposed to new ideas. A neighbourhood manager reflected that sometimes 'we do not know what we don't know'. Appreciative practice, for example, helps to look at things differently and bring out solutions, not problems

- **Benefit to communities**. Community activists felt that these skills would benefit communities and their capacity to achieve change

- **Helping make cultural change happen**. Participants noted that organisations are often risk-averse and action research helps build relationships, and enables people to work with different worldviews or paradigms and weave visions together

A number of the participants have gone on to become strong advocates for the Thinking out of the Box workshops. An important aspect of the seven workshops is that they gave form to the often intangible nature of action research. As a result, they were easier to explain and fitted more accessibly within our product-oriented culture.

Conclusion

I have described part of my journey to build skills and learning for sustainable communities by bringing my learning from the MSc in RBP to bear. It shows the length of time and the depth of skills needed to transfer action research into the language and practice of the public sector and how support from the MSc community, my line manager and a few key peers was important. The results point the way for wider transformational learning in neighbourhoods and communities in order to help sustain progress during the coming reductions in public sector finance in the UK.

Postscript

There is now a stage beyond the Thinking out of the Box series, which seemed at the time such a leap into the future. It feels now that my collaborative action research work is flourishing, with appreciative practice integrated into a regional empowerment programme, a project to map action learning/research with Lancaster University, and a workshop with Etienne Wenger integrating our practice with theory.

References

Berry, T. (1988) *The Dream of the Earth* (San Francisco: Sierra Club).
—— (1999) *The Great Work: Our way into the future* (New York: Bell Tower).
Scharmer, O. (2007) *Theory U. Leading from the Future as it Emerges: The social technology of presencing* (Cambridge, MA: The Society for Organisational Learning).
Swimme, B., and T. Berry (1992) *The Universe Story: From the primordial flaring forth to the ecozoic era—A celebration of the unfolding of the cosmos* (New York: HarperCollins).

Choose Life[4]

James Barlow MSc8, 2004–2006

I am a sustainability manager in the European division of the world's second largest food and beverage producer, PepsiCo. I predominantly work with the environmental challenges we face, trying to reduce our impacts on, and risks from, the environment. I consciously chose to continue working in a transnational food corporation when I joined PepsiCo as a supply chain manager in 2002. I believe there continues to be a place, working from the inside, slowing down the train (Macy and Brown 1998). I simultaneously accept that our current system inadequately values ecosystems services, potentially catastrophically. Working as a 'tempered radical' (Meyerson and Scully 1995), trying to mix science and business in action has provided moments of intense joy, when it feels as if my colleagues and I really are having a positive effect on one of the world's most powerful institutions, and moments of intense self-doubt, guilt, sadness, anger and frustration when we are not! Thriving as a human being in this environment is one of my biggest challenges. How can I balance personal integrity and my belief in interdependence with the reality of where I find myself? How much can be pushed, how and when?

I have chosen to work here. I am very grateful for the trust, development and opportunity I am afforded. I experience what is possible, and what happens when the (many) tensions are tested, when the (many) lines, the current realities of capitalism, are crossed, often inadvertently. With my tiny contribution, I hope to help our society move on to more fruitful structures—more just, more worthwhile, less seemingly short-sighted. I draw hope, and a certain amount of self-justification, from the words of Porritt (2007: 19) that capitalism seems 'the only overarching system capable of achieving any kind of reconciliation between ecological sustainability on the one hand and the pursuit of prosperity and personal wellbeing on the other'.

In these eight years my place in PepsiCo has changed from supply chain manager in 2002 (during which time I was sponsored on the MSc), through times of being an activist for sustainability with other volunteers and having a part-time role on environmental sustainability (ES), to my appointment in 2007 to a full-time environmental sustainability role, with a full-time ES boss and colleague, and, indeed, by 2010, a small team reporting to me. In addition I have changed family circumstances; in 2002 we were three, now we are five!

---

4 'Choose Life' from *Trainspotting*, 1996

During this journey, one especially visible indication of growing organisational commitment to ES was putting the world's first Carbon Reduction Label on Walker's Crisps in March 2007. This was developed from our first life-cycle assessment (for which I had scraped together funding to commission a University of Bath project) and a relationship with the Carbon Trust, based on a joint spirit of experimentation, nurtured at grass-roots level and later cemented at the top. This labelling now commits us to carbon reduction action, shown for example in holding large-scale supplier summits to improve our environmental performance, and supporting the Carbon Disclosure Project Supply Chain Programme, designed to help make visible the climate change strategies and greenhouse gas emissions (GHG) of supply chains. These consumer- and supplier-facing developments have contributed to internal debates, explicating, for example, agriculture's pivotal role in sustainability and awareness that we are an 'agricultural' business, as much as 'market-led'.

Yes, in January 2007, we were accepted as having a place and a voice worthy of a proper, named, hierarchical team! We were helped greatly from the start by working alongside a new corporate affairs director and his team who both knew how to communicate this new lens on the business, and saw the strategic importance of it, not just its 'PR value'! This continued corporate awareness also allows us to act in dialogue with NGOs in ways we hadn't traditionally before. This is all fostering a belief that we can help change the food and beverage supply chain, leading to increased ambition, public voice. This year our UK business president stood up in the Houses of Parliament, calling for effective carbon pricing, government incentives for business to drive GHG emissions down to the scientifically demonstrated less-damaging (to our business too!) levels.

And the challenges are huge, since we are working in the glaring chasm between ecological requirements for absolute carbon reductions and the societal algorithm that depends on increased material use from businesses such as ours to deliver increasing returns for the 60% of citizens that hold a stake in a pension fund. How could my boss, team, other colleagues and I promote this urgent, fundamental argument while retaining personal credibility, and not alienating our VP (my boss's boss) to the extent that we were silenced or discredited right from the start? Several factors proved important. My boss needed time to establish a perspective for himself (which he did with relish: reading, attending conferences). And we needed to invest heavily in our relationship, developing trust and openness, so that we could support one another through the challenges inherent in roles designed to enable institutional change. This is particularly important since any voicing of the current devastating scientific understanding of our ecosystems seems to lend itself to shooting the messengers.

We have been extremely lucky, in that one of our team can consistently deliver resource reduction programmes that have paid for the team several times over. There is also a growing realisation that external expectations on sustainability performance of large companies are stronger, so we need resources to meet them. Perhaps these things allowed our VP to defend the team against shrinkage, even through a corporate restructuring 18 months ago, and the increasingly short-term focus with the economic crisis. He has recently articulated this as:

> I am also fortunate that within our organisation I have two or three people who are absolutely leading thinkers on sustainability and I let them educate me. They stretch me and drag me along. We have great debates—they are change agents who help me (quoted in the *Guardian*, 26 May 2010).

Distanced support from internal champions, sometimes purposefully opaque, even apparently in conflict, has been key. As has the language from our global CEO, Indra Nooyi, in her 'Performance with Purpose' vision for the corporation; the need to deliver action with this language has helped justify some of our actions and investments at a local level, such as resourcing the team more appropriately.

What I have learned is that, just as an individual's first rule of change agency is to 'stay alive' (Shepard 1975), then the same is true of a corporation. There is little point, if you believe the corporation is a possible catalyst for an industry, in the pace of environmental/social sustainability changes leading to economic ruin. For what kind of example would we have delivered?

Alone, I cannot honestly claim to have been the cause of much change, if any. I have worked very hard, sometimes long. I have been very lucky to have appreciated some of the opportunities afforded me, for example that of being part of the tiny team to write our first ever external report (PepsiCo 2008) on the UK business, and having people's trust and support to recommend some very stretching, public targets, such as getting all of our manufacturing and distribution operations to be fossil-fuel-free by 2023! Crucially we have been given the freedom, indeed encouragement by the two PepsiCo UK Presidents in this time, to 'bring outside voices in' to the business to expose our senior teams to progressive ideas.

In this situation, I conclude that I can only continue to be open, and vulnerable; to question, to listen, to understand, not just seek to be understood. Recently my boss and I trialled a new sustainability 'educational' tool in front of 500 people at our European operations conference. It was the first time we'd used it. We framed it as such, and made a point of using 30 minutes of our allotted 75 for live feedback. We were trying to demonstrate how important it was to listen, by doing it ourselves, there. Perhaps leadership is then allowed from a different place. Much of (corporate) life seems lived out in 'advocacy' and 'illustration'. Top leaders seem great at 'framing'. But it is a rare person who consistently, actively, lives out 'inquiry'. In terms of Torbert's four parts of speech (Fisher *et al.* 2003; Torbert 2004), I wonder how much this balance helps or hinders *progress*.

A word on tensions, frequently embodied

Patience seems needed to accompany the 'working through others' we are engaged in. Three years ago my vice president, responsible for our European Environmental Sustainability strategy, repeatedly reminded me not to scamper off over the horizon without everyone, or attempt too much in one go. On good days I find this need for slow, considered steps sensible, and find his counsel invaluable, and I think of how the means cannot justify the ends (Freire 1972). On bad days, I fear (know?) that we don't have the luxury of time, and my impatience is crushing, with the anger, despondency and frustration it brings.

Distance and a gentleness of grip. In the last year, I wonder if I have perhaps reached a personal chaotic, near-crucifying crescendo of sorts. The cumulative negative emotions of trying to work within the power structures of our organisation, of attending to relationships with others whose drivers, fears and senses of responsibility are so apparently different, while holding the seemingly irrefutable facts (are they?) about our societal relationship with our only planet, have brought me into periods of mild depression, and have severely tested those close to me. The exhaustion and numbness have meant I have simply *had* to let go a little, loosen my grip and try not to believe too much depends on a particular sequence of actions. As my wife would readily tell, I am continually questioning my place. Whether this is ultimately a generative inquiry, or a destructive one, only time may tell.

The MSc

I *think* I am a very much more competent operator for change as a result of the RBP MSc. The discipline of action inquiry, the incredibly rich, safe, challenging network of peers to learn, draw confidence and comfort from, and the seeming luxury of a semi-academic hinterland of practice to call on have all contributed to my self-belief, competence and drive.

I was encouraged to be myself, be *james*, when on the MSc. Well, I love being outside, so decided to try to hold certain crucial meetings outside, walking alongside someone with whom I wanted to develop a deep, often very fleeting, relationship. It meant we could not rely on the signals that came from the meeting room, or written forms of communication. There was an intentional lack of eye contact, since we had to ensure we didn't trip up! This was freedom, noticeably different from a normal meeting, especially when the horizons being scanned were further than the three metres a meeting room typically affords. Form mimicked content in this way. In addition, I was having fun; I was being paid to walk and talk. The walks literally were exploring new territory together. And they recognise that we are bodies, physical, in the world. Our broader team now sees walking together, reflecting, or just being, as valuable work time, accepted in the middle of the agenda of an important meeting. Feedback from two of our business's general managers suggested that this form of meeting helped them immensely, and was appropriate as the scene-setter to really broad thinking and, dare I say it, *reflection*, on ES—this in a corporate culture that has an incredibly weighted value on action, looking forwards.

The MSc also taught me to accentuate skills of *noticing* and *networking*, bringing them into my daily business life. Paying attention to others, with whom I meet, those forming external opinions, those acting in other organisations. As an example, when our previous UK business president spoke of 'bringing the outside in' to our corporation, this proved to be invaluable as a justification to choose to introduce certain executives to NGOs whose ideas needed a voice in PepsiCo. This, like so much, couldn't have happened without the joint-driving with our corporate affairs team. So listening, aligning here, too, was absolutely vital. There is a lesson here, too, I think: seek friends to work with and continually appreciate the commonality, not bemoan the difference! This is humbling; it is an **admission of my scale, influence and sheer inability to act, really, alone**. It is liberating too.

In PepsiCo, we talk of Performance with Purpose. As David Whyte (2002: 287) says, 'It takes tremendous energy to keep up a luminescent front when our interior surface is fading into darkness'. The challenge continues to be to realise that our generation is so privileged. We are the first to have enough power to act on the information. I continue trying, perhaps more kindly now, to help us have the will to engage to transform ourselves to consciously become interdependent humans.

References

Dunphy, D.C., A.B. Griffiths and S.H. Benn (2007) *Organizational Change for Corporate Sustainability* (London: Routledge, 2nd edn).

Fisher, D., D. Rooke and W.R. Torbert (2003) *Personal and Organisational Transformations through Action Inquiry* (Boston, MA: Edge/Work Press, 4th edn).

Freire, P. (1972) *The Pedagogy of the Oppressed* (London: Penguin).

Macy, J.R., and M.Y. Brown (1998) *Coming Back to Life: Practices to reconnect our lives, our world* (Gabriola Island, Canada: New Society Publishers).

Meyerson, D.E., and M.A. Scully (1995) 'Tempered Radicalism and the Politics of Ambivalence and Change', *Organization Science* 6.5: 585-600.

PepsiCo (2008) 'Environmental Sustainability Report 2008'; www.pepsico.co.uk/environment, accessed 3 December 2010.

Porritt, J. (2007) *Capitalism as if the World Matters* (London: Earthscan, rev. edn).

Shepard, H.A. (1975) 'Rules of Thumb for Change Agents', *OD Practitioner* 7.3 (November 1975): 1-5.

Torbert, W.R. (2004) *Action Inquiry: The secret of timely and transforming leadership* (San Francisco: Berrett-Koehler).

Whyte, D. (2002) *The Heart Aroused* (New York: Doubleday).

Leadership for change in USA public food procurement: people, products and policy

Karen Karp MSc3, 1999–2001

As the president and founder of Karp Resources,[5] a food industry consultancy based in New York, I have engaged in hundreds of projects over 20 years with leaders in government, social service and private industry, to change food 'for good'.

This is a story about an engagement with the second largest government food buyer in the USA, the New York City Department of Education's Office of School-Food, to procure local food for school meals. This project took place over the course of three years (2006–2009) and was hailed by many in the 'farm to school' world as a dazzling achievement. The project and its results catapulted me and Karp Resources into the national spotlight as leaders in sustainability as that relates to public food procurement, food policy and local food strategies. This article attempts to describe how an action inquiry approach provided a survival strategy to a very challenging consulting assignment.

There are 1.2 million children in the New York City (NYC) School System. With 8,000 unionised employees the department itself purchases, prepares and serves approximately 860,000 meals per day during the school year (and over 200,000 meals per day during the summer) from 1,200 kitchens that supply 1,500 schools. They purchase US$125,000,000 of food per year, which does not include donations and subsidies.

In the USA public education system, children from households with incomes less than 185% of the government's officially designated poverty level can eat lunch at school for free or at a reduced price.[6] More than 80% of the children in NYC schools qualify for price reductions. The United States Department of Agriculture (USDA) reimburses school districts for meals served, sets strict nutritional requirements, and donates thousands of pounds of subsidised agriculture commodities to enable the schools to provide low-cost meals. SchoolFood also has a snack programme and a 'universal breakfast' programme, through which all children (regardless of family income) may eat breakfast at school for free, to encourage higher educational performance. Some of the city's poorest children receive 90% or more of their daily calorie intake at school, a responsibility SchoolFood does not take lightly. Their focus is to make sure that nearly 1 million children are fed safely, to high nutritional

---

5 www.karpresources.com, accessed 31 December 2010.
6 For more information: www.fns.usda.gov/cnd/Lunch/default.htm, accessed 31 December 2010.

standards, on time, at 1,500 locations throughout the five boroughs. And they do this well. Few food-borne illnesses have been attributed to school meals since the Second World War, when the National School Lunch Program began.

Our work was initially funded by The W.K. Kellogg Foundation, and later by the New York State Department of Agriculture and Markets. It was part of the School-Food Plus Initiative, a broad school food reform project with three overarching goals: (1) improving school meals' nutritional qualities; (2) educating children about agriculture, food and nutrition through classroom curricula; and (3) procuring locally grown foods for new cafeteria recipes. Karp Resources was originally an evaluation partner of this initiative. When progress on local food procurement was perceived to be lagging behind the others, Karp Resources was asked to lead those efforts.

Several consultants before us had attempted myriad versions of school meal reform: ranging from replacing the entire menu to retraining school foodservice workers, to outsourcing school meal services to a contract caterer. SchoolFood rejected each of these attempts, and the consultants' tenures were cut short. So when we were engaged to drive lasting institutional change within that system, I was less interested in what hadn't worked with the prior change *concepts* and more interested in *how* our predecessors had approached change. This 'looking at the how' was a new technique for me. Understanding its importance and knowing how to apply it was a significant result of working as a programme evaluator, where observation and analysis were the job, replacing our typical role of 'doing' a particular set of tasks. This work would require us to fuse the two.

It quickly became evident that prior attempts had failed because of the consultants' refusal to acknowledge what SchoolFood was doing well. The prior interventions dismissed the enormous task it is to serve this many meals each day on time, safely and within budget.

Further, the previous consultants had been drawn from advocacy groups who for years had demonstrated against SchoolFood, staging public campaigns on the steps of City Hall and, on several occasions, filing law suits against the Department of Education. With SchoolFood Plus and its US$3 million purse, these same advocates were back at SchoolFood's door, this time proposing 'partnership'. Good intentions were met (understandably) with wariness and scepticism. Our evaluation had revealed that trust and respect were only barely emerging after several years in this new relationship.

My prior experience as a foodservice manager enabled me to see the complexities of their system and to speak a shared language of logistics, supply chains and the food industry's notoriously slim profit margins. Armed with this experience, I constructed a new approach based on appreciation, patience and a commitment to remaining squarely within their procurement and operations parameters. We told SchoolFood staff that *we* knew that local procurement was not their priority, perhaps not even their interest, and that we simply wanted to understand how to fit potential new products (or new suppliers of old products) into their process and menus. We didn't want any special treatment, and we hoped that this approach would help them warm to us. We were empathic and, to an extent, they appreciated it.

A number of other factors guided me toward a deliberate approach of balancing process and results orientations. This was the largest system we had ever engaged with as lead consultants. As evaluators, we intimately knew the system's labyrinthine bureaucratic layers and entrenched hierarchies, which included oversight by federal, state and city regulations. We were privy to many internal interpersonal dynamics among leadership, and its reluctance to engage with outsiders.

This insight rendered us extremely cautious. For perhaps the first time since completing the MSc, I reached back into the literature for a refresher on inside-outside dynamics and tempered radicalism. In both, I found comfort in knowing there were theoretical precedents for the magnitude of change we would try to take on. I struggled with the sense that we might not be successful; that is, we might not actually get any local foods into their system. This possibility sharply rubbed against my nature (and reputation) as one that achieves tangible results. Though I never entirely gave up actual food procurement as an outcome, the project's scale allowed me to accept the assignment as an opportunity to apply an action research framework. I rationalised: even if the practical (food) outcomes were not achieved, there would be some experience outcomes here (process) that would inform how to implement sustainable food strategies at scale, and thus would inform Karp Resources' future work.

As a leadership story, this project's lasting success in establishing new directions in local food procurement is accompanied by bittersweet regret that leadership development *within* the department (that institutional mind-set shift our client had been seeking) was not achieved. Three department heads, the executive director, the executive chef and the director of technology, were our primary contacts. We engaged one-on-one with these high level staffers on product selection, nutritional and product specifications, and pricing requirements. We also relied on them to create agency for us with other SchoolFood staff and with the food manufacturers, brokers and distributors who were additional gatekeepers to moving new product into this system.

About nine months into the work we noticed something that ultimately proved to be a dominant and debilitating trend. The more we followed leads and instructions and identified local products that met every possible requirement, the more push back we got from the executive director. (Although frustrating at times, our progress was steadier with the executive chef and technology director.) Time and again, we made real strides, finding seasonal food items that SchoolFood purchased in significant volumes at times of the year when our region could produce those foods (such as plums, watermelons, frozen vegetables processed by a major New York brand, pears). Time and again, the executive director decided not to purchase them or stalled until the seasonal window had closed, often undermining hundreds of hours of work (ours, his staff's, his suppliers') as well as the goodwill of farmers and other industry actors we'd engaged in this work. The executive director frequently changed his mind about our overall strategy and product priority, demanding that we source items that simply were not in season when requested. These out-of-season demands were a frequent reminder of our lack of success in developing their leadership in the area of local procurement.

This dynamic haunted us. Why would the executive director so blatantly and frequently mistreat a resource (i.e. us) amenable to working within every specified limitation and to meeting every noted condition? Why would he reject assistance someone else paid for that could enhance his reputation and that of the district, and position them as leaders in a burgeoning national trend of farm-to-school?

Eventually we concluded that it was *precisely for these reasons* that we—and our results—were rejected. We were private sector consultants, hired by foundation sector funders, to affect change in the public sector. And, in a male-dominated office and industry, we were women, which we felt factored into the equation. He didn't choose us, didn't want us there, would have preferred to use the money for any number of other purposes, and therefore seemed intent on proving local procurement was a distraction and a waste of time and money by, literally, stopping local food from being purchased.

We realised that the executive director was our work's intended beneficiary, but he was not our *client*. This was a critical point of awareness for us about what could be achieved. We raised this several times with the funder and with other initiative stakeholders, but ultimately neither they nor we were able to overcome this power dynamic.

Nevertheless, we continued to identify high potential local foods and push for their inclusion in school meals. We worked closely with SchoolFood leaders, but shifted our focus to producing data-driven opportunities for future purchases based on current product uses and forms. For example, we expanded the farm-to-school concept to include minimally processed and frozen products in addition to fresh items. Ultimately we were successful in engaging SchoolFood's distributors— the real purchasing decision-makers for fruits and vegetables—to substitute local products for ones they were purchasing on the open market. As a result of these efforts further 'up the chain', more than 135,000 lbs (61,000 kg) of local peaches, nectarines and pears were purchased from New Jersey growers; an upstate New York processor secured a US$4.2 million contract to provide NY-grown, -processed and -packed apple slices to NYC schools; and more than 80,000 lbs (36,000 kg) of frozen vegetables grown and processed in New York made it onto NYC schoolchildren's trays.

We hoped that these tangible successes, in the form of both high-quality local product and new reliable suppliers, would help SchoolFood 'institutionalise' local procurement after our contract ended. And sometimes, we can see these results. For instance, the organisation's executive chef routinely appears at food-related events and speaks in an informed way about our region's food and agricultural infrastructure. Though 'local' is still not SchoolFood's purchasing priority, the vocabulary of local foods has become mainstream within the organisation. Nationally, the results of our work influenced USDA policy, permitting institutions purchasing food with federal money to specify desired geographic origins.[7]

The SchoolFood project was a perfect storm of challenges and opportunities that required every tool I had as a leader, and which was successful in part through elevating the process of inquiring to a possible end in and of itself. The project came at a time when my company's experience (and some daring) converged with industry trends and resulted in a new leadership framework for me. Luckily, there were tangible results as well, because while many of our projects now focus on policy and process, I am not sure I could ever fully give up the aspect of being a leader in food that is the most deeply satisfying. That is, to know that beneficiaries of our efforts have tasted something better, or have simply had a new experience with food.

7 www.usda.gov/farmbill, accessed 31 December 2010.

Two worlds?

Mark Gater MSc9, 2005–2007

> All I've learned and all
> I've felt—when the dawn sky clears,
> It's only snowdust.

This story is about two things: my inquiry with the directors of a UK-based retail financial institution into what sustainable banking might look like, and the impact on me of being an inquirer.

The story starts on the evening of Boxing Day, 2005. As an antidote to Christmas, I had hiked out to one of my favourite places, a hill overlooking the town where I live, and camped there for the night. The previous year, my first on the MSc, had been difficult. I had gone into the degree thinking I understood the problems of sustainability. I was wrong. The whole thing was far scarier and more depressing than I had thought, the web of complex systems binding the human race in its current destructive ways more intractable than I could have believed. I had moved towards the end of this first year both obsessed and deeply depressed, on the verge of quitting the course. I doubted that I could face another year with one foot planted in a world where contemplation of potential ecosystem collapse brought with it a sense of utter powerlessness. Near the end of this year, then, I awoke and stumbled out of my tent. While I slept, a light snow had fallen, and the countryside around me was glistening under a clear blue sky. As I looked out across the hills, I was struck, not just by the beauty of the scene, but by the fact that within an hour at most, the snowdust and that beauty would be gone, melted by the winter sun. And somehow it was okay. Things pass. Somehow the scene, and the snowdust, crystallised in me a realisation that maybe I could contemplate ecosystem collapse with a degree of equanimity, and that doing something was better than doing nothing. The first version of the haiku at the head of this piece started to come together in my head.[8] And I completed the degree, and carried out the inquiry described below.

The inquiry was based on several assumptions and an uncomfortable realisation. My assumptions were (and are): first, that the current money system, in which money is created as debt by banks, necessitates economic growth (Rowbotham 1998); second, that economic growth cannot be decoupled from material

---

8 I was taught how to write an English variant of the Japanese 'haiku' form on the MSc. It was one of several methods of writing that we used to understand and distil thoughts, perceptions and emotional responses to the world.

consumption (Jackson 2009); and, third, that there are limits to material consumption imposed by the Earth's ecosystem (Meadows *et al.* 2004). The uncomfortable realisation was that, as an employee of a retail financial institution, I was part of a system that is driving unsustainable growth. My discomfort was heightened by the fact that I had been working in that system for almost 20 years without ever previously giving this a thought. So, my inquiry, started as the focal point of my MSc project, and continued afterwards, was 'How do I engage the directors of a large financial institution in a conversation about the inherent unsustainability of the business that they run?'

The process that I went through involved multiple cycles of group workshops and individual conversations with the directors over a period of two years. There is not space here to describe the whole process; what I will do is pick out a few key points and then reflect on a couple of questions.

At the beginning of the first group session I ran with the directors, I asked for their responses to the pre-reading (including the executive summary of *Beyond the Limits* [Meadows *et al.* 1992] and various papers on the problems of economic growth and the money system) that I had given them. These included the Foreword and Introduction to *The Ecology of Money* by Douthwaite (2000) and a paper entitled *The Problem with Growth* by the same author (1997). In terms of the view of the world I was asking them to consider, their comments ranged from: 'Don't know which data to believe. Is there a disaster waiting to happen? Or is it alright?' Through: 'Economic growth—is the analysis correct? Is a crash inevitable?' To: 'Is our "world economy" inherently unstable as currently constituted?' And in terms of how they and the business might respond: 'A feeling of impotence—not able to make any real difference', 'If governments cannot fix things, can we realistically do anything?', 'significant unease about the way forward', and 'how do we engage the rest of the business?'

In the subsequent individual conversations, there was an almost universal view that what we were getting into here was outside the realm of what people in their position normally expect to deal with. In comments such as, 'This is not a normal business decision', and 'we are challenging a set of beliefs and assumptions, rather than operating within them', lay both evidence that they were truly engaged in the inquiry and the seeds of what would eventually bring it to an end.

As well as looking at the role of the money system, the early workshops had focused on environmental impacts, especially the topic of climate change. One visible result of this was an increase in environmental consciousness and action across the business, heavily supported by the directors. By the end of 2007, most of the obvious practical steps a business like ours could take to reduce its direct impact were under way or planned. At a review session in April 2008, we agreed to refocus on the impact of the money system and our role in it. We discussed the concept of the 'tempered radical' and there was a view that we could perhaps be a tempered radical business, supportive of the system in general, but wanting to change some damaging elements of that system from within. At the meeting in July, I proposed an attempt at a conscious co-operative inquiry into the current money system and its impacts, so that we could better understand our impact on sustainability and therefore what there is that we might want to be 'tempered radical' about. The meeting itself was difficult; there was no clear concept of what this 'inquiry' would look like in practice, and I got a strong sense of most people wanting to get on and do things, not inquire into them. We agreed that I would pursue the question in the next round of individual conversations.

The answers I got ranged from 'the inquiry is vital for all sorts of reasons', through 'can we do anything about it if there's something we need to change? Not a lot. But we should inquire into it and understand it', to 'stop inquiring and fast-forward to what an alternative would look like'. In the end, that is what I did. In the last workshop I ran with them, I went through my view of what 'sustainable banking' might look like. The session was lively and interactive, with high levels of involvement from them. And it was the last conversation we ever had on the topic.

Of the many questions that arise throughout this story, two stick out for me: why did people even listen; and why did the inquiry end as it did?

Feedback that I got as part of the process provides some practical and replicable answers to the first question. One key factor was that before I got engaged in sustainability questions, I had been visibly successful in a 'real' job (managing a multi-million-pound IT systems replacement programme), and at the time of my inquiry, as well as having responsibility for CSR across the business, I was also running a group-wide 'customer experience' programme reporting directly to the chief executive. As a result of all this I had developed some personal capital with him and the rest of the directors. As one person put it, if I took this stuff seriously, there might be something in it! Another important factor was my deliberate attempt to make myself vulnerable, in the belief that this might allow them, too, to open up. The covering note that accompanied the first set of 'different' reading that I sent out began with the words 'Here is a truth about me. I don't know what to do.' This must have been shocking, coming from someone who had previously been seen by them as an expert in his field, a person who could be relied on to come up with good answers, not just good questions. And in the first workshop that I ran with them, I shared the story of how getting involved in the MSc had been difficult and depressing for me, concluding with the 'Snowdust' haiku at the top of this piece rolling up on a screen over a picture of a snow-covered landscape. Again, feedback that I got after the session revealed the difference that this sharing of a relevant personal story had made.

As for the eventual end of the inquiry, reflecting on the final workshop session, I got a strong sense of two worlds co-existing in the room, in our relationship, and in the inquiry that I was trying to conduct with them. They were, for two hours, visiting me in the world that I spend most of my waking life in, engaging with the issues and priorities and imperatives that I was talking about, respecting my position, and understanding the conclusions I was reaching. And I could visit them in their world, understanding the issues, priorities and imperatives that drive them in fulfilling their responsibilities as directors of a substantial financial institution, respecting their position, and, based on the way that world works, agreeing with their conclusions. In retrospect, I think that this is a valid metaphor for the whole inquiry, right from those first individual conversations and the view that 'we are challenging a set of beliefs and assumptions, rather than operating within them'. That was exactly what I was encouraging (challenging?) them to do. What we eventually jointly failed to do was find a way, despite what I see as honest intent on both sides, to bring these two worlds together and start to construct an alternative shared world, an alternative set of shared beliefs and assumptions within which to operate. And I think that this became starkly obvious (though never stated) as a result of that final workshop. I think we all silently realised that we could not imagine bringing the two worlds together in any practical way without doing significant damage to the business as they saw it (and were expected to see it), and perhaps even to the fundamentals of doing business as they understood them.

There is another question: was my inquiry 'successful'? Has the whole banking system changed as a result of my intervention? Not that I've noticed. But what I set out to do was to find a way to engage a bunch of senior managers in a meaningful conversation about something that matters deeply to me. In this, yes, I succeeded. Even throughout the difficult period of 2008 when the full impact of the credit crunch that began in 2007 was being felt, and other huge business imperatives were soaking up time in executive diaries, I still got time with them to pursue the inquiry. I will never know what effects the inquiry may eventually have. And it's only snowdust.

Which brings me back to me, and the effect on me of being an 'inquirer'. Two of the things that the snowdust helped to crystallise at the end of 2005 were a presentation on complexity theory delivered to the MSc early that December, and the essence of a quotation from Wendell Berry. My take on complexity theory led me to believe that I could never be sure of the outcomes of my actions, and that therefore the best I could do was to live my values. The quote from Wendell Berry (in the context of protest, but easily transferable to my ongoing inquiry) was this:

> Much protest is naive; it expects quick, visible improvement and despairs and gives up when such improvement does not come ... Protest that endures, I think, is moved by a hope far more modest than that of public success: namely, the hope of preserving qualities in one's own heart and spirit that would be destroyed by acquiescence (Berry 1990).

Application of these ideas, and a deliberate memory of 'snowdust', sustained me through my inquiry. The work was difficult and time-consuming (I spent more time, per page, on the initial presentation to the directors, than I ever have or ever hope to again on any presentation!), and sometimes very frustrating. I found it very difficult to hold a position of inquiry, to avoid being the 'expert'. Sometimes I doubted my ability to find a way to keep meaningful conversations going. Eventually, the thing ended, signalled, perhaps, by my finally feeling compelled to take up the 'expert' role I had been trying so hard to avoid. But it was okay—I had done what I could do as well as I believe I could have done it, and that had to be enough.

However, in the background, something else had been creeping up on me, a pernicious sibling of my original depression. I increasingly found during 2008 that whenever I looked at something alive and beautiful, a landscape, a tree, whatever, I would instantly imagine it, *see it*, dead, rotten and spoiled. A constant debilitating vision of eventual ecosystem collapse sat behind whatever I looked at. Rational attempts to stop this, to let myself see just the beauty as it was, failed me. This was not a rational thing, and it would not go away. By the end of 2008, three years after the start of my story, this had started to wear me down. One night, in January 2009, I was walking home with my partner. It was very cold. We approached our house, and our car, a black hatchback. Ice had formed on the car; not hoar frost, but beautiful, swirling crystalline patterns on the black roof. I stared at it in wonder for a long moment and then went inside the house. It struck me the next day that I had seen only the fragile, ephemeral beauty of the ice, not its certain dissolution. And for some reason, ever since then, I have been able to regard natural beauty without unconsciously and automatically picturing its death. There's another haiku in this somewhere. I just haven't found it yet.

References

Berry, W. (1990) *What Are People For?* (New York: North Point Press).

Douthwaite, R. (1997) *The Problem with Growth* (Dublin: The Foundation for the Economics of Sustainability).

Douthwaite, R. (2000) *The Ecology of Money* (Totnes, UK: Green Books).

Jackson, T. (2009) *Prosperity without Growth? The transition to a sustainable economy* (London: Sustainable Development Commission).

Meadows, D.H., D.L. Meadows and J. Randers (1992) *Beyond the Limits: Global collapse or a sustainable future* (London: Earthscan).

——, J. Randers and D. Meadows (2004) *Limits to Growth: The 30-year update* (White River Junction, VT: Chelsea Green).

Rowbotham, M. (1998) *The Grip of Death: A study of modern money, debt slavery and destructive economics* (Charlbury, UK: John Carpenter).

Putting my learning into practice

Prishani Satyapal MSc9, 2005–2007

For all of my adult life I have had a yearning to understand how to most effectively harness the power of business to change the world. I have long believed that there is potential for business corporations to use their economic clout and cross-cultural people power to organise for a shared purpose.

I suppose, in many ways the cards have been stacked against me in this quest. I am a South African, and I work for a global gold-mining corporation in Africa. Recently I took over as head of Environment and Community Affairs for our operations in Ghana, which sees a company of just six years old taking on and managing mining complexes that have been around for 120 years.

My experience of community and environmental management or 'sustainability' was very limited until I arrived at the start of the MSc. Early course discussion was strongly based on the environment and, in particular, climate change. I thought that I had chosen the wrong degree. I thought, 'They don't get it—we can't worry about the environment in countries like South Africa, we need to make sure people get out of the poverty trap first.' I remember saying in class, 'Surely the social leg of the triple bottom line comes first?' (Elkington 1997).

Well, yes, in my worldview then, it did. In my mind I held what Argyris and Schön (1996) would call a 'governing variable': a central belief that to influence the behaviour of business so that it was positive and responsible was a noble and honourable goal. I did not question this but rather continuously tried to change how I went about trying to achieve it.

The new information I was learning about climate change, Earth systems science and the implications for business (Lovelock 1979; Porritt 2005; Harding 2006) resulted in my engaging in 'double-loop learning': I began to question my assumptions. My life to this point had been rearranging how I did things, not what I was doing it *for*. Senge (2006) refers to double-loop learning as unpacking the 'story behind every action'. This story, he goes on to say, 'exists not only in our rational minds, but in our emotions and our full bodies'.

I was constantly trying to do things differently because I felt I was not being effective, and I could not understand why. In my professional life I was engaging with 'sustainability' yet sometimes thought about feeling unfulfilled. I was frequently reminded to leave my emotions out of it, that this was a business and, to be effective, I had to be rational *only*—there was no place for the so-called 'soft stuff'.

Gradually, I began to explore what the story behind *my* actions contained, and to connect my emotions with my beliefs. My 'governing variable' shifted from thinking that a sustainable planet comes from managing the 'triple bottom line' to understanding that the economy and society depend on a complex natural environment that sustains our existence. We cannot 'manage' the environment; rather we have to work with the Earth to sustain ourselves, other beings and that same enabling Earth. My purpose has been reframed from *helping business to save the Earth* to helping business understand that the Earth is giving clear signals to say that our way of living may no longer be supportable.

This knowledge and reframing has given me much more confidence in my ability: I know that I have the skills to deal with the complex issues of gold mining. I believe it is the combination of ecologist + sociologist + business knowledge and skills that develop the appropriate level of thinking for roles such as mine. I believe that companies often wrongly identify environmental managers' ability as that of technical environmental specialists. These specialisations, I believe, have created myopic silos of environmental management (water separated from food security, separated from biodiversity, etc.). While we need specialist knowledge, we also definitely need people who can consider the bigger systemic implications of our practices and strategy. I draw on this insight in the strategy that I have developed for my role in Ghana (see Fig. 4.1).

Figure 4.1 **Thinking systemically**

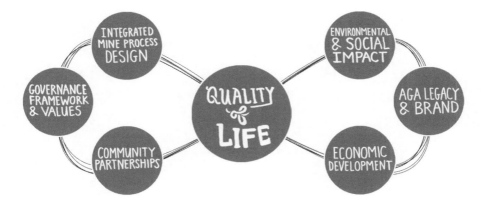

Learning about complexity in the MSc helped me know that the strategy I developed could not be a 'tick-and-move-on' action plan; rather an ongoing process, an infinite process of success and re-evaluation. The strategy is based on the symbol of the infinity curve, highlighting the facts that our approach will need to adapt to, and that we will adapt with, our ever-changing environment. Furthermore, infinity is used to show the never-ending interconnectedness and interdependence of the environment, society and the economy. Right at the centre of this is 'Quality of Life', a concept that integrates the business goals, and reminds us what this work is for.

I continue to believe that the social, environmental and investor benefits of mining can and must be balanced and that I can play some part in helping that happen, by bringing a more systemic way of thinking.

References

Argyris, C., and D. A. Schön (1996) *Organizational Learning II* (Reading, MA: Addison-Wesley).

Elkington, J. (1997) *Cannibals with Forks: The triple bottom line of 21st century business* (Oxford, UK: Capstone).

Harding, S.P. (2006) *Animate Earth* (Totnes, UK: Green Books).

Lovelock, J.E. (1979) *Gaia: A new look at life on Earth* (London: Oxford University Press).

Porritt, J. (2005) *Capitalism as if the World Matters* (London: Earthscan).

Senge, P. (2006) *The Fifth Discipline: The art and practice of the learning organization* (London: Random House).

5

Establishing sustainability practices in organisations and industries

- **Alison Kennedy**. Working below the parapet . . .
- **Kené Umeasiegbu**. Protesting and engaging for change
- **Vidhura Ralapanawe**. Building an iconic eco-factory

This chapter brings together three accounts of significant initiatives that have each changed the rules and influenced their sectors more widely. In their stories we see: collaboration, and its challenges, choices about how overt or covert to be, the roles of personal passion and commitment in motivating and communicating change, how people worked through inquiry and dialogue, and the arduous, detailed work required to turn visions into practice. The initiatives they developed are beacons that can influence systemic change more widely, thus we need to take a long-term view in judging effectiveness. These stories show the grit and determination that an individual has to show, even in orchestrating collaborative action.

Working below the parapet . . .

Alison Kennedy MSc11, 2007–2008

I would like to tell a story that started before I joined the MSc, but has taken on more significance since I have been able to put it in context and understand more about the approach to change I have been instinctively pursuing.

What do you think of when you think about books? I suspect that the content will come to mind before anything else. Occasionally you may consider them to be beautifully or badly produced. But few people consider the implications of the manufacturing of a book, unless like me you have been responsible for putting ink onto paper for various published items for many years. I hope that you are now looking at this book with more respect for its physical entity as well as for its written messages.

As a publisher of children's books, I must also think about safety—some titles more closely resemble toys than conventional books. Then there is the responsibility for the factory and factory workers' conditions, and here I join with a group of like-minded publishers to use the ICTI (International Council of Toy Industries) CARE standard to assess and audit the factories we use around the world. As a production and distribution director I must also observe the commercial criteria to purchase at the best price, to meet and exceed the schedule requirements, and to produce the materials to the best possible quality within the technological capabilities available. But my personal passion, above all, lies with my responsibility for the forest sources that make up the paper that we use in our books.

During the first years of the new millennium WWF campaigned to make major retailers (and therefore us) aware of the issue of forest-fibres in paper. I felt this was to be applauded, but that it was not enough, since it required retrospective reporting and only applied to pulp. But, it was the prompt I needed to begin a search for a tool that would allow me to proactively choose sustainable papers. The more I searched for such a system the more helpless I felt. There seemed no differentiation other than the beginnings of the Forest Stewardship Council (FSC) accreditation that had begun with sustainable wood sourcing and which was slowly being applied to a very limited range of papers. The only way to show sustainability was to use FSC or 100% post-consumer recycled paper.

I was wary of making others aware of the time and energy involved in my search, so I operated 'below the parapet'. After several false starts with environmentally passionate, but commercially naive partners, I was overjoyed when I met by chance an environmental consultant who spoke about the environment (or what we might now call sustainability) from a commercial standpoint. Since my experiences on the MSc, I have learned to recognise and respect such encounters as signs of 'synchronicity' (Jaworski 1996). I had at last found someone who had the skills and the patience to help me define my idea as well as the ambition to look beyond the very apparent difficulties of putting it in place.

We set about creating a grading system which would allow me to understand the sustainability of all my papers, which we later published and copyrighted. It defined a set of criteria which would allow someone to apply a grade to any paper based on each species and forest location within it: grade 1, with illegal sources, through grade 2, with missing sources, to grade 3, baseline sustainability, through 4 to 5 which is FSC or 100% post-consumer recycled.

The next step was to engage with the long supply chain from printer back through paper broker, merchant, pulp mill, paper mill and a number of other levels to forest. I brought together ten of my suppliers (accounting for over 95% of my manufacturing base) for a workshop where I shared my ambition to remove all unwanted and unknown tree sources from my paper supply. This was ambitious, since each paper may be made up of anywhere between 1 and 15 pulps, and each pulp itself may be made up of anywhere between 1 and 15 different tree sources. At this workshop I explained that, for me, it was not, nearly, enough to have a few books on FSC or recycled paper; I wanted to know that everything I produced was at least legal (not logged from protected forests), something that I, or any other publisher at that time, would be unable to claim. I implored the suppliers to provide me with the information I needed to use the grading system so that I could both make informed decisions and allow them to be part of a more sustainable supply chain.

My passion for this work enabled me, I think, to really drive home my idea. The workshop was a great success and our suppliers left London keen to provide the information. However the reality of seeking this information down the supply chain proved frustrating and long-winded. With dogged determination I pushed the suppliers to keep up the pressure on their supply chains. Each time that I thought that we would fail, I resorted to the 'final' chasing email suggesting that I would give up on the paper (and therefore the supplier) and there would be a final push to provide the information. In the end we were able to grade enough at grade 3 and above to make sustainable decisions on our purchasing. Two years on from the workshop I was able to claim we did not have any unwanted or unknown forest sources in any paper, in any of our books. It was only at this point that I fully shared what I had been doing with the board and the decision was made to make this work on sustainable paper sourcing a defining part of our brand, along with product safety and ethical factories.

So we enjoyed some good publicity from all this, but soon it was time to ask 'what next?' I became uncomfortable at telling the story of the grading system over and over again. I knew that we had a powerful tool and that we had reached a place of comfort for ourselves. But, I constantly questioned what difference we, as just one company, were really making to change the face of sustainable paper sourcing.

It was then suggested that a truly ethical approach would be to share the tool with other publishers. After all we had a system that worked, and we knew from our own experience just how much illegal paper was being unknowingly used by suppliers to the UK publishing industry. So, in June 2006 I invited ten publishers to our offices for a presentation about the work, and what it had enabled us to do, and to establish whether it was of interest to others. After four meetings, in as many months, we had formed a group, PREPS (Publishers' Database for Responsible Environmental Paper Sourcing), which had agreed to establish a secretariat to build, populate and maintain a database of papers which would be graded using our copyrighted grading system.[1] Three years on PREPS now has in excess of 4,000 papers in the database, an annual third-party audit of our system, and a membership of 19 publishers, including publishers from Germany, Norway and the US as well as UK members. We regularly engage with the mills and other key stakeholders such as the environmental NGOs to ensure we keep our joint purpose of being both commercial and sustainable.

I don't intend to stop there. I have instigated a couple of other initiatives, but they are too ahead of their time to be brought out into the light and will stay 'below the parapet' until the time is right, and the appropriate partners are in place. I have learned not to give up but simply to look for that synchronicity which will confirm that the time is right to move forward.

Reference

Jaworski, J. (1996) *Synchronicity: The inner path of leadership* (San Francisco. Berrett-Koehler).

1   See www.prepsgroup.com, accessed 31 December 2010.

Protesting and engaging for change

Kené Umeasiegbu MSc11, 2007–2009

I took part in one of the 2009 G-20 protest marches in London, marching for action on climate change and social injustice. We were a mixed group: faith groups marching for aid to Africa; socialists marching for job security and tighter regulation of banks; pacifists demonstrating against the wars in Iraq and Afghanistan; anarchists protesting against all authority. There was much passion in the air. But when the bullhorn-wielding guy chanted that protest mantra: 'What do we want?' there was an amusingly awkward mumble as we tried to give an answer. A fellow marcher asked my views on the efficacy of protest marches. I reflected that most of us march partly to achieve some results and partly to satisfy our conscience that we have done our bit: a quest for effectiveness, or for vindication. Our conversation got me thinking anew about the relationship between protesting and engaging. How best might one act to bring about change in society: protesting at the gates or walking through to engage in a boardroom? Exploring this relationship strongly inspires my career.

I protest, so I engage

My view today is that protesting and engaging are both important in driving change. Public demonstrations crucially raise the profile of an issue and rally people around it. Yet having made the case for change, engagement must follow—connecting key actors to create a new reality. In other words, an effective social change strategy needs the tactics of both protesting and engaging. Various actors may be drawn to one or the other as their preferred vehicle for change, depending on their world-view, circumstances, action logics and emotional drivers.

Public protesting has an admirably dramatic and courageous quality about it which engagement appears to lack. All change agents start from the point of 'protesting' about the world as they see it. However, those in search of vindication alone find fulfilment in the cathartic experience of protesting without ever engaging, while those in search of effectiveness often need to endure the assiduous exercise of engagement to attain the same fulfilment. Protesting requires resolve and courage in the face of opposition. Engagement also demands resolve and courage, but this must be combined with collaboration, diligence, focus and optimistic resourcefulness—all sustained over the long term. This makes engagement quite an arduous tactic. But, as an essential ingredient for change, it cannot be ignored.

For many campaigners in the West, social and environmental injustice is important, yet distant. Unlike them, as an African, I know people in my extended family
whose lives are directly impacted by this injustice. This places the cost of ineffec-
tiveness in stark human terms. So my interest in this subject needs to evolve further than political posturing or intellectual sparring, to seeking tangible solutions.
Against this background, simply pursuing the catharsis of protesting could become
self-indulgent.

My interest in understanding the balance between vindication and effectiveness,
as well as my inquiry into 'ethical globalisation' led me to Cadbury plc, a global
confectionery company based in London. Over six years, I navigated my career
through the company's corporate responsibility agenda; nurturing along the way
my idealism and cynicism, disappointments and optimism—and new convictions
about the prospects of an ethical globalisation. Perhaps my biggest surprise working in a corporation was the number of employees who long for a better world, but
who respond to this only in their private lives because their jobs offer little platform for action. My experiences also taught me to appreciate the vital contribution
of campaigners who challenge the status quo, thereby bolstering those of us who
engage from within. My inquiry also led me to the MSc course in Responsibility
and Business Practice which, in offering tools to engage others in a shared inquiry,
proved invaluable to my subsequent roles.

My last role at Cadbury (until my departure in mid-2009) was setting up the Cadbury Cocoa Partnership, a £45 million investment established in 2007 to address
social and environmental sustainability issues affecting cocoa-growing communities in Ghana, India, Indonesia and Dominican Republic. These issues—which epit-
omise an 'ethical and sustainable supply chain'—include sustainable agriculture,
labour practices (especially addressing child labour), farmer livelihoods and community development. Since Cadbury lacks the capability to address these issues,
it established a partnership comprising organisations with the requisite expertise, including the United Nations Development Programme (UNDP), Care International, World Vision, Anti-Slavery International, International Cocoa Initiative,
Nature Conservation Research Centre and Voluntary Services Overseas. Together
with Cadbury, they form the partnership's international board which oversees its
programmes. An implementation board in Ghana (comprising government, farmer
representatives and local chapters of three international charities) manages on-
the-ground project delivery. I was responsible for programme implementation and
governance, and for facilitating the engagement of partners on the international
and Ghana teams. In this role, I had to maintain the drive for results, while balancing the diverse interests of partners.

Facilitating engagement with others

Building engagement starts with fostering the right conditions for various parties
to work together toward a shared goal. In practice, this is not easy.

In my personal assessment of the Cadbury Cocoa Partnership, all partners are conceptually inspired by the vision of an ethical supply chain, yet each retains some core interests that must be accommodated. These range from clear business outcomes for Cadbury, to advancing the Millennium Development Goals for UNDP while demonstrating their expertise at partnering with companies. The charities want funding for their projects while safeguarding their reputation from accusations of 'selling out' to a corporation. Politicians want immediate results for their constituencies. Farming communities want to learn better farming techniques, earn more income and improve their social conditions. From these diverse interests, we were able to agree concrete shared goals around empowering and improving farming communities.

Nevertheless, the partnership faced some challenging power dynamics and conflicting egos—including mine. All too often, our shared goals were relegated to the background in the clash of peripheral interests (partners' competing pet projects, debate over administrative charges, rivalry between charities, and so on). Additionally, in order to ensure that Cadbury's interests do not override other partners', international board members spent three months haggling over the partnership charter and concentrating power around themselves. They decided that the Ghana board—the only team with farmer representation—would not be competent enough to run its own affairs, therefore all key decisions were made in London and handed down. Sometimes ideas that would benefit farming communities were disregarded unless proffered by the more powerful board members. I thought this led to a squandering of resources and attenuation of some programme goals. Also, as the only African at international board meetings, I felt uncomfortable with what I perceived as an attitude of condescension among these well-meaning partners towards the communities they were seeking to help. In moments of frustration and powerlessness, I found myself craving the cathartic experience of protesting. I did lash out on a number of occasions, sternly criticising some decisions and attitudes! Although it felt good to protest, it tended to alienate those I needed to engage for results. By contrast, I felt we managed tensions better and maintained focus on our shared goals when I facilitated our meetings like a form of action inquiry—including investing in one-on-one engagement with key partners (Martin 2006).

Expanding my view

The Cadbury Cocoa Partnership illustrates what it takes to turn personal commitment into action within a corporation. The partnership is partly a response to pressure from campaigners to end child labour in cocoa farming, but partly also, an expression of the personal commitment of Cadbury's leadership to building a more ethical supply chain. Granted, this commitment is secondary to the goal of growing shareholder value, but it is genuine nonetheless, as Cadbury rightly argues that creating long-term shareholder value requires a sustainable supply chain.

Ignoring my personal frustrations, I think the partnership is achieving more results than any of the parties could have done in isolation. After its first year, the partnership led to Fair Trade certification for Cadbury chocolate, keeping the spotlight on the ethical sourcing of cocoa. This in turn, motivated other major chocolate manufacturers in the UK to review their cocoa supply chains and seek independent certification. In all its imperfections, Fair Trade's approach of empowering farmer cooperatives, in my view, strengthens the farmer's voice in supply chains and enhances implementation of sustainable agriculture initiatives. The partnership also illustrates what can be achieved when charities go beyond protesting, to engage with companies. Some campaigning charities declined to join the partnership but those that did are directly influencing Cadbury's cocoa supply chain.

The ability to see the big picture, balance seemingly conflicting interests and be motivated by longer-term objectives requires at least a 'strategist' action logic according to the leadership development framework (Fisher *et al.* 2003). In demonstrating how personal development can drive organisational transformation, this framework is supporting my ongoing quest for effectiveness.

When to engage; when to walk away?

I believe that to achieve viable and lasting change, protesting must lead to the genuine engagement of possibly conflicting parties. The ability to engage effectively depends in part on the balance of power among actors, and in part on their willingness and competence to participate in co-creating a new reality. Yet there are occasions when the results of engagement do not justify the effort. Engagement occurs over the long term; therefore there is always a risk of getting comfortable in the order that one set out to change. There is also the possibility of creating the illusion of engagement, while only the powerful actors actually define the new reality. These are the risks that discourage many activists from engaging with governments and corporations.

So I hold these questions as I continue to cultivate my ability to facilitate engagement: how to know when protesting must give way to engagement; how to prepare all parties for genuine engagement; how to retain the optimistic resourcefulness to keep experimenting with new solutions. Equally, how do I know when engagement is failing, when I should return to protesting? These questions inspire the next stage of my inquiry. For now, I have come only as far as acknowledging that craving vindication is not a sufficient basis for choosing how to act. That feeling tends to lead me towards protesting—even when it is clearly ineffective.

References

Fisher, D., D. Rooke and B. Torbert (2003) *Personal and Organisational Transformations through Action Inquiry* (Boston, MA: Edge/Work Press).

Martin, A. (2006) 'Large-group Processes as Action Research', in P. Reason and H. Bradbury (eds.), *Handbook of Action Research* (London: Sage Publications, concise paperback edn): 166-75.

Building an iconic eco-factory

Vidhura Ralapanawe MSc2, 1998–2000

In January 2007, Sir Stuart Rose, CEO of Marks & Spencer (M&S), launched Plan A, the company's widely acclaimed sustainability plan, which listed 100 initiatives under five pillars, of which climate change was the most significant. As sustainability plans go, it was remarkable in its reach and depth. Of the 100 commitments, one referred to building a green factory to supply apparel to M&S. Sri Lanka had been identified as a possible location for this venture, owing to its reputation in the apparel industry both for ethical manufacture and also as open to new ideas. MAS Holdings (MAS), the largest apparel exporter in the region with a workforce of 45,000 and annual revenue of US$800 million (2009), was well placed to respond to the challenge.

The apparel industry in Sri Lanka contrasts with the general industry stereotype. Owing to tighter national labour laws and practices from progressive companies such as MAS, the Sri Lankan industry provides higher worker well-being and pay than the neighbouring countries. This and better standards of living in Sri Lanka create a higher cost base for the manufacturers, threatening their survival in the fiercely price-competitive global apparel markets.

The green factory 'competition'

In February 2007, an M&S team approached the three largest suppliers in Sri Lanka, MAS, Brandix and Hirdaramani, to explore building a 'green' factory. Owing to my background in sustainability, I was part of the team from MAS that took part in the meeting with M&S representatives, led by Dian Gomes, Managing Director of MAS Intimates.

The discussion revolved around 'what is a green factory?' And it was clear that the answer to that question must also emerge from the project. Within the meeting I found myself playing the role of an expert—drawing on my knowledge of green buildings and the Sri Lankan energy market. The discussion touched on possible KPIs (key performance indicators) for a green factory, the challenges of converting existing facilities vs. new constructions, and carbon neutrality.

This meeting set the stage for what was to come. It was a confidence builder for M&S, demonstrating that MAS had the knowledge and capability to deliver. It also built confidence with Dian, that we could successfully do this internally, and led to my eventual leadership of the project.

MAS was aspiring to become a strategic vendor to M&S, and a green factory supporting Plan A would strengthen the relationship significantly. The MAS business model is relationship based, not transactional. While M&S was clear that there would be minimal financing coming from the UK, and that there are no guaranteed orders for the factory, these were not considered as serious challenges. If MAS builds a worthy facility, M&S is unlikely to move away from it. Additionally, it gives MAS a solid foundation on its journey to position itself as the premier *ethical* apparel manufacturer globally. The timing is right; the organisation is in an expansionary phase looking to enhance its bra manufacturing capacity.

M&S framed the agenda by offering the 'M&S partnered green factory' to all three manufacturers, leveraging the hyper-competitiveness among the three players in the local market. And that played well at the end for M&S, with all three manufacturers coming up with 'green factories' within a two-year timeframe.

The beginning of the journey

In April 2007, Dian decided that we would take on the challenge. He felt that sustainability is an imperative of the future, and a host of 'green factories' will follow. MAS culture, which Dian was instrumental in shaping, is based on aggressive competition and pursuit of excellence; this imposed twin demands: to be the first, and the best. We targeted a three-year window; the factory, MAS Intimates Thurulie, has to be the best in the world for at least three years.

Dian assigned three key people for the project. I was to head the design phase of the project and Ushaan Abeywickrema was appointed general manager of the plant. Having played multiple roles in the company, Ushaan had a reputation of 'getting things done' irrespective of complexity and timelines. He was to take charge of the construction as well as ensuring that other elements of the factory (people, processes, equipment) were in place when we opened. Sanjeewa Lokuliyana was to be the lead architect.

We brought together a team from the University of Moratuwa in Sri Lanka to add the technical expertise—led by Professor Rohinton Emmanuel. While the consultants had the knowledge and experience in the industry, this was their first 'green building'.

The factory was to be located in MAS Fabric Park, an export processing zone managed by MAS in Thulhiriya, 60 km north-east of Colombo. Out of the available sites in the park, we selected one with a water body and lush greenery.

My initial role was to set the context within which the design was to take place. The building should educate (a 'model'), inspire and influence the future. The focus was on the *story* as much as the KPIs. We deconstructed the typical factory—trying to understand what parts of the operations are open to new interpretations and solutions. As a company with over 25 factories in Sri Lanka, MAS has 'a way of doing things'—a socio-technical regime (Geels and Schot 2007) that can often be a barrier to innovation. My task was to keep the group in a mode of inquiry, to always ask why, and how can we improve on things.

Professor Emmanuel drew up a philosophical framework that encompassed our approach: honour the space and location, the worker and nature. MAS was already fundamentally rearranging the way its operations were run, moving into a lean manufacturing model. The way work is organised within factories was being redesigned, shifting from 'lines' of machine operators performing the smallest sub-division of the production process, to self-managed teams. This required a new team culture and a new approach to work at all levels.

Our challenge was to find ways these changes in the socio-organisational sphere could be enabled through changes to the structure and fabric of the building. Thus we opted for multiple compact spaces where people get to know each other, away from a large hall where the individual is anonymous. We looked at worker well-being more holistically; in addition to thermal comfort (the *only* domain traditional manufacturing facilities focus on), the team set its sights on indoor air quality, outside views, daylighting, aesthetics and the outdoor environment as critical elements of the design.

A building is more than a mere collection of spaces; it plays an important role of building community. Thus walkways and gathering spaces (cafeteria, etc.) become important beyond the 'functionality', inviting us to look at where to place them and their aesthetics. We also looked at spaces for creativity and contemplation. The ability to be closer to nature was within 'our interpretation' of a green building; and it would also mimic the lush green environment the employees come from.

Tackling energy and thermal comfort

Thulhiriya is located in the wet zone of Sri Lanka with a tropical hot-humid climate. Providing low-carbon thermal comfort to approximately 1,300 people working in the facility was a challenge. Air-conditioning, the obvious solution, consumes about 45% of the energy load of a typical apparel plant in Sri Lanka. Evaporative cooling, a system that sends cooled air with higher humidity, is an alternative, with 75% savings on energy, but does not work well in humid environments. Worker discomfort would contribute to lower efficiencies and high staff turnover. Sweating would create stains and quality issues.

We looked at thermal comfort beyond the single value indicator (temperature) to a more nuanced definition that included temperature, humidity, air velocity and adaptation of local populace. The solution also had to meet international comfort standards, which was critical for the highest 'Platinum' rating of the LEED (Leadership in Energy and Environmental Design) green building certification the plant was aiming for. A green building is more than an assortment of 'green features'. We needed to design an *integrated system* where interdependent components come together to create multiple synergies.

An elegant four-pronged design emerged:

1. A building that minimised passive heat gain (orientation, green roofs, cool roofs, courtyards, overhangs)

2. A cooler micro-climate (over 400 trees planted in the surrounding area, specifically selected to create canopy forest conditions)

3. Behaviour modification (breathable light attire and change in certain work habits)

4. A ducted evaporative cooling system which provides cooled air at higher velocities

Whether the solution could move beyond theory had to be proved *before* the final implementation. A staff training facility was set up in an existing building; system testing and optimisation for six months preceded the actual deployment.

The evaporative cooling system, daylighting and high-efficiency lighting system that we designed promised a 40% reduction in energy use. On-site solar installation took 10% of the remaining load, with the first net metering arrangement for Sri Lanka. A mechanism to buy green power from the grid, which did not exist before, was created with the government energy regulator. MAS signed the first green power purchase agreement of Sri Lanka with Hydropower International, a small hydropower producer, making Thurulie the first 100% renewable powered manufacturing facility in Sri Lanka.

The translator and the enabler

The success of the project depended on the ability of multiple groups—the Thurulie project team, the consultants, the construction company and the MAS business team—to learn and work together. The teams came together easily because of a shared ideal: building the world's first eco-factory. This was all the more attractive at a time when Sri Lanka was searching for 'good news'.

Yet the teams also occupied different territories. The consultants drawn from academia were focused on technical excellence, and the business teams were looking at the financial issues. M&S wanted a story that would resonate with their consumers, especially as an early success story of Plan A that demonstrated its aims visually. Each group viewed the project from its own lens, and I found myself straddling multiple domains: a translator, able to speak in a multiplicity of languages and reframe as the situation demanded.

My engineering background and time spent on learning about green buildings helped me understand and influence the theoretical aspects of the design. I understood the business context from my engagement in the company, and for the construction teams I became the primary interface and the 'specialist' on green design. I opted to spend time talking about our vision and the role of the factory in the larger context, and this found resonance among many, including the contractors, enabling the group to coalesce for a shared vision.

Ushaan was the ultimate enabler, pragmatic and action-oriented, counterbalancing the 'dreamers' among the team (including me). It was ultimately his responsibility that the factory became a reality. It needed to open fully staffed—having recruited and trained staff and management, put systems and machines in place— and be ready to begin operations.

Our relationship was the axis around which the project revolved. We had worked together before, and had deep appreciation of the strengths each brought to the table. We both understood that we were shaping industry, and within it, MAS.

We still had to sell the design to the company; the project had to be signed off by a wider audience including finance, manufacturing specialists and the Chairman, Deshamanya Mahesh Amalean, who took a personal interest in the design. We had to go back to the drawing board twice, to ensure business needs were met and costs managed, resulting in a much more robust design, still staying true to the original vision. We used all the skills in our arsenal, backed by passion and sheer doggedness to get the project approved. We had full backing from Dian, which ensured that the project stayed on track.

The timeline was bordering impossible; Dian wanted the factory to be operational in early 2008. We needed a construction partner who could deliver the resources to complete the project swiftly and who would not shy away from trying out new concepts and methods.

Captain M.G. Kularatne, CEO of MAGA Engineering, the largest construction company in Sri Lanka, became an early enthusiastic supporter. Though the project was much smaller than they normally handle, they were keen to be part of the 'first eco-factory for apparel'. We were able to tap into similar sentiment with all other building service providers and suppliers.

The team was able to retain its innovative spirit beyond planning into the construction phase. This was partly because the core team that planned was also the team tasked with execution. Not all ideas worked but the spirit of innovation was infectious. Even the masons came up with ways to improve.

Even with a large number of specialist subcontractors and heavy timeline pressures, the team was able to keep the culture of inquiry alive. Asoka de Silva, the Project Manager from MAGA, commented,

> At the end of the day what struck me was . . . this is the first time I'm having site meetings of this nature. It's usually far more aggressive . . . Here it's not like that, here even if something is not done we sort it out in a reasonable way.

This approach benefited MAS in the end when we were requested to finish and open the plant one month before the planned completion date halfway into the project.

Serendipity and reflections

The plant was officially opened by Sir Stuart Rose, CEO of Marks & Spencer, and Deshamanya Mahesh Amalean, Chairman of MAS Holdings, on 25 April 2008, less than 13 months from the first planning meeting. The factory was widely profiled globally including a piece in *The Economist*. Thurulie also received the coveted LEED Platinum certification from the US Green Building Council, making it perhaps the first purpose-built factory to do so.

Many factors played to the success of the project. MAS as an organisation is better poised to tackle breakthrough projects. There is a strong subtext of the hero myth within the organisation, and a strong culture of empowered agency with wide room to act. Yet culture is merely an enabler; the strong strategic sense of the decisions—not only to build a green factory, but also to do one that is radical in its approach—taken by Dian and Mahesh was critical. Dian, especially, in his role as 'protector' of the team, ensured that the project streamed ahead without issues.

Getting the correct team was also important. The management team of the factory were its co-creators, with a strong sense of ownership, which kept the 'spirit of Thurulie' alive.

Thurulie was not an end in itself; it was an event that prompted larger changes in the apparel industry. It also helped to coalesce a larger movement within MAS, which is addressing sustainability at a much more radical level. An important step in a long journey.

Reference

Geels, F.W., and J. Schot (2007) 'Typology of Sociotechnical Transition Pathways', *Research Policy* 36: 399-417.

6

Paying attention to everyday practices of sustainable living

- **Helen Sieroda**. Like a river flows: how do we call forth 'a world worthy of human aspiration'?

- **Jon Alexander**. Sport as inquiry: safe escape, activism and a journey into self

This chapter brings together two accounts that focus on the everyday attentions and practices of living with sustainability in mind. We have called them 'micro-practices' elsewhere in this book, and see them as significant and political—the detailed forms in which new possibilities are created, enacted and disseminated. Helen and Jon's concerns are widely shared among MSc course participants and graduates, and many people have a parallel story of this kind to tell. We caught glimpses, for example, in the stories from Christel Scholten, James Barlow and Mark Gater in Chapter 4.

These two stories have common themes in embodiment, subtle attentions and reflective action. They are also distinct, reflecting the different lives from which they emerge.

Like a river flows:[1] how do we call forth 'a world worthy of human aspiration'?[2]

Helen Sieroda MSc11, 2007–2009

We face an uncertain and fragile future. How to respond? Where to intervene? With such complex interconnected challenges, when so much needs fixing so urgently, how to act in ways that are helpful rather than harmful? This story gives a taste of how I've been coming to grips with these questions.

Often I feel caught between worlds. At work I'm 'important', a respected senior practitioner, a 'leader' who earns a good fee. At home my activities seem invisible. I hadn't paid much attention to this split at the heart of my life until the MSc brought home how our economic system only values activities that go through the market-place. Much is excluded from this world: unpaid work; community; the environmental and social costs of consumer goods. If something can't be measured, it's invisible—as if it doesn't exist. How can I honour different strands of my life: mother, community member, global citizen, not just the professional? Partly in defiance, partly affirmation, I decided to examine everyday actions and interactions—things in my life that don't 'count': gardening; parenting; being in nature; conversations; the list goes on—all unpaid and officially 'of little or no importance' as depicted in the UN System of National Accounts (Waring 1995). I say I value these things; I wanted to challenge myself to 'walk the talk' by giving them full attention.

I began on my allotment; I sowed and weeded, pondering the challenge of sustainability, wondering about the rootlessness of modern life. What might it mean to have one's identity and behaviour shaped and nourished through participation in a specific place? I reflected on the layers of meaning in local landscape: geology, ecology, history, a sense of the sacred, making place both 'geographical terrain and a terrain of consciousness'.[3] One summer, ignoring all things human, I set out to explore my bioregion, eager to learn about wildlife, moors and rivers. I soon realised that treeless 'wild' Dartmoor, with its Bronze Age remains, recent trackways, leats[4] and farms, speaks of 6,000 years of human involvement. Nevertheless, it seemed normal to view nature as separate from being human; I stood on the moors, map in hand, a spectator stranded inside a human body, living a deeply

1 From the poem 'Fluent' by John O'Donohue.
2 Reason and Bradbury 2006: 344.
3 www.heartoftheearth.org, accessed 31 December 2010.
4 Leats, common on Dartmoor, are artificial watercourses, usually used for irrigation, to provide drinking water, to supply water to a mill or for tin mining.

rooted conceptual disconnection between *human* and *nature*. I'd read about the Cartesian split between thinking mind and embodied matter; discovering how it coloured my relationship with place shook me. My previously abstract view of our prevailing paradigm became painfully real. Clearly, my investigation into the value of personal, local micro-practices needed to include a deeper understanding of worldviews and whole system macro-perspectives.

How to address this disembodiment? Looking for physical, connected knowledge, I continued gardening and walking. Philosopher Freya Mathews (2005: 55) argues that, with steady, patient repetition and a caring attitude, the world 'makes room for us', so over time we become *native*: 'the people of this place'. The idea is simple: individuals, families and communities in rural, urban or suburban contexts can participate as long as they can commit to a place and make it home. For example, opposite our house is a granite wall. Last spring, invisible behind ivy and bindweed, a bird made its nest. Quietly listening to the chicks became a daily routine with my son on the way to and from school. Developing proximity and love for the particulars of place is one practice that reconnects.

Another involves engaging with 'what is'. It's easy to idealise nature as always pleasant and abundant, without flood, drought or imperfection; in reality Dartmoor can be hazardous and harsh. I 'soldier on' captured by an *ideal* of how things should be while denying the *actual*; a quagmire makes a gateway impassable; today the soil is too wet to work; badgers inevitably guzzle unprotected sweetcorn. When plans fail I can try harder, throwing more of the same at a problem, or instead try 'bending': aligning activities 'with the grain of the given' (Mathews 2005: 26); accommodating unpredictability; working with what presents itself—one's stamina, the terrain or weather. Learning to adapt to what is available *here* has far-reaching implications. Every day we participate in what Thomas Berry (1999: 59) calls a 'humanly constructed wonderworld', manipulating the world to serve individual ideals and interests, and in the process inadvertently creating a 'wasteworld'. Because we are embedded in infinitely complex systems, even with the best of intentions, intervening for sustainability from 'outside'—while denying reality or holding unexamined preconceptions, preferences or prejudices about how things *should* be—could carry similar unintended consequences. Rather than making decisions abstractly, I try stopping to connect with my surroundings (inner and outer) letting a subtle sense of what is emerging from within the connection guide action. Pondering the tension between 'letting be' and the need to intervene leads to some simple questions: How to live well in *this* place? What are its constraints, gifts and potential sources of energy? What grows well here? What's in season? What helps this community flourish? Physical environment interweaves with human community, mapping deep accumulations of memories, dreams and evolving relationship between people and place.

Next, I turned my attention to seemingly inconsequential commonplace human associations, interactions with local traders or neighbours and conversations at the primary school gate. Increasingly the latter became my focus; the head resigned, precipitating a wave of complaints. For years the school has lurched from crisis to crisis. Earlier I'd set up a 'Parent Forum', a parent–community partnership intended to help the school succeed, as well as work to support eco-literacy projects. Now I found myself criticising, as a familiar cycle took hold. As I attempted to understand what was happening systemically I drew a feedback diagram (Fig. 6.1).

Figure 6.1 **'Here We Go Again'**

When the school is seen as failing, those who can will remove their children. The roll falls; funding, morale and performance (teachers' and pupils') nosedive. Less obvious and longer term is the impact on community—removed children grow up not belonging here. Commitment to place is eroded, young adults trickle away; the community loses resilience.

As individual parents we feel powerless to change the situation, but if the situation is viewed as an open system shaped by all kinds of 'insignificant' daily interaction then perhaps we precipitate change in unforeseen ways. By sharing stories we shape awareness of the issues, influencing the agenda. When I criticise do I actively contribute to an adversarial complaints culture, co-creating the *idea* of a failing school? Am I part of the problem? But what if parental revolt is not a bad thing? I worry that this educational system isn't serving our children with its stressed teachers, narrow curriculum and obsession with testing. Is it failing to prepare them for the future? Should I stop adapting to (and thus creating) the status quo? Increasingly, I believe this kind of critical awareness or 'inquiry' is needed to address the complex challenges of sustainability. The questions are uncomfortable, and 'right' answers aren't obvious.

Paradox runs through this narrative: intervening and 'going with the grain of the given'; allowing events to unfold yet holding clear intent; working to revive the school while questioning the system; trying to intervene in the world by attending to small, personal activities. This last point raises uncomfortable questions about how to gauge the effectiveness of actions. Am I doing enough? It's easier achieving 'out front', gathering accolades for heroic 'world saving' deeds. In contrast this approach demands humility: I can't take credit; I don't get 'strokes'. Feedback is crucial; the problem is how to get it? I began recording everyday unsolicited comments that I usually don't absorb and was surprised at how much accumulated over the weeks.

Here is a sample:

> I wouldn't have done this grant application if it hadn't been for initiation sessions around your kitchen table.

> You don't realise how important your input is—you hold the space.

> You have a gift for being there when needed. Unobtrusive. I couldn't have done this project without you.

> You're often quiet, just listening; then come in with a few words that capture things, taking the discussion to another level. You get to the heart of the matter, and make it look effortless.

Slowly I began to appreciate the value of 'just being there' as a sounding board, helping develop strategies, encouraging, commiserating and sharing countless conversations.

Where does leadership for sustainability begin and end? I'm beginning to see leadership not as a thing but a process. I'm learning the value of vulnerability, yielding, silence, clarity, humility and 'heart'. This feels like a process of getting out of the way and allowing something bigger than me to unfold. Perhaps my greatest learning is that tending the allotment, raising my son, cultivating a sensuous, aesthetic and spiritual connection with the natural world are not trivial side issues in the race to a low-carbon society, but the foundation of a flourishing, just, resilient world. For me this is the ground of inspired personal action.

Nevertheless, I detect an urge to share how this process extended into my working life where I occupy a 'proper' leadership role. Might this enhance my credibility? This is a raw learning edge . . .

References

Berry, T. (1999) *The Great Work: Our way into the future* (New York: Bell Tower).

Mathews, F. (2005) *Reinhabiting Reality* (Albany, NY: SUNY Press).

Reason, P., and H. Bradbury (eds.) (2006) *Handbook of Action Research* (London: Sage Publications, concise paperback edn).

Waring, M. (1995) *Who's Counting? Sex, lies and global economics* (DVD; Montreal: National Film Board of Canada).

Sport as inquiry: safe escape, activism and a journey into self

Jon Alexander MSc12, 2008–2010

In many ways, action research has not come easily to me. By the standards London culture seems to set, I am as successful as a 27-year-old man could hope to be. I have achieved beyond my years in academia, sport and business, and in order to do so I have played by the rules, played to win, and often won. And yet beneath that I have carried deep doubts about the very rules by which I played. My first workshop on the MSc in Responsibility and Business Practice was—in the best possible way—a traumatic experience, in which all those doubts were allowed their first breath of air. For the first year of the course, however, while I dug wholeheartedly into the academic side of the degree (new economics, globalisation, climate science, and so on), I struggled to find ways to experiment practically, with my own lived experience. It was only in the second year that I began to find a way to direct this new questioning self, and to identify a setting in which I could play with making my own rules for the first time. That setting was sport, and in this short piece I attempt to show how by inquiring into a personal passion I've found a new sense of my own power in the world, and gained a deeper understanding of myself.

Sport as safe escape

'The cause of our apathy, however, is not indifference. It stems from a fear that lurks beneath the tenor of life-as-usual. Sometimes it manifests itself in dreams of mass destruction, and is exorcised in the morning jog and shower' (Macy 2007: 92).

As of March 2009, this is what I thought was the extent of the role of sport for me, an act of exorcism separate from and in service to my 'real work'. My theoretical critique of advertising was deepening and becoming more damning as I studied. I was coming to see advertising as a whole as a pervasive force, reinforcing and enhancing the increasingly materialistic values and behaviours of our society which I believe are at the root of so many of our problems (see Crompton and Kasser 2009 for a powerful discussion of these issues); yet in practice I was a miserable breed of tempered radical (Meyerson and Scully 1995), failing to find any agency for this thinking, any way to bring it into my lived experience. Physical exercise was in this my coping mechanism; at best an exorcism of demons that allowed me to maintain a veneer of sanity, at worst a regular physical self-flagellation that allowed me to forgive myself for my perceived sins.

Going deeper

In June 2009, I took part in my first 'middle distance' triathlon event in Weymouth, Dorset, which consisted of a 1.9 km sea swim, 90 km cycle, and half marathon (21.1 km) run. By this point, my tutors' gentle but insistent rebukes had succeeded in teaching me at least one action research practice, that of freefall writing. Freefall is a beautifully simple technique: you simply write what is in your head, following the train of your thought persistently, while at the same time pushing that train in the direction of the greatest emotion. It is a technique I try now to employ whenever I feel intense emotion—and this was such a time. Here is a taste of what I wrote.

> I will always remember the feeling . . . a feeling of total simplicity, oneness, and ease of mind. I had a certainty throughout that I could complete the course, a certainty that this was something my body was almost built for . . . It released me from myself, made me open to the world around me. This feeling began during the swim, with the half audible world and less than half visible sea, where I yet felt myself completely safe, my rhythm taking me ploughing evenly through. This was an incredible sensation, a true loss of self in the finest sense of the word, because the loss became a gain somehow. I hardly know what it is I am saying but it is true, this was flow, everything moving on around me, breathing, place push drive, place push drive, place push drive, breathe, again.

Reading this back to myself a few days later, it was abundantly clear to me that there was something beyond exorcism in the experience of sport. For almost the first time since starting the MSc, I wanted to explore something further in practice, not theory. Almost by accident, I had started inquiring properly, after months of agonised conscious effort to begin.

There was one more barrier to overcome, however. To inquire into sport felt like self-indulgence, a distraction from the 'real work' for which I had started the MSc. No matter how much my tutors insisted it was fine, I needed to come up with an approach which I would give myself permission to undertake.

Sport as activism

The idea was not long in coming once I knew I was looking—I would try to do the world's first 'Eco Ironman' triathlon, an event double the distance of the Weymouth triathlon, renowned as one of the world's toughest sporting challenges. I would aim to raise a significant amount of money for charity; I knew also that there was a possibility of getting hold of a bamboo bike, which would be a great hook for press coverage to build awareness among the sporting community of the possibilities of a more environmentally friendly approach to our passion. This idea offered the possibility of extending the inquiry beyond myself, to do it in a way that might offer some inspiration or learning to others who read or heard of it, what is known in action research terminology as third-person inquiry. With the opportunity of a broader intervention if done well, I could give myself the green light.

On 4 October 2009, I completed the Barcelona Ironman in 11 hours, 32 minutes and 28 seconds. I didn't have a bamboo bike, but I did train on a vegetarian diet, travel by train rather than plane, and sport a limestone-based wetsuit for the swim and a pair of running shoes made of recycled fibres for the run. I raised over £3,000 for the Wilderness Foundation's TurnAround programme, which uses wilderness experience and skills training to reintroduce young offenders to society. And there has been a strong appetite for the story in triathlon circles; several magazines and websites have run the story, and this has resulted in opportunities to work with event organisers, coaches and even the British Council to start spreading the word that you don't have to have a high environmental impact to be high performance.

It has been a real release to be an activist in this way, to set aside advertising for a while and realise that is not all of who I am; that I can act in the world without it having to be through my day job. It has been a wonderful thing to feel I am doing something positive, rather than focusing all the time on the fear of my day-to-day fight with my career self.

Unexpectedly, though, I think finding my agency, my ability to act in this alternative way, has also helped me find more space for myself in advertising. Since starting to train for the Eco Ironman in July 2009 I have achieved infinitely more in my 'real work' as well. I have started working with different clients in different ways, experimenting rather than trying to do the one right thing, and I have started to find ways to express my critique of the industry more openly—I am currently working with Crompton and Kasser on a report on advertising and the psychology of consumerism for WWF. It is never as simple as linear cause and effect, but these are things I do not believe I would have found the cognitive space to do without the Eco Ironman, without embracing the idea that there is more to me than my work.

Sport as spirituality

As wonderful as all of this has been, the most significant lesson my experiment into sport has taught lies elsewhere, in my understanding of my deepest self. It is an understanding I find difficult to express appropriately in words, but it is something I touched on in that freefall writing after Weymouth, and felt again often in training for the Eco Ironman.

The best I can do to express it is to talk of a visceral understanding of myself as animal, before human or ad-man or brother or lover or anything else; an understanding of what it is to be utterly empty physically yet utterly full emotionally; of what it is to lose your conception of the physical borders of yourself in a bizarre cocktail of fatigue and elation.

This has changed my worldview at a profound level. This shift too I find hard to explain in words, but the closest I can come is something Arne Naess wrote: 'One may speak of beautiful and of moral action. Moral actions are motivated by acceptance of a moral law, and manifest themselves clearly when acting against inclination. A person acts beautifully when acting benevolently from inclination' (Naess 1989: 85).

When I saw myself as human first and animal a distant second, many of my benevolent actions were moral. As animal first, my inclination changes, subtly but distinctly. And I believe my actions have gained a new beauty as a result, a beauty which has given me new resources of energy and new bravery in every part of my life, from sport to 'real work' to my relationships with my loved ones.

It comes from a knowledge I refresh by running as often as I can.

References

Crompton, T., and T. Kasser (2009) *Meeting Environmental Challenges: The role of human identity* (Godalming, UK: WWF).

Macy, J. (2007) *World as Lover, World as Self* (Berkeley, CA: Parallax Press, 1st edn).

Meyerson, D.E., and M.A. Scully (1995) 'Tempered Radicalism and the Politics of Ambivalence and Change', *Organization Science* 6.5: 585-600.

Naess, A. (1989) *Ecology Community and Lifestyle: Outline of an ecosophy* (trans. D. Rotherberg; Cambridge, UK: Cambridge University Press).

7

Seeking to shift systemic rules and awareness

- **Charles O'Malley**. Lessons from the entrepreneurial path
- **David Bent**. Creating places to stand and the levers to move the world
- **Jen Morgan**. Leading by nature
- **Paul Dickinson**. The practice of making business responsible
- **Roland Widmer**. The gap between discourse and practice: holding promoters of Amazon infrastructure projects to account

This chapter brings together five accounts of people seeking to contribute to systemic change. As this was the purpose of all graduates, there is considerable overlap between this and other groupings. In these five stories, we see the diverse intellectual models of change informing graduates' attempts to shift systemic patterns and mobilise energies. These people are deliberately outside mainstream business in independent, non-governmental and charity organisation roles. They use these positionings to work for rule-change in various spheres. Their stories show: dilemmas about whether change requires meeting people where they currently are or offering radical innovation; consideration of how to create alternative contextual conditions, especially financial drivers, to enable different forms of behaviour to arise for people and organisations; working through inquiry and through partnerships; emotional dimensions of change work and of living with uncertainty; graduates' career decision-making; and reflections on effectiveness, impact, scale and timescales.

Lessons from the entrepreneurial path

Charles O'Malley MSc5, 2001–2003

I was 34 years old and it was as if I had just woken from a deep sleep. I found myself on a beautiful and fragile spaceship floating through the infinite expanse of the universe. A spaceship dominated by competing fiefdoms at war; running out of key supplies; and where the inhabitants were critically undermining the life support systems—Spaceship Earth.

I was a few months into the MSc, recently made happily redundant with a pay-off of six months' salary. My heart had been opened to a wider circle of compassion. I keenly felt the pain of the world and the urgency of the crisis. But what should I do? What exactly was needed? And what was I capable of?

I had a degree in history and 10 years of mostly unfulfilling experience in finance and venture capital. I also had a wife and our first child on the way. Torn between, on the one hand, a newly dawning sense of responsibility for the whole that offered purpose in life, but also risk, sacrifice and uncertainty, and, on the other hand, my existing responsibilities to the family that seemed to urge precaution, safety and security.

Eventually, after much deliberation, I decided that it seemed wisest to build on my existing experience. I turned therefore to the entrepreneurial path. My reasoning? I dislike bureaucracy and politics. I like to make quick decisions and get on with things. I thought I knew something about entrepreneurship.

In addition, I believe that younger, small, more entrepreneurial organisations tend to be more innovative—both through disposition and necessity. They are less constrained by existing realities than larger organisations, have less vested interest in the status quo and have less to lose and more to gain from innovation.

If we are to achieve a smooth transition to a healthier economy and society, we must move quickly to establish the credibility of alternative ways of doing business and challenge the legitimacy of the status quo. We must develop new business norms and an expectation that businesses should create and not destroy social and environmental value.

We need alternative models, which can demonstrate the viability of a different way of doing business and raise the expectations of the public at large—in terms of the standards they expect from the companies they buy from, and in terms of what they expect from their politicians, thereby giving governments greater confidence in raising legal minimum standards and undermining corporate lobbying attempts to prevent this. We need to demonstrate that purpose-driven lives can be more rewarding than consumption-driven lives, and that there are options to live such a life. We need to change the story that shapes our culture and ultimately help change the rules of the game we live by.

So much for the theory. What about the practice? It is said that you learn more from failure than from success. I have learned a lot! These have been both the best and the worst years of my life. But at least now I know that I am alive!

Over the past nine years, with varying degrees of success, I have launched: a community finance fund for the *Big Issue*; an annual conference for socially responsible entrepreneurs; a consultancy business providing strategic advice and investor introductions to social and environmental businesses; an incubator for green businesses; and now an online community for social and environmental innovation.

The following lessons I have learned along the way are personal—and not in any way intended as the key success factors for sustainable entrepreneurship. I offer them in the hope that they may have wider relevance for other entrepreneurs or more broadly for other initiatives focused on social and environmental change.

Lesson 1: Vision must be balanced with pragmatism

Despite many years of experience in advising and investing in entrepreneurial businesses, my own early adventures suffered from an excess of idealism. For this I blame mostly the evangelical zeal that can come from waking up to the critical issues of our time. I learned that while vision and mission are essential, they must always be grounded in reality.

In 2004 I launched a consultancy to advise early-stage, mission-driven businesses on strategy and fundraising. Our clients were companies with a clear social or environmental mission. In the majority of cases they offered a financial return competitive with other early stage companies. However, some of the companies we advised were offering investors a 'blended return', where higher social or environmental impacts were offset by lower financial returns. I imagined that this sort of investment would make sense to investors who were also active philanthropists, if the social or environmental impacts met their philanthropic objectives.

In fact, most of the investors we found (even socially motivated ones) still saw the world through two different lenses: their investment lens (driven by the likely financial return relative to the level of financial risk); and their philanthropic lens (driven by social impact, 100% loss of donation taken as given). A typical investor wants to know: is it an investment, or is it a donation? An investment will be evaluated by one set of criteria and a donation by another. Anything in between is likely first of all to confuse and, second, to fail both sets of criteria.

To me this makes no sense. It is illogical. But I have come to understand that for most people who are both investors and philanthropists, these are two different games, just as different as tennis and golf. They do not mix. So to raise investment successfully, I have generally found it important to make sure that the rules (and language) of the game of investment are met.

The reality was that we didn't have enough people willing to buy what we were offering at a price that made sense for us to deliver it. I learned through this that I must meet the world as it is, not as I would like it to be.

Lesson 2: You learn most by trying things out

When you bring strong convictions into the business planning process it is highly likely that you will fall into the trap of 'confirmation bias', whereby you seek the evidence that confirms your original hypothesis and ignore the evidence that contradicts it.

Savvy entrepreneurs spend less time theorising and more time trying things out in deliberate experiments to test their assumptions. This was a lesson I learned from an experienced and successful entrepreneur and investor when he was evaluating one of the investment opportunities we brought to him.

The world is complex and when we interact with it in new ways, it is difficult to know how it will respond until we've tried it. Now when I am setting up a business, I try to identify the principal uncertainties and figure out cheap, quick and low-risk ways of testing them. Then I learn through trial and error. It seems obvious but, when trying to change the world, start small, and build through iterations.

Lesson 3: Build a living system

My definition of a successful business is one in which the founders have become redundant. Traditionally this has meant building a well-oiled machine capable of producing the same result time and time again. The businesses of the future, I believe, will be living systems, where people and resources self-organise around the business objective. A business is made up of two key elements: (1) a holding idea; and (2) organising principles. Think of Wikipedia, or eBay, or Linux, or Transition Towns: they all demonstrate in various ways that if you can design the right self-organising system, 'there is nothing so powerful as an idea whose time has come' (Victor Hugo).

In retrospect I realise that, in my early entrepreneurial attempts, effectively there was no business apart from me—making me less a business owner and more an independent consultant. In my attempts to launch a green business incubator (killed off by the credit crunch), I had learned that lesson and was focused on recruiting management and raising investment for new businesses where we would be just controlling shareholders. In my current endeavour, launching an online community for open innovation for sustainability, our aim is to provide a means of connecting companies to thousands of innovators worldwide who can address their social and environmental issues through online challenges. We will be successful to the extent that we can create a living community that has its own life and its own momentum.

Lesson 4: Think long-term

My greatest learning has been that large-scale social and economic systems are not created or maintained by any single individual or group—they are driven by their own internal logic, beyond the control of any person, company or government, and constantly co-created and perpetuated by all the participants in the system.

Changing systems is hard and it takes time. However, I have come to realise that failure and success are all a matter of perspective. My short-term outlook for the planet (the next 100 years, say) is not rosy, because I don't think we are moving fast enough on the critical issue of greenhouse gas emissions and because as yet not enough people are seriously questioning the fundamental flaws of our economic and monetary systems. However, in the longer term (a few million years), this will probably all seem like a storm in a teacup. On Spaceship Earth, new life is born out of the death of the old.

This may seem inappropriately philosophical, but the entrepreneurial journey has shown me that you never quite know when failure or success are just around the corner, so it pays to keep calm and carry on.

Closing thoughts

Choosing to act as an entrepreneur from within the current system, but trying to push its boundaries, I am aware that I am, to some extent, colluding in a system that is accelerating an unprecedented ecological collapse. Sometimes the most we can hope for is to make a small contribution towards exposing the flaws of our current system, questioning its legitimacy and pointing the way towards alternatives that are more socially just and environmentally sustainable.

As Václav Havel said in his seminal essay *The Power of the Powerless*, written in communist Czechoslovakia in 1978:

> We do not know the way out of the miasmas of the world, and it would be an expression of unforgivable pride were we to see the little we do as a fundamental solution, or were we to present ourselves, our community, and our solutions to vital problems as the only thing worth doing.

We can simply do our best with the limited knowledge and skills we have. The rest is out of our hands.

Reference

Havel, V. (1985) *The Power of the Powerless: Citizens against the state in Central-Eastern Europe* (New York: Palach Press).

Creating places to stand and the levers to move the world

David Bent MSc4, 2000–2002

> I was involved in the intellectual masturbation on climate change. Then I heard other chief executives saying they were making money. So, I decided we needed to get a piece of that (Chief Executive of one of the largest consumer brands in the UK 2008).

> Give me a place to stand and with a lever I will move the whole world (Archimedes of Syracuse).[1]

Since 2003 I have worked at Forum for the Future, a leading sustainable development charity. Over that time, I have participated in a shift in business mind-sets, illustrated by the Chief Executive's words above. Using Archimedes' metaphor, the places that Forum might stand, where we actually chose to stand, and the levers I subsequently used all changed.

In 2003 the debate was still about 'responsibility', meaning the impact of business on society. Now the key word is 'sustainability', and is more about the impact of particular issues—especially climate change—on business. Forum was part of creating that shift. Our activities evolved from, primarily, raising business leaders' awareness of sustainable development issues to working with many more companies on the commercial opportunities of sustainability. In turn, I played a role in shifting Forum, and my work shifted, from working on green accounting to putting sustainability into business strategy, engaging in a fast-evolving field.

So, what was possible, using responsibility as the place to stand? How was 'corporate sustainability' created as a new positioning? What levers do I now use? What are the limits of this position? What might be next?

Limits of responsibility

March 2003 was an important month for me. I handed in my dissertation after two stimulating years studying for an MSc in Responsibility and Business Practice. I left PricewaterhouseCoopers after four and a half frustrating years auditing big companies. I started a job at Forum for the Future.

---

1 Quoted by Pappus of Alexandria in *Synagoge*, Book VIII, according to en.wikipedia.org/wiki/Archimedes, accessed 31 December 2010.

The job title was 'Green Accountant', a combination of the master's and my old skills. My former bosses at PwC could not understand why I would throw away my career to work on corporate social responsibility (CSR). Most business people in 2003 had not heard of climate change. They associated CSR with stand-alone reports and community programmes—a regrettable cost of protecting the company's reputation from people who didn't understand that the business of business is business.

Joining Forum, I inherited an experimental technique called environmental shadow cost accounting, which calculates the extra annual cost of being environmentally sustainable (Howes 2002; Bent and Richardson 2003). My job was to sell and deliver projects with corporate partners.

Forum was founded in 1996 on the notion of partnership: long-term, trust-based relationships with companies and public sector organisations to create positive solutions to difficult problems. At the time this was a radical step away from adversarial campaigning, the favoured mode of environmentalists. Of course, partnering with already-successful companies risks being co-opted by the status quo, but Forum believed the potential for change is worth that risk.

At first I thought companies should want to know the scale of their negative impact on the environment. But projects proved difficult to sell, and often relied on the charm of my boss to get started. And projects were even more difficult to progress. Time and again there would be long delays and limited enthusiasm. I became frustrated. Gradually I realised that the shadow costs method was a flawed lever for change. The technique emphasised the costs involved and did not give useful information about alternatives. It rubbed people's noses in the damage business imposed. Not surprisingly, companies did not want to listen.

Whatever their personal values, business leaders have to prioritise shareholder value because of the legal, investor and ideological context. Unfortunately the only substantive connection between responsibility and shareholder value is to protect reputation. This led to the business response of 'CSR as PR': trivial annual reports; the prominence of community and volunteering programmes; and lots of lobbying, often through trade associations who could run counter to their members' caring image.

The responsibility mind-set failed to make companies more responsible. It was a limited place to stand. Fortunately, the terms of the debate and Forum were both changing.

Creating a new place to stand

Considering how political transformation happens, Michael Jacobs draws an historical parallel with the adoption of the welfare state (Jacobs 2006). He proposes four factors to enable political action on climate change: huge disasters; an intellectual economic case; a significant fraction of businesses believing they would benefit; and a great moral uprising.

In 2006 some of these factors were coming into the mainstream context for climate change in particular and sustainability in general. The *Stern Review of the Economics of Climate Change* provided an intellectual case (Stern 2006). The popular success of *An Inconvenient Truth* hinted at possible moral uprising.[2] There were signs that business people could see the benefits, for instance linking competitive advantage and CSR (Porter and Kramer 2006).

There was significant change in Forum, too. A new chief executive prompted a full strategic review resulting in a much simpler focus matching the changing mood of the times. Our work with companies was to 'prove that sustainable businesses are more successful businesses' by applying futures, innovation and leadership approaches.

I was pleased that these approaches made stronger connections to shareholder value. Futures techniques, like scenario planning, show how the future success (and so current value) of a business will be affected by sustainability issues. Business people are taught that innovation is the only way of renewing their edge in a fiercely competitive, globalised world. They also want to be leaders, as successful individuals in organisations that win.

The accounting work was cut. I was glad, and was asked to lead an internal development project called Future Business with grand aims: 'to catalyse a revolution in how business makes money, and to keep Forum at the leading edge of practice as the agenda evolves'. I ran with this, enjoying the researching and serious thinking involved.

In retrospect, I see the project as having a delayed success. It stimulated the 'Expert' in me (Torbert 2004), and I wanted to get to know everything myself. Not only is that impossible, but by researching intensively alone I made it difficult for Forum to run with the results, and Forum did not have mechanisms for embedding it into our futures, innovation and leadership techniques. So, the overlaps between 'my' project and other areas became sources of internal conflict. I allowed the pressure of time to make publication of the research, called 'Leader Business Strategies' (Bent and Draper 2008), the end of the project.

Nevertheless, after that faltering start the tools and thinking generated in the project are central to our work with companies on strategy. My job has evolved into the 'Head of Business Strategies'. I return to the project's insights for a lot of my work (including the structure of this contribution).

One successful output was a pair of contrasting statements which I used to create a dividing line in our aspirations. I consistently gave a particular message: 'our partners used to ask Forum "What should our CSR function strategy be?" but they are now asking "What should our business strategy be, in the light of sustainability?" ' As a statement this was partly true and partly a hope. It has stuck, and helped people in Forum define our work on sustainability and business strategy. It now forms part of the messages Forum sends to the outside world. In this way the

---

2 en.wikipedia.org/wiki/An_Inconvenient_Truth, accessed 31 December 2010.

Future Business project has had a tiny role in shaping the debate, and turned the hope into more of a truth.

I now spend most of my time challenging and supporting companies as they try to integrate sustainability into their business strategy. I experience these projects as stimulating both intellectually—lots of analysis of data—and creatively—designing and holding open spaces for others to make their own difference.

Throughout I also experience a tension: having my own strong point of view but holding that space open. The privilege and responsibility of Forum's charitable status is that we must challenge our corporate partners, even if that closes down the participants' space. For me, that tension is multiplied by needing to hold back the intellectual in me who believes I already have the 'right' answer—an issue I addressed in my MSc dissertation, but a lesson that can be nearly learned a thousand times.

Living as well

My time at Forum is almost half of my adult life. There has been a lot of living, and one death. All this living affects and is affected by working.

On the living side, I got married and had two children—committing to a life with family, and all that comes with it.

Work-wise, I have committed to the particular career domain of specialising in 'sustainability and business strategy'. Fortunately for my intellectual curiosity this is still a large terrain, and fortunately for my ambition it is relatively young. I have therefore started to deliberately create platforms (such as the outputs from the Future Business project) that I know I will test and improve (or junk) in future years.

My mother died in 2009, after a three-year battle with cancer. This brush with my mortality has had numerous effects. In a work context it gets tangled up with the need for urgent action on sustainability. The science tells us that if we continue as we are then the natural world will struggle to support a large, complicated human society. To put it another way, Mother Nature is going to die after a long battle with a mutation from within. We have no time for delay or error, but there is an enormous gap between the required and actual action.

Through 2009 I experienced despair, for instance seriously discussing with my wife which country we would move to in anticipation of runaway climate change. My despair is heightened by Forum's necessary positioning that 'we can do this'. I have to be professionally optimistic, even as I am personally pessimistic.

For me, getting beyond the despair starts with articulating the reason for the despair—the gap between required and actual action—and finding some new places to stand that will close that gap.

Limits of corporate sustainability

Over the last few years, I have worked with plenty of companies who accept the proposition that sustainability is a normal driver of business context—rarely accepted in 2003. They have tried to improve their own business strategy, with cascading improvements in their innovation of products and services, capabilities, cultures, supply chains and more. Truth be told, however, these sustainability strategies affect the business only a bit. A few partners are toying with committing the whole company to sustainability, but they are few. Why?

In my view this is because companies are 'resource dependent' (Bower and Gilbert 2005) and have to fit a particular niche in the current economic ecosystem (Beinhocker 2006). Incremental innovation is possible but few companies are prepared to risk initiating disruptive change.

The corporate sustainability approach requires lots of individual large companies to initiate change, to replace their familiar context with something more sustainable. The approach does not fit with the theory of how companies work or my experience of the last five years.

Forum's progress reflects this. Forum's strategy-in-practice assumes that companies are the masters of their own fate, can change their behaviour and so change the system. Only our tourism work has systematically impacted the context that determines shareholder value creation.

Five years into the 'corporate sustainability' framing we can see it is failing to make corporations more sustainable. It is a limited place to stand.

Creating the next places to stand

The transformational moment when the credit crunch raised questions about 'the future of capitalism' (to quote the *Financial Times* essay series in 2009) has passed. So, I assume a world that continues to prioritise shareholder value. This narrows the available levers and places to stand.

Forum undertook a strategic review in 2010. In my moments of despair, I see this as Forum's last opportunity to create a strategy that catalyses a sustainability society—because action from 2015 might well be too late. So, it is Forum's last chance to question meaningfully our fundamental assumptions and practices (do some double-loop learning), and come up with new places to stand.

At the personal level, we had our second child in February 2010. So, there will certainly be more living, much of it in the dead of night. Professionally I feel two developmental needs. First, to ground, systematise and broadcast all the propositions I am generating through my work with companies on the leading edge of sustainability and business strategy. Second, to develop the skills—from technical ones such as quantification of business strategy to non-technical ones such as charisma—for the next place to stand.

If business is going to play its part in creating a sustainable future, then change initiators like me need to find the levers that then enable companies to initiate change themselves. A company will only act for a sustainable future where it can see how it will be more successful. We—change agents with business—will have to play with the things that determine shareholder value, including regulation and incentives, consumer behaviour, competitor pressure, new and deployed technologies, and investor expectations. Simply having a better strategy process is not, by itself, enough. But it can be the way a company responds to wider changes in the system.

References

Beinhocker, E. (2006) *The Origin of Wealth: Evolution, complexity and the radical remaking of economics* (London: Random House).

Bent, D., and S. Draper (2008) 'Leader Business Strategies', Forum for the Future; www.forumforthefuture.org/library/leader-business-strategies, accessed 31 December 2010.

——, and J. Richardson (2003) 'SIGMA Guidelines—Toolkit: Sustainability Accounting Guide'; www.projectsigma.co.uk/Toolkit/SIGMASustainabilityAccounting.pdf, accessed 31 December 2010.

Bower, J., and C. Gilbert (2005) *From Resource Allocation to Strategy* (Oxford, UK: Oxford University Press).

Financial Times (2009) 'The Future of Capitalism', *Financial Times*, April–May 2009; www.ft.com/indepth/capitalism-future, accessed 31 December 2010.

Howes, R. (2002) *Environmental Cost Accounting: An introduction and practical guide* (Amsterdam: Elsevier).

Jacobs, M. (2006) 'RSA/Forum for the Future: The economics and politics of climate change'; www.thersa.org/__data/assets/pdf_file/0018/657/The-economics-and-politics-of-climate-change-jacobs-221106.pdf, accessed 31 December 2010.

Porter, M., and M. Kramer (2006) 'Strategy and Society: The Link between competitive advantage and corporate social responsibility', *Harvard Business Review* 84.12: 78-92.

Stern, N. (2006) *The Economics of Climate Change: The Stern Review* (Cambridge, UK: Cambridge University Press).

Torbert, W.R. (2004) *Action Inquiry: The secret of timely and transforming leadership* (San Francisco: Berrett-Koehler).

Leading by nature

Jen Morgan MSc9, 2005–2007

Nature as our guide

I often wonder what the world would look like if humans and the social systems we created related in a way that was reflective of living systems. How would this shift the way we stimulate and enable change for sustainability?

As a lover of nature and someone who works for WWF, I am frequently exposed to the natural world. I am very aware that each species and life form has a unique purpose. To be alive means to interrelate and have a relationship to the world around us. Nature and ecosystems are in constant flow, movement and action. Life is always giving birth and creating something new. Living systems are naturally intentional, relational, active and emergent. These themes of behaving authentically as nature does through 'intention', 'relationships', 'action' and 'creating the new' are strands that inspire my daily practice as a change agent and also permeate through the multi-stakeholder programme I lead at WWF called the Finance Innovation Lab.

The Finance Innovation Lab is a programme which involves a wide range of stakeholders of the financial system such as activists, economists, academics, bankers, policy-makers, designers, religious leaders, entrepreneurs and investors. Over time, these diverse people, organisations and networks will build resilient relationships and work collectively to develop innovation experiments that will help to shift the global financial system so that it serves society and the environment.

The process will be convened through the practice of the Art of Hosting, which supports conversations and action that are based on purposeful, participatory and practical approaches which help to enable personal and social change.[3]

Through sharing my story and that of the evolution of the Finance Innovation Lab, which will continue to be developed over the next few years, I hope to help to inspire a way of relating that is reflective of living systems and one that enables others to work towards transformational change for sustainability.

3 www.artofhosting.org, accessed 31 December 2010.

Inspired by intention

> A living system pays attention to that which is meaningful to it—here and
> now (Art of Hosting).

The Finance Innovation Lab's intention is to address some of the systemic flaws of
the financial system that are preventing a transformation to a One Planet Future
in which humans live in harmony with the natural world. For example, although
the majority of the financial value of the London stock market is ultimately owned
by UK citizens through their savings and pensions, many people are unaware that
their money is exacerbating climate change by being held in large oil and gas companies. What systemic interventions could be made to awaken the UK public to
the impact of their money so that they hold the system to account and invest their
money in a way that makes a positive impact on the world? Or what systemic interventions, such as a change in laws, processes or business models, might be needed
so that our savings could be invested in local communities, social enterprises and
innovators of the future?

From the summer of 2010 onwards, the participants have worked collectively
to identify the areas of potential change and have also formed smaller groups to
create, develop and test prototypes. These prototypes might include testing new
business models, policies, products, education programmes or campaigns. We are
providing a space where all current and future stakeholders of the system can take
part, including mainstream players and new pioneers. Because of this we expect
the outcome to be a spectrum of ideas—the majority of which are likely to be disruptive and some of which will be more palatable for mainstream players. However, we are clear that we are not interested in trying to 'convince' organisations or
people to change. We are working from a basis of engaging those who have energy
and enthusiasm for change from the outset.

Our role at WWF, along with our other co-convening partners, is to 'host' a space
for Innovation Lab participants to co-create a process which enables the conditions required for change. We are beginning this work with about 100 people who
range from divisional directors of investment banks, strategists in management
consulting firms, spiritual leaders, senior accountants, students, scientists, policy-
makers, serial entrepreneurs and recognised academics. Most importantly we have
developed a community of people who have a personal commitment to change.

These participants will be supported by a broad faculty base who will act as
coaches, mentors, content supporters and networkers. During the year, the participants and faculty will come together in quarterly cycles to expand their growing
knowledge and relationships. They will also be given the opportunity to connect to
their deeper personal intention, which will inspire an even greater sense of energy
not just from themselves as individuals but also from the collective group. With
ideas, relationships and capacities for change developed, the group will then have
the resilience to be able to inspire and demonstrate practical examples to the wider
world.

Throughout the process some people have felt uncomfortable with what we are doing and others, including some preliminary convening partners, have walked away, not wanting to challenge or disrupt the status quo. What has helped us gain successful momentum for this programme has been the steadfast commitment to wanting to stimulate transformational change despite not knowing if we'll succeed, who will join us or if we'll make any impact. Being rooted in intention is energising and inspirational not only for ourselves but also for others around us. As a result, we are succeeding in building a community who also have this 'itch' for something different and for something that connects them to a deeper sense of meaning and values which relate to caring for people and the world around them.

Relating for change

> A living system participates in the development of its neighbour. An iso-
> lated system is doomed (Art of Hosting).

Becoming more grounded in my intention has also helped me become more aware of my own interactions and relationships with other people. How people relate to me is often more of a reflection of how I relate to others through my own values and behaviours. Being aware of my 'relating' provides me with a good mirror to learn how I can better inspire change in the world. I have noticed that if I relate in a way that is true to my values and purpose or if I am positive and appreciative it is more likely that others will relate back to me in a way that is enabling and inspiring.

Relating with authenticity builds a deeper level of trust, understanding and commitment. These are required in dealing with the nature of our severe global challenges which are very complex and messy. The solutions to these challenges will require people to work together in new ways, which are uncomfortable in that they test assumptions, mind-sets and embedded behaviours. What will carry us through will be resilient and deep relationships that will steward a more radical and accelerated change process.

Building strong and healthy relationships in the Finance Innovation Lab has been core to our process and will be one of the key factors that determine our success. As an NGO we have limited resources and, when you compare this to the scale of the work that is required in addressing natural resource destruction, climate change and free-falling biodiversity loss, it is essential that we build relationships with other stakeholders in order to collaborate and innovate for change. This means that we need to work with those who have existing power and resources to bring to bear and who are often the incumbents of the existing system such as investment banks. However, even more importantly, we also need to be working with the innovators of the future system such as entrepreneurs, designers and students. Engaging at a strategic systemic level and in a way that is experimental in generating new types of behaviour with varied stakeholders, is certainly a new way of working even for our own organisation, especially as it requires us to abandon a 'control and manage outcomes approach'. It has challenged us to build our capacity and adapt our internal decision-making processes, programme measurement, brand ownership and fundraising strategies.

The nature of the change that we are seeking to stimulate is also requiring strong relationships, not just with the convening partners but also with the participants, faculty and funders. We have been keen to start by appreciating the potential of each person and organisation that is seeking to become involved and to work with them individually to explore their personal interest and level of commitment for change. We have invited hundreds of people to help contribute to co-creating the Lab and have spent time and energy growing relationships and social capital which we hope will help to build a resilient community of change agents. Taking this approach has certainly required more time, patience and emotion than we had probably anticipated; however, it has certainly been very effective and has given us reassurance about our convening process.

Enabling through action

> A living system is in constant change (Art of Hosting).

My purpose as a change agent in helping to solve our global challenges is calling me to take action. As in nature, there are many forms of interaction and action—some are forceful, some are passive and some are enabling. The enabling forms of action are the ones that have interested me the most over the past few years as it seems like the best way to harness and develop human potential in order to make breakthroughs for our future. The MSc helped me to develop my practice in enabling change through the discipline of action research.

Action research is a continuous cycle of inquiry, action and reflection. It involves curiosity, experimentation, making sense of situations, testing assumptions and being open to failure. It is core to the project management as well as convening processes of the Finance Innovation Lab itself. We are including elements such as dialogue interviews, learning journeys, reflective retreats, prototyping and sense-making sessions as well as ensuring that we have learning historians who will be capturing our collective learning in a way that is fun, experiential and inspirational.

The Lab is about people coming together in a way that co-creates the change process and creates experiments for change. Over time, the Innovation Lab teams will give birth to multiple innovation initiatives which could shift the financial system so that it better serves society and the environment. These may be in the form of new business models, processes, policies, products or education programmes.

Over a year, participants will work together to prototype their ideas; not in the form of research papers or reports but rather in real practical action such as creating and testing a concept for a new type of bank or new mode of exchange of 'value' in a local community. For example, one of the innovation groups is seeking to explore a pilot in a UK town in order to experiment with a new local currency, 'L', which is based on learning and education. Another innovation group is seeking to develop a new risk model for finance that focuses on measuring risk in terms of resilience, which is based on a future that is emergent and unpredictable. Getting involved in day-to-day action through experimentation and practical action will allow the participants to sense and determine what is actually required to shift the system. They will build physical models of the change they would like to see, test their ideas with faculty who will offer coaching, mentoring and support, spend time with businesses, government and local communities, grow important relationships, and learn and adapt their ideas and test and try again. They will pursue action that helps to put conditions in place to enable systemic change to happen—including building their own personal and organisational capacity for change.

It is likely that some prototypes will fail; however, what is most important is that some will certainly succeed. What has been key to the process so far is not only to act in a way that is framed and authentic to our purpose and values but also to act in a way that is open to learning, emergence, failure and enabling of opportunities.

Creating something new

> Living systems cannot be steered or controlled and are not intent on finding perfect solutions (Art of Hosting).

When I think about the moments in my life of deep, meaningful and enduring personal shifts, they have often come about as a result of seeking opportunities to create something new. Or, in other circumstances, which have been both personal and societal, changes have come about through disruptive moments or events.

It is this creative and disruptive type of change that will help us move more quickly and effectively to transformational behaviour. Systems of food, mobility, housing and finance are very much stuck social systems held in place by those actors who are powerful and have a vested interest in maintaining the existing paradigm. To leapfrog ahead, we need pioneering and brave people, communities and organisations who are willing and able to challenge that status quo and to experiment for change.

As with ecosystems, our approach with the Lab is to connect wide-ranging communities so that something may spark and virally spread through networks. In this regard, it has been important to be externally focused and be open to the possible.

The Lab's process is one that encourages innovation through bringing diverse actors together and then helping them to build coherence around how change will be enabled. As we have seen in several events so far, when bankers, activists, scientists, investors, academics, policy-makers and religious leaders work collaboratively—in a way that is trusting and challenging—something new and unexpected comes about. It is also plausible that what comes about is systemically more effective as it takes into account multiple stakeholder perspectives. Diversity of values, views and experiences help people to look at the world from an alternative mindset and to see it in a way that can offer new insights, breakthroughs and solutions for our future.

An emergent leadership

I have hope that humans will soon meet our collective global challenges. My hope stems from a new form of leadership that is truly emerging; one that is reflective of the natural processes that enable and bring out the best in life and communities. I am inspired by a growing number of people in the world who are catalysing change in this way through connecting to their purpose, valuing the importance of relationships, learning through action and innovating disruptive solutions. I would like to take this opportunity to thank the MSc course founders and tutors for helping to spark this new leadership and for enabling me to make a personal shift which has been fulfilling, energising and life-giving.

The practice of making business responsible

Paul Dickinson MSc1, 1997–1999

The MSc course was pivotal in directing me towards an appreciation that climate change was an unprecedented global emergency. It was the subtle but effective comments of Stephan Harding at Schumacher College that forced me to recognise that there might be an unpleasant discontinuity between my happy childhood, and the life experience of future children.

The carefully constructed curriculum also gave me the opportunity to test theories I had previously developed regarding the role and impact of corporations, and the potential for new forms of accountability and democracy to emerge from the global interconnected business system.

I believe it is extremely important to consider what one might reasonably call the big picture.

For many millions of people, the Second World War is still a living memory. The loss of 50 million lives in six years of horrendous fighting is an intolerable disaster that must never be allowed to happen again, yet few consider climate change in these terms. Many films have been made, from 1945 through to 2010, celebrating the heroism of soldiers who fought to protect the lives of innocent people. Fifty million people seem like a lot to have their lives prematurely curtailed by ill-judged human activities, but let's consider the loss of life that dangerous climate change will probably deliver. The World Health Organisation estimated back in 2005 that 150,000 die each year as a consequence of climate change.

Over the next 100 years I am afraid we may see loss of life on a completely unprecedented scale. It could be a billion people, or more. The distinguished scientist James Lovelock foresees perhaps 80% or more of us dead, with the remainder thirsty and starving (Lovelock 2006). This is, therefore, the defining global crisis of our generation, and very likely the next couple, too.

It was entertaining recently, to have a leading business school interview me for a case study on the Carbon Disclosure Project (CDP). The draft they wrote up tried to create a balanced tension, along the lines of 'Why did Paul decide to work to do good?' This was a stupid distortion of what I really said. If a billion or more people are going to die, you have no choice. There is no 'why'. I do my job 7 days a week and 365 days a year because I have no choice. If you can read a graph, you have no choice either. We are on the brink of an absolutely unprecedented catastrophe. And like the Second World War, there have been many, many warnings, all largely ignored.

A critical problem is the relatively brief span of an average human life. Consider my life. I am 46; what have I seen? The Berlin Wall fell. The northern ice cap disappeared. This is all very exciting. And in a very few decades, I will shuffle off to my grave considering that I have seen a lot of important things. But these events are absolutely not comparable. The Berlin Wall lasted 28 years, and the northern ice cap about 2 million.

In 1988 I abandoned a degree in politics to work in corporate communications. At the age of 24 I came to realise what many others are now coming to appreciate; namely, that business runs the world. But the vast, dominant global business system has some terrifying characteristics:

- It is not organised to protect itself from systemic environmental risk

- It is not self-aware, it is unconscious and uncoordinated

- National governments have no mechanism to control global business

I believe our great corporations are really very mysterious. My underlying opinion is best communicated through the title of the book I wrote, *Beautiful Corporations* (Dickinson and Svensen 2000). Think of Coca-Cola or L'Oréal. They are each more than 100 years old, bigger and stronger than they have ever been before. Their senior executives have some control over them, for a while. But ultimately they themselves are driven by processes and structures that have transcended human generations. The corporation is an emergent life form that is so ubiquitous that it cannot be understood by humans. We can no more understand corporations than fish can understand water.

Well, what to do about it?

The management thinker W. Edwards Deming stated that a system is defined by its objectives: 'A system is a network of interdependent components that work together to try to accomplish the aim of the system. A system must have an aim. Without the aim, there is no system' (Deming 1993).

So the purpose of business in law is to make money. But the growing scale of corporations is creating a disconnect between the management and owners. This fascinating phenomenon was brilliantly described by the academics Berle and Means, who observed in their 1932 book *The Modern Corporation and Private Property* (Berle and Means 1932) that the legitimate authority for the conduct of corporations has evaporated between capital providers and management control groups; but this creates an opportunity.

> The control groups have cleared the way for the claims of a group far wider than either the owners or the control. They have placed the community in a position to demand that the modern corporation serve not alone the owners or the control but all society. It remains only for the claims of the community to be put forward with clarity and force. When a convincing system of community obligations is worked out and is generally accepted, in that moment the passive property right of today must yield before the larger interests of society (Berle and Means 1932: 312).

To understand the nature of the problem of climate change, all you need to do is comprehend the following sequence of events:

1. Scientists state there is a serious problem

2. Governments come up with plans to take action to reduce the problem

3. Business lobby groups successfully oppose government plans that may limit their operations

4. As a consequence, nothing happens

It is important to notice that this intolerable state of affairs has persisted for a couple of decades now.

The Carbon Disclosure Project launched in 2000 to accelerate solutions to climate change by putting relevant information at the heart of business, policy and investment decisions. We further this mission by harnessing the collective power of corporations, investors and political leaders to accelerate unified action on climate change. We operate the only global climate change reporting system. Climate change is not a problem that exists within national boundaries. That is why we harmonise climate change data from organisations around the world and develop international carbon reporting standards.

Some 2,500 organisations in 60 countries around the world now measure and disclose their greenhouse gas emissions and climate change strategies through CDP, in order that they can set reduction targets and make performance improvements. We act on behalf of 534 institutional investors, holding US$64 trillion in assets under management and some 60 purchasing organisations such as Dell, PepsiCo and Walmart. This data is made available for use by a wide audience including institutional investors, corporations, policy-makers and their advisers, public sector organisations, government bodies, academics and the public. Since we sent out the first request for climate change information in 2003, the number of disclosing companies has grown tenfold.

We are a UK registered charity. On our website you can find out how organisations and public sector bodies around the world are responding to climate change by taking a look at the individual corporate responses to CDP or by reading our reports.[4] Our reports provide detailed analysis of the information supplied each year to CDP and indicate important trends and developments.

Lord Adair Turner, Chairman, UK Government Financial Services Authority and Chairman of the Committee on Climate Change has observed:

> The first step towards managing carbon emissions is to measure them because in business what gets measured gets managed. The Carbon Disclosure Project has played a crucial role in encouraging companies to take the first steps in that measurement and management path.[5]

4 www.cdproject.net, accessed 31 December 2010.
5 Keynote speech at the Carbon Disclosure Project launch event at the Museum of London, October 2006.

The driving force behind the creation of CDP was to achieve two objectives:

1. To assert the collective authority of the previously suicidal supine share-holder over the very powerful but unrestricted corporation

2. To encourage the better instincts of corporations to compete to deliver human survival. Corporations love to compete; it is in their DNA

In answer to the question—the incredibly stupid question—does it make economic sense to take action on climate change, there is a simple answer. Yes.

The budget that parents will expend to keep their children alive is equal to 100% of their potential expenditure. Like the relentless onset of an inescapable dawn, public awareness of climate change grows each year. The great corporations are starting to talk about CO_2 in their advertising. This kind of sustainability product marketing is an incredibly good sign. The sleeping giants are waking up and they will help us protect ourselves. It was Malcolm McIntosh who first presented to my mind the extraordinarily brilliant and illuminating phrase: 'when I shop, I vote'. Speaking at the first CDP launch event in New York in March 2003, former US Secretary of State, Madeleine Albright, said: 'our business is to help investors vote with their money'.

In 2010, our eighth year of operation, CDP wrote to corporations requesting detailed information on greenhouse gas emissions, technology and strategy, on behalf of 534 investors with US$64 trillion (a figure similar to world GDP, US$64,000,000,000,000).

That is a lot of votes.

It has been pleasing to see many high-profile politicians support our work. German Chancellor Angela Merkel wrote in her foreword to the CDP German report: 'It is extremely important for investors to take account of climate change in their decision making. I wish the Carbon Disclosure Project success with its further efforts both in Germany and worldwide'.

UN Secretary-General Ban Ki-moon commented in his introduction to the CDP Global report:

> The Carbon Disclosure Project's detailed reporting is helping persuade companies throughout the world to measure, manage, disclose and ultimately reduce their greenhouse gas emissions. No other organisation is gathering this type of corporate climate change data and providing it to the marketplace.

Bill Clinton was more succinct in his keynote speech at our 2007 launch in New York: 'The Carbon Disclosure Project is vital, and we have got to get everyone involved, and there is nothing to be afraid of'.

I was asked to describe the internal culture of our very successful organisation, and my leadership style. First, I think we all need to learn that the idea of leadership in isolation from the direction in which you are travelling is irrelevant. My charisma is limited, and I cannot give rousing speeches. In this sense, I am the opposite of Adolf Hitler. But maybe that is a good thing.

In terms of the culture of our organisation, I would say we encourage honesty, we like to discuss mistakes, and we always think we could do what we are doing a lot better. As the CEO I try to get out of people's way. I am at best the second-best sales person, and am frankly proud to be considered a peer of most people I work along-side. We don't have senior management, we call it central management. Hierarchy is a tiring irrelevance. Authority is taken, not given.

I hope that is how CDP runs, and how we can perhaps help the global business system steer away from the looming cliff edge. Every time I feel myself spiralling into a cold terror of hopelessness, I remember that the preceding generation were very nearly wiped out in an hour by ICBMs carrying hydrogen bombs. At least climate change is not as bad as that!

One of the MSc tutors, Gill Coleman, told me that she believed in the transformative power of education. I do. I have seen it with my own eyes. Of the 50 employees at CDP, seven completed the MSc in Responsibility and Business Practice. We were not given a meal, but instead taught how to fish. So now we can feed ourselves, forever. That is the essence of transformative educational power.

References

Berle, A., and G. Means (1932) *The Modern Corporation and Private Property* (New York: Transaction Publishers).

Deming, W. Edwards (1993) *The New Economics for Industry, Government, Education* (Cambridge, MA: MIT Press, 2nd edn).

Dickinson, P., and N. Svensen (2000) *Beautiful Corporations* (London: Pearson Education).

Lovelock, J.E. (2006) *The Revenge of Gaia* (London: Allen Lane).

The gap between discourse and practice: holding promoters of Amazon infrastructure projects to account

Roland Widmer MSc8, 2004–2006

Working for change through sustainable finance

Sustainability is the centre of gravity for my professional practice. In particular, I have been involved with sustainable finance since the 1990s. Capital allocation decisions are crucial, and finance enables and guides activities in all spheres; hence my decision to take leadership within a civil society organisation to work for change through sustainable finance.

Since 2008, I have been coordinating the Eco-Finanças Program at Amigos da Terra—Amazônia Brasileira (AdT), Brazil. The objective of Eco-Finanças is to promote public interest in relationships between finance, the environment and society. Eco-Finanças is a member of the international networks BankTrack and BICECA. Launched in 2000, it continues to be unique throughout Latin America.

The Eco-Finanças team consists of three people, and I report to the director of AdT. Our work combines proposing action—such as offering assistance to banks in integrating socio-environmental dimensions into their credit policies—with attempts to exert social control on finance: for example, by confronting violations of relevant guidelines. These lines of action are designed to be mutually supportive.

In my practice, I benefit from the legitimacy of acting through a respected environmental NGO. My position allows me to openly promote public interest. This entitlement makes a big difference.

In this contribution, I would like to provide insight into my work by presenting a practical case of taking leadership for systemic change and by inquiring into the learning gained. I start with a few words on how I approach this work.

Acting for systemic change

Notions of systemic change learned through the MSc in Responsibility and Business Practice (RBP) inform my approach. While ultimately I intend to contribute to systemic change, my immediate focus is geared towards goals that match with the reach of my programme.

Given resource restrictions, Eco-Finanças works on emblematic cases. An ideal case reveals systemic problems, communicates to specialists and the wider public, and provides chances for success and personal and organisational learning.

Hereafter, I focus on one such case: the construction of two large hydropower dams on the Madeira River, the main tributary of the Amazon, in the western Amazon Region.

Box 7.1 **Madeira River hydroelectric project**

The Madeira River Complex includes the Santo Antônio and Jirau hydropower plants (reservoir size between 530 and 1,000 km², combined 6,500 MW, under construction), and a 2,450 km power line, at a total cost of approximately US$17.3 billion. A system of navigation locks and two additional hydroelectric dams along the border region between Brazil and Bolivia are projected. The area of indirect impact measures 1,000,000 km².

Necessary as economic development is, the challenge is to address it with appropriate solutions, and mega-dams are not part of them. Negative environmental and social impacts of the Rio Madeira Complex are flagrant and irreversible. The planning and implementation of the Rio Madeira hydroelectric project has been characterised by a long catalogue of violations and deficiencies:

- Irregularities in the environmental licensing process, associated with enormous political and economic pressures
- Violation of rights of indigenous groups and peoples, lack of minimum guarantees for ensuring the quality of life of riverine families and other affected communities
- Underestimation of the influence of various crucial elements, including negative impacts on biodiversity and fish migrations, mercury accumulation, malaria, problems related to the huge amount of sediments carried by the Madeira River, illegal deforestation
- Diplomatic tensions between Brazil, Bolivia and Peru due to cross-border impacts that were not appropriately considered
- Violations of environmental and labour legislation and non-compliance with financial sector self-regulation initiatives such as the Equator Principles[6]
- Lack of consideration of mutually reinforcing social and environmental impacts between the Madeira Complex and other regional infrastructure projects that are part of the Initiative for the Integration of the Regional Infrastructure of South America (IIRSA)

When I took over Eco-Finanças, the Rio Madeira case had already begun. When embarking on a project, I have found the following exercise to be very helpful. It grew from my practice, and is informed by action inquiry skills I learned through the RBP MSc.

---

6 www.equator-principles.com, accessed 31 December 2010.

First, I make explicit to myself what could be easily overlooked in the frenzy of project execution. I examine how the project relates to larger objectives, to my worldview and to my values. From there, I try to discover: what is needed now, what would be the best intervention and what can I and Eco-Finanças contribute in this respect? I also check how the project fits into the portfolio of work and the overall objectives of my programme and my organisation. I anchor the project in my own and the institution's biographies.

From a practitioner's perspective, this exercise provides direction from a principled perspective; it motivates and unleashes healthy energy; and it creates something I can refer to in critical circumstances, for example, when the project experiences difficulties. Appreciating how the project fits in the broader picture provides comfort and patience. From an action-inquiry viewpoint, this practice prepares the ground for single-, double- and triple-loop learning (Torbert *et al.* 2004).

Over time, this exercise has turned into common practice in all my projects. It helps me with what appear to be paradoxes: being committed while avoiding being tangled up or attached, and providing a sense of urgency while preventing panic and despair.

On this basis, I set the ball rolling. In the Rio Madeira case, the coordination I have provided includes the following:

1. Creating an enabling environment and obtaining the mandate to act. This meant gaining project plan approval from donors and my boss

2. Defining objectives and planning how to best attain them. I evaluated and redefined initial project objectives, developed a strategy that aligns resources, instruments and products with targets and objectives

3. Building alliances. We entered into partnership with other organisations and networks to create mutual support synergies

4. Checking in with opponents. We reached out to selected project promoters (such as construction companies and banks), shared our concerns with them and investigated how they saw the issues at stake

5. Starting to deliver the work plan. A first concrete phase usually consists of doing research and developing the products (such as reports) we need later as campaign tools and reference points

6. Publicising products, creating impacts. In the Rio Madeira case, we lodged several lawsuits, sent notifications to financiers regarding their responsibilities, published reports and press releases, and encouraged journalists to write articles about the violations occurring

7. Continuously: monitoring progress, questioning governing variables and adapting action strategies when necessary. This sounds like any other project management recommendation for 'continuous improvement'.

However, there is more to it: to the extent that I connect my action back to various levels of learning, I practise action inquiry (Fisher *et al.* 2002)

After this glimpse into my practice in the chosen case, I will present a line of argument that has proved particularly helpful in my change agency.

Exposing the gap between discourse and actual practice

Exposing the gap between discourse or 'espoused theory' and actual practice can be an effective campaign tool. It can be considered a transposition of Argyris and Schon's (1974, 1978) contribution from the personal to the organisational realm. For example, most companies nowadays claim how sustainable, green or responsible they are. Meanwhile, they keep breaching company policies and industry-specific self-regulation standards, and are often complicit in violations of the law. Exposing such gaps is powerful and leaves little room for interpretation. The bigger the gap, the bigger the reputational risk and possible damage; hence the incentive to close the gap between discourse and practice.

In practice, we use non-compliance with such standards and the gap between discourse and practice in various forms, including legal actions and disclosure of information through media, reports and case studies.

Results

I will now describe and review selected results of our work in the Rio Madeira case.

The use of legal action

Having selected legal actions (e.g. against government agencies) as a crucial means of action, we were confronted with judges that were not impartial, but had yielded to political pressure. Through their sentences they created jurisprudence that counters public interest. This directly opposes our intentions and could be used as negative precedent in the future. Therefore, we appealed. The process is still ongoing. In addition, we adapted our strategy.

We have not achieved immediate goals such as the paralysis of the construction sites, and the initial aim of avoiding destruction has not been reached. Wider goals such as the setting of positive precedents through jurisprudence seem distant. Meanwhile, tangential progress was made in that:

- The cases are in the judicial system, and they could be reappraised in the future

- Evidence of the lack of independence of members of the legal system is now available to wider public scrutiny

- Pending legal cases can be referred to in other realms of action, and serve as input for campaign work, for example when unveiling collaboration between financiers

- The experience gained in this case improves our practice in new cases

Holding financiers accountable

Indicators of our impact include:

- Financiers have become more careful in the design and financing of new projects

- We have had successes in exposing the co-responsibility of financiers in infrastructure projects and their non-respect for relevant guidelines. This created reputational damage, which is an indicator of success, but not an ultimate goal of our action

- Our intervention showcases the lack of effectiveness of self-regulation initiatives in the financial system such as the Equator Principles and the Green Protocol

- Brazilian banks call on Eco-Finanças as a key civil society stakeholder when reviewing their investment policies

Other forms of action

One recent successful experiment in terms of exposing the responsibility of project promoters is the use of the Public Eye, a sort of 'anti-Oscars' for the most irresponsible companies in the world.[7] For its 2010 edition, we nominated GDF Suez, majority owner of the consortium that is building the Jirau dam. Despite strong competition, GDF Suez almost won the Public Prize. The fallout of this distinction is ongoing. So far, it includes several articles in leading newspapers, an intervention on Jirau at the 2010 Annual General Meeting of GDF Suez, an exchange of letters between a group of NGOs and the CEO of the company, a review of investments by institutional investors, and plans for the first lawsuit on the case in France.

Assessment

A look at the evidence might suggest that, from a narrow and immediate perspective, our legal intervention almost failed, while other lines of action proved more successful. Our (and others') actions unveiled the illegitimacy of the project. However, as one would expect in asymmetrical power relations, the dominant interests of the promoters of the Rio Madeira Complex have prevailed. Illegitimate mega-

7 www.publiceye.ch/en, accessed 31 December 2010.

projects advance despite violations of laws (let alone self-regulation), while affected peoples (including isolated indigenous people with radically different worldviews) and the more-than-human world bear the brunt.

While this is the type of analysis that is most pertinent from a short-term perspective, I would like to turn to questions from the perspective of systemic change: how do we define and measure success, and in what (time) frames?

The idea in this case was to prevent or mitigate negative impacts and contribute to positive systemic change. Such change does not happen overnight and goes beyond a single project.

Considering the non-linearity of systemic change, it is difficult to assess completely which of the seedlings we planted will grow. In general terms, one can point to factors that may prove important in the future: we helped form the opinion of specialists and the wider public; the cost of non-conformity increases; the lawsuits lodged may be reconsidered; we inspired other civil society actors to act; new lawsuits in other cases were successful and so on. Importantly, we stood up, took leadership, and acted in keeping with our values and best understanding. This last point may be an inspiration for present and future self-elected practitioners. It is certainly part of what I gained from my engagement: the encouragement to continue crossing over from 'understanding' to 'acting', and lots of learning that will inform my future practice.

References

Argyris, C., and D. Schön (1974) *Theory in Practice: Increasing professional effectiveness* (San Francisco: Jossey-Bass).

—— and D. Schön (1978) *Organizational Learning: A theory of action perspective* (Reading, MA: Addison Wesley).

Fisher, D., D. Rooke and W.R. Torbert (2003) *Personal and Organisational Transformations through Action Inquiry* (Boston, MA: Edge/Work Press).

Torbert, W., and Associates (2004) *Action Inquiry: The secret of timely and transforming leadership* (San Francisco: Berrett-Koehler).

8

Connecting up stakeholders for more sustainable outcomes

- **Jo Confino**. Katine

- **Nick Pyatt**. Challenging the system with the success of inquiry

- **Simon Hicks**. Collaborative conservation

This chapter brings together three accounts of people working on international projects through approaches of inquiry and dialogue. Two are independent consultants; one is with a major media organisation. In all three cases, issues of power are apparent, as those from the privileged world seek to work alongside people elsewhere in the globe and act for systemic change without exerting inappropriate control and dominance. Detailed attention is paid to processes and everyday aspects of interaction, to the practices and crafts of relating to others with respect and mutuality. In the case of Katine, told by Jo Confino, how the project is conducted is open to searching public scrutiny through the media. We see the need for persistence, patience and working with emergent timing. The stories elaborate key aspects of relational practice. They show how people can work to create the conditions for different things to happen and different sorts of awareness to be developed. Nick Pyatt's and Simon Hicks's stories show some of the challenges of taking care of themselves that those taking leadership for sustainability often encounter.

Katine

Jo Confino MSc10, 2006–2008

The *Guardian* has always been internationalist in outlook and passionate about development issues. At the heart of its values are social justice and giving a voice to the voiceless. With this in mind, we set ourselves a challenge in 2007: how could we use emerging web 2.0 technology to tell the story of development in a new way? We joined forces with the Nairobi-based NGO Amref and Barclays Bank to develop an integrated development project in one community in Africa over three years, which we would report on using everything from videos and picture galleries to audio and live web-chats. The community we chose is Katine, a rural community of 25,000 in north-east Uganda which suffers from extreme poverty and the after-effects of civil war.

One of our aims was to break away from the marketisation of development, whereby NGOs feel the need to present only success stories in order to ensure donations keep flowing in. We wanted to show the extraordinary complexity of development, as well as being honest and transparent about why it is so difficult to create sustained progress.

The creation of the project coincided with my participation in the MSc, and the learnings from my studies proved instrumental in the design and implementation of the project. At the heart of the MSc in Responsibility and Business Practice was a recognition of the importance of different worldviews; that a Westerner looking at Ugandan development issues, for example, would have a very different set of cultural references than a Ugandan. Bringing those unconscious judgements to the surface was something of a revelation. I was also influenced by reading development literature, such as the work of Robert Chambers (1997) who highlights that the voices of the affluent North often dominate.

It therefore became abundantly clear that it would be a mistake to involve only our own journalists, experienced as they are, in the telling of the Katine story, and that we needed to also bring Ugandans' own perspectives to the fore. I therefore formed a partnership with the media NGO Panos to employ two Ugandan journalists so that much of the reporting would come from an African perspective.

Another learning from the MSc programme was that the voices of the poor and oppressed are rarely heard directly, and are far more likely to be mediated by professionals, whether from the worlds of development or journalism. To seek to change this, I ensured that one of the Ugandan journalists lived full-time in Katine and that one of his key responsibilities was to train members of the community so that they could directly voice their own views on how the project was going and how it was impacting their lives. We built a media centre in the village so that the villagers were able to read what we were writing about them and also post their comments on the website. The first time one of the villagers posted a comment on an article was actually one of the most joyous moments of the whole project.

It was not only in the writing of the project that I sought to ensure participation from the Katine community. The decision to work with Amref was in part based on its commitment to involving the community fully in the decisions that would affect their lives. For example, when we were deciding whether to extend the life of the project to a fourth year, I worked with Amref to develop a two-day stakeholder conference near Katine that sought to break down traditional hierarchies and power structures. This meant that local political leaders, bureaucrats, Amref staff, villagers, *Guardian* colleagues and I, all sat together debating what we needed to do to achieve sustainable change. In more traditional projects, the villagers themselves would not have been involved in such a process.

From a journalistic perspective, the project has been an excellent way to challenge how the media covers development, which is often to arrive in a community, find a story, and then quickly move on, often never to return. Even when covering disasters, such as the South-East Asian Tsunami or the Haitian earthquake, initial blanket coverage soon gives way to a loss of interest.

However, perhaps the most important lesson for me is how transparency leads to greater responsibility. The Katine project has been unique in making public the process of development. Amref's work has been monitored and challenged, not just by *Guardian* journalists but also by the many bloggers who have been watching the process, and by our expert independent evaluator. As a result of this level of continual scrutiny, Amref acknowledges it has needed to be more flexible and open to changing direction. For example, when a blogger pointed out that the cost of building a school seemed on the high side, Amref was forced to admit that it had unwisely used a contractor from the capital Kampala and agreed to switch to using local builders, which had the added benefit of creating wealth and employment in the area.

What else have I witnessed? Development is slow, sometimes painfully so, and complex. Also, it is extremely fragile and vulnerable, especially to external political, economic and environmental shocks.

From the outset, I recognised the importance of ensuring projects fit within local and national government objectives and that local political leaders are involved in the whole process, to ensure the best possible chance that they will 'own' it when the NGO pulls out. When I first visited Katine, I saw the perfect example of the opposite approach: a state-of-the-art health clinic opened by the Ugandan First Lady the year before, paid for by the Japanese government, and containing operating facilities and a dental suite. All the still unused equipment relied on electricity, yet the nearest energy supply was five miles away. Beyond this, it was impossible to find a doctor prepared to live and work so far away from a main town.

Part of the MSc involved looking at different theories of development, but watching the Katine project unfold, I recognised that what really counts is the quality and commitment of the staff working in the field. Also, while much can be achieved while an NGO is involved, what hope for continued progress when it pulls out? From Katine, it is clear to me that sustainable change cannot be forced through in a few years, but can take a generation to embed. This is why I have been working with Amref to agree long-term legacy funding to help maintain community structures such as water and education committees and the village health team network.

While much effort has been made to create change in Katine itself, the *Guardian* has also put enormous emphasis on using the project to influence the development debate. Two events spring to mind. One is a presentation I made to the director-general and directors of Europe Aid and other major donors based in Brussels, who wanted to learn from us how to communicate development. The other was two half-day workshops I ran with NGOs under the challenging title: 'How honest can you be with donors before they stop giving money'.

The Katine project has been watched closely and admired by development experts across the world and has won numerous journalism awards as well as the prestigious International Coffey Award at the 2010 Business in the Community awards for excellence. Perhaps most important, though, it has been a spur to reinvigorate interest in development issues within the *Guardian* and has been the catalyst for the launch of a major new Global Development website that will be tracking the Millennium Development Goals to 2015.[1]

Reference

Chambers, R. (1997) *Whose Reality Counts? Putting the first last* (London: Intermediate Technology Publications).

1   www.guardian.co.uk/global-development, accessed 31 December 2010.

Challenging the system with the success of inquiry

Nick Pyatt MSc10, 2006–2008

My story relates to an initiative to create a company in India's poorest state, Orissa. The company is to be owned by 8,000 poor farmers and produce forest products for timber, paper and fruit industries. The business would generate £50 million over 20 years for a community which currently has 90% of its population living off less than US$1/day.

To this work I brought 27 years of experience from managing development projects and running a large forestry production company. I knew that poor farmers have a lot of experience and wisdom which, when captured, can make interesting things happen. I knew that conventional ways of promoting forestry development were not working.

The journey has been one of inquiry, exploring ideas that seemed to have the potential to work but were not yet supported by donors or other enablers who would be needed to make them work in practice. It illuminated the conundrum of why very poor farmers with sub-agricultural land that is good for growing trees were not taking up generous incentives that paper and other industries, desperate for local supplies of trees, were already offering them.

I started from the assumption that there was something wrong and that it should be possible to put it right and enable the farmers and factories to trade to mutual benefit. Conventional development sector tools such as participatory rural appraisal (PRA) seemed to have been unable to find the solution, even after strong consultation with the stakeholders. (Despite PRA's best intentions, typically, external experts deeply immersed in Northern developmental theory perspectives still control the questions asked, interpretations made and actions taken.) I also assumed that, while I did not have a methodology to achieve this, it would emerge if I was open to it and worked with the partners I found around me.

At its heart the way forward seemed to call for: balancing power where it was widely disparate, addressing the dignity as well as the wealth of the weak, providing people with the capacities to unlock their potential, and putting experts in enabling rather than leadership roles. However this would have to emerge from an intervention that neither farmers nor factories had overtly asked for. The answer to opening up the potential for change seemed to be deeply based in stuck systems and power relationships. Initiating inquiry and dialogue seemed to offer elements of a solution, since action could emerge as a result of stimulating reflection among the farmers, businesses and other stakeholders. As these ideas formed I became increasingly conscious that they could be very powerful, yet were not conventional development approaches and indeed not necessarily ones of which the development aid delivery system would approve. Since conventional approaches seemed to me to be dramatically under performing, challenging the system with an effective approach felt worth doing. If it could work, maybe, just maybe, the system could be changed.

The breakthrough came during an MSc Workshop in 2009 when Peter Garrett presented his Implicate Change dialogue approach developed with David Bohm, based on notions of implicate and explicate order. It has a strong track record of delivering improved performance, having released a number of corporations and public sector organisations (including prisons) from systems that have served them badly. An important part of the solution has been evening out the power between the voices of all who have an impact on a desired change, particularly enabling the perspectives of the weakest to be heard, going beyond what PRA achieves. These elements connected with an intuitive analysis that I had made of my situation, although I would not have easily articulated it.

Peter was invited into the project and the dialogue approach immediately made an impact. Quickly our engagement with stakeholders was conducted with a greater purpose and acknowledgement of each whole person in the system, not just their position. Power was more effectively dealt with, especially the unfamiliarity of poor farmers with the processes that would unfold. Talking to power on an equal basis would be new for them, let alone expecting a win–win outcome. The farmers were supported to consider what they wanted from the process and prepare plans. After work with individual stakeholders, a gathered event was held. Care was taken to ensure that the event balanced power between the stakeholder groups, with detailed attention paid to: seating arrangements, timetable and facilitation. The farmers were supported to develop their own vocabulary for each step of the dialogue process, also to prepare presentations to the businesses and advisers.

The event was very powerful. Invited observers described how the farmers changed from beneficiaries of charity to business people. A key moment that transformed understanding and appreciation of the way forward came when an old farmer stood and shouted at the business people: 'We know how to be hungry, we do not mind that. What we do not accept is the way we expect to be treated if we accept your money'.

The expectation by farmers that they would be treated badly was later given weight by the CEO of one of the participating paper companies who described the poor treatment that farmers received from staff and middlemen. Also he felt unable to stop it. The forest business assumption that access to affordable money and technical support was the barrier to farmers growing trees was undermined. While these were important, dignity was a business-critical issue for the farmers.

As dialogue continued, the desire between the farmers and businesses to trade grew, though they did not trust each other any more than before. A 'social business' framework that was introduced for consideration received growing support, as the stakeholders tested each other and found both opportunity and protection in the design.

Following the event the stakeholders began to commit themselves to action. The broad vision was clear. It was also clear that the farmers needed to own the business structure to strengthen their trading relationship with forest industries. Achieving that would be a patient process, empowering them to understand their options and make effective decisions. Once again our dialogue approach would be at the heart of the process.

This was a slow and initially costly process; the businesses would not fund all of the initiative, though they did contribute. But the projected returns to the 8,000 farmers make an exciting prospect. It would appear a logical investment for continuing the development aid that funded the initial activity.

A notable absentee from the process was the appointed donor contact, the gatekeeper to institutional support, including funding. As the programme progressed, his opposition grew and he remained disengaged from the dialogue process. I am sure that on some levels he was aware of the challenge that the approach posed. From his perspective, an inquiry process that keeps revealing new understanding can look as though it keeps changing the picture. Well, it does. Doing that in a world that takes confidence from certainty can be a challenge. I found Alexander Ballard Ltd's (2008) organisational responsiveness framework helpful to understand this situation. Our approach is a breakthrough project (Level 4), seeking a new way of doing things where the orthodox approach is not enough. Our gatekeeper acted firmly in efficient management mode (Level 3), wanting us to simply tweak the existing system. For example he repeatedly asked why we didn't work with the businesses to refine their incentive systems for growing trees. Yet the dialogue approach made it clear that it was how the farmers expected to be treated that mattered, and tweaking the existing system was unlikely to change that. Changed power relationships that delivered mutually beneficial outcomes probably would.

No matter how many times we discussed this, the gatekeeper could not hear the analysis. To me this connects to the organisational responsiveness framework, spiral dynamics (Beck and Cowan 1996) and leadership action logics (Rooke and Torbert 2005). These frameworks acknowledge that people sometimes just cannot hear what others at different positions are saying. To overcome the gatekeeper we had to build constituencies of support for our perspective to enable the gate to be opened, because he seemed unable to do that by himself. Simply being able to use these sense-making frameworks helped me to work out what to do. Yet I found the power of the gatekeeper's inaction transfixing. A temptation is to make a fuss. But the project team found that if we challenged him as a civil servant, the system would move to protect him, even if his colleagues disagreed. And that happened even though the gatekeeper's boss is a great supporter of our partner organisations. This makes reaching him very difficult. And as time passes our resources have dwindled, and we need to put time into other things. Yet, slowly, things move in our direction.

The journey has been powerful and has challenged my personal behaviours. There have been long periods where things have not succeeded because of them. Learning and adapting has required moving into unexpected realms to be personally and financially sustainable, and finding more riches than I could have imagined.

My key drivers have been the value of the inquiry approach and the call to 'go fear-wards' that were key learnings from the MSc.

Currently, my time and emotional energy need to be channelled into trying to make this initiative work, and to attending to economic viability and responsibility for my family. Just now these are challenging. Yet pausing briefly to write has reconnected me to the inquiry approach from the MSc, reminding me of its power and of how it has provided ways of making sense that have guided my action in this story.

Have I been using single-, double- or triple-loop reflection during this process? It feels as though on one level I've tied myself in knots with reflection, and it is great. I find, though, that it is hard to reflect richly when things are moving slowly, which is what this initiative currently feels like. I need the dynamism of challenge that pushes back the boundaries of my imagination so that what we need to do becomes clearer. One of the high-level, triple-loop reflections is: 'is it worth it? Do my family deserve what I am putting them through to persist with this?' The answer remains clear, yes, but the internal cringe is hard to live with among the family. Yet the vision of the initiative is consistent and so far seems to enable us to attract enough supporters to feel as though it is worth keeping going. And holding the initiative by being open to deep reflection has allowed the key moments to happen.

Choosing the overall approach to use involved such questioning. Finding a dialogue approach which goes beyond participatory rural appraisal and balances power between stakeholders was vital, although it was deeply threatening to experts, and initially puzzling to business people and farmers.

In all of this I aim to act with what Rooke and Torbert (2005) call a Strategist action logic. But I know that under pressure I can be an Individualist, somewhat preoccupied with first-person inquiry. The Strategist seeks to also enable second-person inquiry. But, if I were too concerned about the thoughts of others I could not have done this. To be a champion, to try to be a Tempered Radical (Meyerson and Scully 1995), it feels as though I have to be a bit selfish. I am never quite sure where the boundaries are, but I am sure that they are beyond those of the orthodoxy that I have lived in for so long. To do this project, I feel I have to follow my own intuition and not necessarily listen to others, though I also know I have a lot to learn from others if this is going to work. (There is a Samuel Beckett quote that goes something like: 'Who could have done this better than I? Thousands of people. But I am the one here, so I must do my best.')

I'm blessed with implementing partners who keep me out there, hopefully enough, who I respect deeply and argue with loudly; forging great outcomes in the furnace of our passion. The exciting challenge some supporters are setting is to make this approach replicable beyond our actions (which would be third-person inquiry). Whatever you call it, it would be brilliant, and I believe we can do it, if the system can be changed to support this sort of initiative, or better ones that come out of it.

What encourages me, despite the challenges, is that I know this is right for the farmers and the businesses; both intuitively and because they keep telling us each time the dialogue continues and we all learn more. I know I will need to learn a lot more to do it right, but as long as we can keep the ownership with the farmers we can achieve a good business model.

I also know that there are two elements of this work that I find challenging and yet, if I try to impose my worldview, that might undermine the initiative:

- So far women have had little voice in the process. Women will do the bulk of the work. We must find a way to give them more voice in the dialogue process

- I get constant warnings that there will be greater harmony if there is religious and cultural uniformity among the member farmers of the business. Yet this is a population with a *range* of religions and cultures. Working only with uniformity of view fits with experience but feels abhorrent. It will have to be raised in the dialogue process and dealt with. It would be easier to sweep it under the carpet and go for uniformity to ensure sustained success for the business

I know I can work this out as I go along with the partners I have.

And now, as we have held on so long, it seems possible that other, corporate and global finance, supporters will join us.

References

Alexander Ballard Ltd (2008) *Adaptive Capacity Benchmarking: A handbook and toolkit* (prepared for Hampshire County Council on behalf of European Spatial Planning: Adapting to Climate Events; Winchester, UK: Environmental Futures Group, Hampshire County Council, www.espace-project.org/part2/part2_outputs.htm, accessed 1 January 2011).

Beck, D.E., and C.C. Cowan (1996) *Spiral Dynamics: Mastering values, leadership and change* (Malden, MA: Blackwell).

Meyerson, D.E., and M.A. Scully (1995) 'Tempered Radicalism and the Politics of Ambivalence and Change', *Organization Science* 6.5: 585-600.

Rooke, D., and W.R. Torbert (2005) 'Seven Transformations of Leadership', *Harvard Business Review* 83.4: 66-76.

Collaborative conservation

Simon Hicks MSc4, 2000–2002

My working life and my passion has been in the service of wildlife conservation. I chose to leave a secure position in my fifties, wanting to develop and apply my experience to greater effect to save more species. How was it, I wondered, that the small conservation organisation for which I had worked for over 20 years could achieve so much on a relative shoestring when the international wildlife conservation industry appeared to achieve so much less? By achievements, I mean species saved, their decline reversed to full-on recovery within their ecosystems.

I visited the Species Survival Commission (SSC), World Conservation Union (IUCN), in Gland, Switzerland. I was welcomed by the coordinator and given access to the chairpersons of all the species specialist groups. I sent them a questionnaire intended to discover what they spent their money on, what proportion of it delivered species recovery and who had funded it. The response I received was too small to be of use and, a little puzzled, I headed for the University of Bath School of Management's MSc in Responsibility and Business Practice (RBP), with the specific intention to gain a better understanding of my task.

Learning to understand patterns, connectivity, appropriate responses . . . and self

The MSc taught me that there are recognisable shapes and patterns in behaviour, in history, in life.

Typically a species recovery project is initiated with a workshop, the output being an action plan with recommended steps to lead the project managers towards a successful conclusion. Job done, the workshop facilitators move on. If something goes wrong, the facilitators and most of the workshop participants seldom hear of it. Those left on their own with a project in trouble can soon lose their way, sometimes meaning the end of a project, even of a species.

From understanding systemic thinking, I learned that 'linear' doesn't work, that information needs to be fed back for adapting and managing. An introduction to Gaia taught me that it was ever thus, since evolution began, and I resolved that anything I learned from now on would be fed back through loops of sharing and showing. I learned that my early efforts to understand *what* was happening in conservation were less revealing than *why*, and to understand *why* required conducting my research *with*, rather than *on*, people. I had begun to inquire. I was ready to begin again.

Applying the principles of action, reflection, learning . . . and more action

Five years later, I can reflect on what happened next. Three interlinking loops of action resulted. My inquiry, to evaluate conservation workshop outcomes, became a long-term piece of research. The research trail led me to half a dozen potential projects, setting a second loop of action in motion. The projects became the foundation for a third loop, a new charitable trust called Conservation Works.

Every project is evaluated using the method and format learned in the evaluation inquiry. The results are fed back into a database used to inform the better selection and management of future projects for funding by the Trust. Thus the three loops—evaluation, project management and the Trust—are linked through cycles of interdependent informing, challenging and developing.

Figure 8.1 **Interlinked action bases for species conservation**

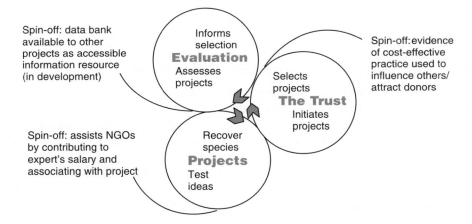

. . . the Trust

Conservation Works is defined by a distinctive brand of project that has the recovery of a species as a measurable objective, and always incorporates a wider implication to advance conservation practice. The project proposer is funded to initiate and monitor each project; its impact to be evaluated later by the Trust. By these means the Trust can be sure that its projects receive the best professional attention; incur no administrative overheads; and require no time-wasting application or reporting protocols. The Trust also repeatedly encourages institutions to work together, in search of new breakthroughs for conservation.

. . . the evaluation inquiry

In pursuit of understanding 'what works' in conservation, I decided against using the questionnaire with predefined options for scoring or ranking, and, instead, set off to visit for myself 30 diverse species recovery projects on four continents. In each case I sought two well-informed participants to inquire *with them* into the real, positive and negative factors impacting on the workshop recommendations, and I asked: 'was it done?' 'did it work?' and 'why?' I addressed the interviewees as members of a community of conservationists across the world who shared many of the same issues, encouraging them to confide their mistakes and problems as well as to describe successes.

I coded the data from 1,500 responses into five general categories, sorted it into over 100 positive and 100 negative 'factors', clustered under nine 'sense-making' fields. It is planned that the results will form the basis of a free, interactive website into which project managers can input their project category, and download the basic operational dos and don'ts that apply.

. . . the projects

The collaborative inquirer in active, and passive, mode

The evaluation inquiry took me to Addis Ababa. While there, I came across a group of black-maned lions, once the private collection of Emperor Haile Selassie. Immediately I saw the opportunity for a national conservation education campaign, the lions having both deep cultural resonance and characterising the top of an African plains food chain and ecosystem. Starting with the lions' keepers, I negotiated a passage upwards through the layers of bureaucracy, collaboratively including every relevant government official en route. Frequent visits were made to Addis Ababa University's biology and genetic departments, the Wildlife Conservation Authority, the Natural History Museum, the city administration, palaces, tourism and cultural ministries, and more. I wove together hitherto inconceivable alliances, in preparation for a wholly Ethiopian-owned project, starting with an international conference of experts, hosted by the city.

At the last moment, an unconnected press event brought the plan to a sudden halt, and new players onto centre stage, including two international zoos and an animal welfare NGO. The various interest groups allied themselves with the country's president, the city administration or the national government, with no communication between the national institutions or the overseas experts. I repositioned ConservationWorks as an independent adviser and tried to maintain dialogue with, and communications between, as many of the players as possible. Prevailing negative influences, for example competition for foreign funds and a fear of accepting responsibility, made this difficult, especially as my own, conservation-driven motivation was little understood.

Realisation dawned that people do not necessarily wish to communicate, nor do they always take 'ownership' of their responsibilities, sometimes even appearing insensitive to their professional territory—unless there are positive financial implications. They certainly found it difficult to comprehend why an outsider would wish to do something of value for *their* country for no apparent gain, especially if he expressed no political alliance with any one faction—except the black-maned lions!

In such a situation, where does the collaborative inquirer stand? This one chooses to visit often, to wait, watch and talk to everyone, with the occasional reminder that the offer of an international conference is still on the table. Sometimes I wonder how often or far I should push the concept of biodiversity conservation in an environment that is fundamentally unreceptive to it. I am assuming that I am right, and hope that, sooner or later, an influential Ethiopian will appear who agrees with me, and active collaboration can begin again. Meanwhile I am uneasy with my foreigner's sense of rightness.

Collaborative inquiry by email

Working with an international conservation NGO led to a realisation that it and another conservation group, the European Association of Zoos, were both targeting the same Kazakh antelope, the saiga, without realising it. I contacted both institutions, and began leading a structured email dialogue between strangers, lasting three months. Using three columns and varying colour and font, I manoeuvred their remarks to address one another, with space for me to facilitate. The result was a presentation by the NGO to the Antelope Advisory Group of European zoos, and a grant to source major funding for satellite tracking. It demonstrated that noncollaboration between conservation sectors, a significant negative factor identified by the evaluation inquiry, can sometimes be reversed to become a positive opportunity.

Defining the issue before attempting collaboration

A project to staunch the flow of illegally trafficked chimpanzees out of Democratic Republic of Congo (DRC) has been successful, so far as it goes. I was appointed as conservation adviser to a local NGO called JACK, which began with the confiscation of a young chimpanzee in Lubumbashi in south DRC. The animal had arrived by train with its carrier, as had more than 400 others over a ten year period, to supply a clearly visible roadside market where they had been photographed and recorded by JACK's founder.

My chief contribution was to guide the new refuge towards a conservation mission rather than a welfare one. In the past, sanctuaries have generally responded to humanitarian sensibilities, motivated by the welfare of the individual animal rather than the conservation of the species. To help differentiate its role of conservation from that of welfare, JACK called its holding facility a Centre d'Accueil or 'refuge' to stress a temporary rather than permanent place of stay, as all those apes that can, will return to the wild.

Other principles that separate conservation actions from welfare include:

- Only accepting confiscated animals. An animal that has been obtained through payment, however little, perpetuates the trade. Viewing each new arrival as an opportunity to learn, teach or develop conservation skills that will bring the illegal traffic of wildlife closer to an end

- Collaborating with a consortium of Congolese authorities. This had already begun with a brave, young inspector of hunting from the Ministry of Environment, who seized the first chimpanzee from a poacher. Others included the directors of national park and zoo garden provincial offices

The strategy worked and now chimpanzees are seldom seen on the 1,000 miles of railway south from Kindu in the north to the Zambian border. Our plan next is to apply the same strategy on the Congo River, east to west, from Kisangani to Kinshasa.

Encouraging unwilling collaborative partners

Kisangani has everything a chimpanzee refuge needs—except funding. It is unlikely that this town has the resources of Lubumbashi and an alternative source needs to be found. This may be exactly the project we are looking for to combine and bond the strengths of two conservation sectors, the professional associations of African zoos and African sanctuaries, which characteristically view each other with suspicion. There is a pervasive and insidious influence at work in conservation, as in other sectors, whereby organisations claiming to share a common mission to conserve wildlife find it hard to share their skills and work together for greater effect. I attended conferences of both associations and asked of a sample of delegates at each, 'Is there a difference between a zoo and a sanctuary?' I recorded and analysed their answers.

As I suspected, most negative perceptions about the other sector—zoo or sanctuary—were subjective and contradictory. However, one response did have substance . . . and I almost missed it. Surprised by the vehemently 'conservation', rather than 'welfare', position one sanctuary interviewee took, I prompted the delegate to confirm if animal welfare was still a principal concern. 'Of course it is!' came the indignant response. The unspoken inference was 'animal welfare is what we are . . . conservation is what we do'.

I realised that the core difference between zoo and sanctuary sectors was the principal purpose for which each had been established: people want to see animals, and some animals need to be rescued. However, both associations also include 'conservation' in their charitable purpose. Zoos that display, and sanctuaries that save animals, are what they are. What else they do—or could do, especially together—represents an opportunity.

A sanctuary and education centre to be built within an old zoo on the banks of the Congo River, funded by zoos in Northern Europe or America, just might be the catalyst required to bury the differences dividing two conservation-driven sectors. The result could be a new strategy for conservation.

Postscript

An unexpected, extra loop has appeared, carving a wide trajectory. I have discovered that the SSC coordinator of ten years ago is now its chair. His office is half an hour's drive from mine, at the University of Bath. A copy of my evaluation inquiry report 'What Works?' landed on his desk a few weeks ago, followed by two hours of rich debate. The start of a new chapter? We shall see.

9

Itinerant change agents to professions and sectors

- **Charles Ainger**. 'Holding up the tightrope'—helping us all act for sustainability
- **Simon Cooper**. Doing things right—and doing the right thing

This chapter brings together two accounts of people who are now working independently and using their access and relationships to promote change for sustainability. Until recently Charles Ainger was part of a global organisation, with which he is still associated, and so could have appeared in Chapter 4. But over recent years he has expanded his attention to influencing the wider professional development of engineers, especially in the water industry, taking up a range of opportunities and positions of influence. He talks about his purposes, practices and challenges. Simon Cooper's story gives insights into the potential opportunities and dilemmas of being a consultant in corporate social responsibility. Will clients want more challenging questioning? What conditions might make radical questioning generative?

In both accounts we see them seeking out and making the most of opportunities, adapting their strategies as they go along, feeding information from one context into others, and working alongside other people to make their contributions to change.

'Holding up the tightrope' — helping us all act for sustainability

Charles Ainger MSc3, 1999–2001

What am I doing?

My RBP MSc thesis title was *Walking the Tightrope* (Ainger 2001) because I felt that I was doing a balancing act between remaining credible in my organisation and my as-radical-as-possible actions for change. It also expressed my emotional tension, between my more radical change aspirations and the too-slow rate of progress. Since the MSc, my roles have developed to include mentoring for others engaged in this balancing act, so I have adapted my title. Here are two examples, within the half-dozen things I am active on.

I've just done a peer review of an engineering management journal article, about how best to use sustainability assessments to improve the sustainability of buildings. Engineers and architects use such tools all the time to make decisions, and the devil is in the detail, in my practical experience, of asking the right questions, of the right people, at the right time in the project development process. Rather than just ask: 'what's the least change that would make this paper acceptable?' I've acted more like an adviser, and asked many questions, to get the authors to revise the paper to extract the very best from their experience, and to make the recommendations as practical and also as radical, as possible.

Shortly, I'm off to South Africa, assisting the Institution of Civil Engineers' (ICE) President in his one-year 'President's Apprentices' campaign. This brings together 12 young engineers from 'developing' and 'developed' countries, to listen to leading edge expertise on how to deliver more effective, sustainable urban infrastructure in developing countries, to help meet the Millennium Development Goals. They then have to generate their own set of advisory documents on how to do this, to be publicised through many engineering institutions round the world. Mine is a part expert, mainly facilitation and mentoring role.

Common threads: how am I acting for sustainability?

There are some common strands here, reflecting a planned opportunism approach. I say 'yes' to working in several different communities, as opportunities arise; but with some common principles for choosing what to accept. No doubt these reflect my personality, as well as a sometimes instinctive, sometimes conscious, intellectual analysis of where I can be most effective.

First, I act as an internal innovator for sustainability. This is an often hidden, but vital, role—now dubbed 'social intrapreneur' (Elkington and Hailes 2008)—helping organisations, from inside, to make practical use of the 'tension for change' generated by those in that other key role, of external activist. Such tension generates a vital 'pull' for change.

Second, my approach is to look for existing initiatives that seem most likely to have an impact, and for which I have relevant expertise. I try to help the people doing them to be as effective as possible, using the systemic, action research lessons gained from the MSc and later experience.

Third, I aim to get involved with the energy and enthusiasm of the younger generation, who have to take us forward; this prompts my mentoring and educational roles.

These criteria mean that almost everything I do is with other people, as colleagues and as those whom I am mentoring: bosses, managers, lecturers, graduate students, engineering front-line practitioners, occasionally regulators and policymakers. I have become a member of several different 'communities', which is a valuable asset. But measuring my own success or failure is difficult, because it is so indirect and dependent on others

How did I get from the MSc to here?

These roles and principles have developed from my momentum when I left the MSc in 2001, in working on two parallel strands. The first was my role as sustainable development director at global engineering company MWH. The second was engaging with students and graduates via my Cambridge University Engineering Department Visiting Professor role that started in 2001.

My MWH role, with very many other people worldwide, helped push the company to a new declared purpose of 'Building a better world', to a 'Climate Change Commitment' partnership with The Climate Group (MWH 2008), and also to a partnership with the International Water Association (IWA), sharing knowledge on water and climate. After retiring from MWH in 2008, I am still involved with the IWA, as a magazine co-editor. One key role in MWH since 2003 has been to act as a public 'thought leader' on water, sustainability and climate change, which has led to keynote talks and papers in several places.

The content of these roles since 2003 reflects a move away from just advocacy for sustainability, to realising the difficulty of actually changing things. My focus has moved on to how to innovate better and faster, in my long-asset-life, risk-averse, engineering infrastructure sector. Systemic learning that started in the MSc has been important for that understanding. Since retirement, I have been able to take opportunities to do advisory work with a few policy-makers and regulators, who can be critical gatekeepers in enabling change.

The visiting professor role at Cambridge has led to all sorts of things. I developed and ran, until retirement, the module on 'Organisational change for sustainability' in the MPhil in Engineering for Sustainable Development. This now has an energetic worldwide set of alumni, making waves wherever they can (University of Cambridge 2009). The academic connection has provided a base for joint paper writing (Fenner *et al.* 2006), lecturing and gaining wider connections for academic and professional contributions to knowledge. One big issue is the need to bridge the gap between the narrow specialisations of people in technology or environment, and the systemic, multidisciplinary and collaborative solutions we need. Everything we do at and through Cambridge aims to develop people who can bridge that gap.

These 'parallel strands' have criss-crossed and connected, in content and in relationships. My March 2010 Australian keynote talk was an update of ideas on how to transform infrastructure, and will help advise the regulator, and feed into books in 2011. I have successfully said 'yes' to synergistic opportunities. My membership of multiple practitioner, academic and alumni communities has allowed me often to play the 'weak link' role (Barabasi 2002) in spreading knowledge across the gaps between specialist social networks.

Successes, failures and disappointments

Because most of what I do is not formally commissioned, and is with others, it is difficult to judge success or failure. There is some feedback on immediate outputs, but not on longer-term *outcomes*. I can sometimes judge successes from unsolicited comments. My MWH retirement plaque says: 'in gratitude . . . for providing us with challenge and inspiration'. And the CEO: 'You've been such a huge contributor, not only your technical base and knowledge about the things you advocate, but an inspirational leader to all of our younger people . . .'. However, I am cautious about such responses, as over-flattering. Because when I try to push boundaries and raise harder questions, some feel embarrassed about not doing enough, or fast enough; and they can compensate by being over-enthusiastic about my own, not so effective, role.

My failures are more like disappointments—in how long change takes, always longer than you hope. So much of the difficulty in change is nothing to do with sustainability practice, but comes from the everyday incompetence of organisations— poor knowledge sharing, short-term thinking, silo cultures, the 'not invented here' syndrome.

One recurring self-critique is that I help others who have started things—so not a leader, always a lieutenant? My response to myself is that in general we have enough inspirational leaders who are good at starting things and showing us a vision to head for. What we need are more quiet leaders, who are the ones who actually help everybody, effectively, to get there.

Key learning on innovation for sustainability

Much of the 'everyday incompetence of organisations' arises from reductionist thinking, dominated by top-down management; from the ideas that technology provides the 'magic bullets' and that economic analysis, often neo-liberal, drives real behaviour. My search for a better understanding of the way the complex world really works leads to many perspectives that started with one of the best surprises in the MSc, the action research approach. This provided a starting point for a series of approaches, beyond the usual technical and economic analyses.

During the MSc, I explored organisations as complex organisms and theories of power in depth. Since then, I have gained insights from complexity and systems thinking, from considering the impacts of informal systems of knowledge sharing, and from appreciative inquiry, as one key to spreading knowledge. One favourite quote is: 'People are much more likely to act their way into a new way of thinking, than to think their way into a new way of acting' (Pascale and Sternin 2005). In particular, the few 'weak links' between social networks can connect different specialisations (e.g. technical and sustainability), or geographies (e.g. learning for water demand management in the UK from Australian experience).

I have informally adopted inquiry as an approach (I have tried, for instance, to turn workshops into ongoing co-operative inquiries), but it has not been a formal practice. I seem to have learned inquiry by some sort of osmosis, and I'm sure that, at best, it has improved my practice.

So the MSc learning has been fundamental to my practice since. But I still find that the complexity of academic languages can be a barrier to widespread use. These ideas are more complex than the simplistic explanations we have to counter. We cannot educate most people (no time, and little inclination in the audience) in the detail of these vital approaches. It is a challenge to bring the essence of their learning to large numbers of people without dumbing down. So the 'Lowcarbonworks' project—*Insider Voices: Human dimensions of low carbon technology* (Reason *et al.* 2009)—is exciting. It takes action research thinking and applies it in understandable language to real innovation challenges.

Motivation, frustrations and support

My motivation is a deep belief, based on science and intellect, plus a love of wild nature, that we must live within the limits of the planet, and that every individual deserves empowerment and quality of life.

I try to pull today's reality towards the sustainability goal, to get the tension right, and not snap. The frustrations are mostly about how long change takes; but as I get older, I seem to have more equanimity about the disappointments. I feel a strong inevitability about the overall journey, particularly because I can see that there are solutions available. My daughter Katharine's writing sums up our power for action very well:

> 'Power to' is the ability to act for oneself, the ability to create rather than to coerce. It is social power, experienced in relationship with others. The great lie in our society is that 'power over' is the route to fulfilment . . . By contrast, 'power to' offers an attractive, abiding route out of powerlessness that everybody can use (Ainger 2003: 11).

As I felt during the MSc, support from those I am myself supporting is important. So is my wife's understanding and fellow feeling, with her fierce sense of fairness and social justice. In 2008 we worked together in a wholesale 'retrofit' of our own house for lower carbon emissions. I'm very much with Rob Hopkins, of the Transition Town movement, on 'the action for sustainability is fun' idea.

I have hardly called on the Bath RBP network for support, because the several other communities I inhabit have kept me busy with opportunities. But conversation on the RBP email list is always there in the background, whispering its familiar language and occasional inspiration, and is a valuable reference point.

Retirees have a duty, a strong role to play, and experience to bring, in enabling sustainability.[1] In April 2010 I talked on 'our personal response to climate change', to the local University of the Third Age retirees' group, wanting to engage them in the sustainability journey. I ended my talk to them with a favourite quote, which reflects my feelings about its do-ability: 'The best way to predict the future is to invent it' (Alan Kay, Apple Computers).

References

Ainger, C. (2001) *Walking the Tightrope: Learning to be a change agent for sustainability* (Dissertation, MSc in Responsibility and Business Practice; Bath, UK: School of Management, University of Bath).

Ainger, K. (2003) 'Keynote Editorial', *New Internationalist* 360: 9-12.

Barabasi, A.-L. (2002) *Linked: The new science of networks* (Cambridge, MA: Perseus Publishing).

Elkington, J., and J. Hailes (2008) *The Social Intrapreneurs: A field guide for corporate changemakers* (London: SustainAbility; www.sustainability.com/library/the-social-intrapreneurs, accessed 31 December 2010).

Fenner, R.A., C.A. Ainger, H.J. Cruickshank and P. Guthrie (2006) 'Widening Horizons for Engineers: Addressing the complexity of sustainable development', *Proceedings of the Institution of Civil Engineers, Engineering Sustainability Journal* 159.ES4: 145-54.

MWH (2008) 'Walking the Walk on Climate Change'; www.mwhglobal.com/MWH/AboutMWH/Climate_Change_Commitment.html, accessed 31 December 2010.

Pascale, R.T., and J. Sternin (2005) 'Your Company's Secret Change Agents', *Harvard Business Review* 83.5: 72-81.

Reason, P., G. Coleman, D. Ballard, M. Williams, M. Gearty, C. Bond, C. Seeley and E.M. McLachlan (2009) *Insider Voices: Human dimensions of low carbon technology* (Bath, UK: Centre for Action Research in Professional Practice, University of Bath; go.bath.ac.uk/insidervoices, accessed 31 December 2010).

University of Cambridge (2009) 'Where are they now?: Former Engineering for Sustainable Development MPhil students return'; www.eng.cam.ac.uk/news/stories/2009/alumni_presentations, accessed 31 December 2010.

1 GreyandGreen website: greyandgreen.org.uk, accessed 31 December 2010.

Doing things right—and doing the right thing

Simon Cooper MSc7, 2003–2005

I entered the MSc in Responsibility and Business Practice full of certainty—that a gradual build-up of facts should lead to a convincing conclusion, that for every question there is an answer, and that the more questions you manage to answer, the more successful you are being.

Two years of the course challenged those views very effectively, and led me down a path where a 'good' question was a thing to be cherished, to be looked at from different directions to see how the light shone through it. I was not alone in taking this path—many MSc alumni find they have a diverse set of questions to enrich their life and work, and I now know it is called 'Living Life as Inquiry' (Marshall 1999).

Part of my need for certainty came from 25 years as a broadcaster, where scripts and news items present a definite view of the world, telling listeners what is going on in an unambiguous way. A career change led to running the press office for the radio station Classic FM, where certainty also seemed to be my friend. To convince a journalist, you first need to convince yourself, and equivocation might be taken as a lack of belief in the story you were putting over.

Against that background, relishing the unanswered question was a big leap. I left the warm embrace of the radio company I had worked for since my 20s, piling financial uncertainty onto all the other uncertainties by joining the world of freelance consultancy, hoping to help people to understand and communicate corporate social responsibility. My wife and I founded a company to help us do this. Our feeling was that some of the big questions—what is a company for, how does the consumption-based economy impact on sustainability and many more—were not surfacing and maybe we could find a way to get these into the open. Perhaps if we could get people to interpret and tell their CSR 'story' in some way, those questions would come out.

I found the path to earning money lay in helping others to answer their questions. A company chairman questioned how his executive team was performing, partners in a law firm questioned how they could reduce their carbon footprint, a charity questioned how it could attract businesses to buy its 'ethical' carbon credits. In each case, there was satisfaction to be had in addressing the question that was being asked—but there was often a richer reward from asking new questions, either unspoken or avoided.

The consultant's life involves being in the right place (in terms of skills, knowledge and contacts) at the right time to answer the right question. As I developed my practice, I quickly learned that, although one can maintain networks, update knowledge and generally 'put yourself about' so that you are in the 'right place', there is almost nothing you can do to influence timing—the 'right time'. The 'right time' is all about context and the wider world's stage of understanding, which means that you have to develop patience.

Patience is also needed when judging the right time to ask a 'new', 'bigger' question. I would start by convincing clients that I could bring an answer to their existing questions with me. My previous career working for a company they had heard of helped, and I chose to put my academic qualifications on my business card. That 'MA MSc' felt immodest, but I'm convinced it got me through doors that would otherwise have been closed. Coming in as an 'outsider', I would usually have something new to contribute, often based simply on my more outward-looking, less introspective approach. As relationships grew with a range of clients, it was obvious that some were happy to consider new questions, while others were not. The only way to find out was to ask the question, often with my heart in my mouth, but I soon found that the worst that happened was that the client's eyes glazed over and they changed the subject. However, sometimes—months later, after reflecting—they would return to the 'big' question themselves. Drop a pebble in the pond, and wait for the ripples to fan out.

Usually, the client's existing question was about 'doing things right', but the new question was about 'doing the right thing'—a bigger set of considerations, requiring that more reflective approach. I found that many people are fixed on solving the problem that immediately confronts them; thinking further ahead or in a broader context could not, I observed, be a real option for them until we had done something to quiet their immediate concerns.

Also it seemed that new questions could be more easily floated in a collaborative context; asking a question of one firm or organisation would make them uneasy, but asking the same question of a group of similar firms or organisations was more acceptable and often led to useful debate. I realised that I was working in the realms of 'second-' and 'third-person' inquiry here, something I had been taught about but which I had not experienced so clearly before. As I experimented I noticed the new questions tended to be framed positively rather than negatively, and were 'bigger' than the existing questions. For example, in the media we were criticised for not reducing our environmental impact: paper for scripts, electricity for continuously operating studios and transmitters, and so on. But the 'big' question was different: what impact were our programmes and news articles making on the minds and lifestyles of our readers, viewers and listeners? How could we encourage them to be better citizens of the world? Using the example of music therapy (which uses the universal language of music to help people with profound communication difficulties such as autism), I encouraged colleagues to go beyond making entertaining and satisfying programmes and to consider the impact their broadcasts were making, or could make. A group of media outlets, including Classic FM and the BBC, worked together to produce output which was environmentally and socially positive and would, we considered, have a much greater effect than any amount of switching the lights off or turning the heating down—although we did that too.

The positive/negative balance troubled me. Firms often seem to start to address corporate social responsibility from the premise that they are doing harm, and need to reduce it. Their questions are around reducing carbon footprints, minimising resource use, solving human rights issues in overseas suppliers and so on. In most cases these questions have answers—through setting the right objectives and putting the right mechanisms in place. But as I was helping firms to answer these questions, I felt weighed down by the 'reducing' objective; every morning they had to get out of bed thinking 'today I will do less . . .' Yes, the eventual outcome would be positive—a more environmentally safe world, for example—but the building blocks seemed to be reducing, minimising actions, telling people to stop doing what they wanted to do. How much more uplifting it would be to think in terms of 'today I will do more . . .'

Such positive questions were rooted in the bigger considerations that were coming to the fore in my work. This usually started with 'so what really matters here?', first as a question to myself and then to others. We went on to consider not only the boundaried, well-defined aspects that could be reduced, but also those positive aspects that should be maximised, expanding the boundaries of the question to ask: what more could be done to improve this situation?

These positive, bigger questions seem powerful. For instance, as the concept of carbon neutrality started to take hold, some law firms became concerned about their CO_2 output. I ran a seminar for a network of managing partners where I asked the question, 'what is the biggest positive impact that you could have on sustainability?' This was a good example of 'group' questioning proving more fruitful than individual inquiry, and the discussion ranged far and wide, from developing new concepts of environmental law to broadening pro bono work among sustainability campaigners. The most interesting idea was the one that few at the seminar could imagine happening in their firms: when giving advice to clients, a firm's lawyers should be encouraged to direct that advice towards an environmentally positive outcome. Since lawyers, the argument went, are usually in the 'expert' role, any advice given, including environmental advice, is likely to be acted on. Some saw this as a logical extension of the duty of care that law firms have towards their clients: if environmental issues represent risks of the medium to long term, it is the duty of the professional adviser to point them out. Others, however, were strongly of the view that lawyers should stick to answering the question that has been put to them, and doing any more was straying dangerously off-piste.

I have not heard of any of the law firms involved explicitly following this path, so the argument has clearly not been accepted—yet. But in its core mechanism—using the expertise of a profession to cause others to act in a more sustainable way—it runs parallel to my second example, in higher education.

Universities that Count is a benchmarking and performance improvement programme which aims to transform the way that universities approach issues of environmental and social responsibility. Funded by the four UK Higher Education Funding Councils, the programme originated in a partnership between the Environmental Association for Universities and Colleges (EAUC), Business in the

Community and our company. The EAUC's members are commonly estates or environmental managers from universities across the UK. Not surprisingly most of the 55 universities participating in the first year were focused on the 'minimising harm' questions, particularly around environmental impact. Early on we realised that this focus, though important, could mask the positive 'what more can be done?' questions. We formed the view that the key positive environmental and social impacts of universities are intellectual: the teaching and learning that leads to graduates going out into the world and acting in a more sustainable way in their lives and careers, and the university research that helps to plot a course to a more sustainable future.

This is a positive set of questions, rooted in the bigger considerations which surround a university's approach to environmental and social responsibility. Our problem was that many of our participants came from the environmental or estates operations of a university, not its academic side, so we devised a specific set of questions on 'Teaching, Learning, Research and Knowledge Exchange' to engage the academic community and, as we go through the second year of the programme, we look forward to helping them to do even better in these important areas. Again, asking these questions of the group of 55 universities seems to be a more fruitful approach than individual inquiry: the opportunity to compare approaches and share practice is welcomed by all who care about this field. I see this as an example of third-person inquiry, trying to influence a system.

So, asking these new and appreciative questions has proved richly rewarding as a field of practice for us and, we hope, for those we work with. However, it also introduces a whole range of difficult questions. If one is expanding boundaries, where does one stop? Is a law firm responsible in some way for the laws it interprets as well as for the effects of the way it interprets them? Is a university responsible for the actions of its graduates after they have left and gone into the world? Asking how to 'do things right' is important, and urgent. But addressing these questions is also the gateway into questions that are more searching and difficult to answer: those about 'doing the right thing'. Addressing the first kind of question puts you in the right place to try to answer the second kind, when the time is right, but only with sensitivity and humility can one hope to identify when that moment has come.

Reference

Marshall, J. (1999) 'Living Life as Inquiry', *Systematic Practice and Action Research* 12.2: 155-71.

10
Working through community and society

- **Ian Roderick**. The journey to CONVERGE

- **Indrė Kleinaitė**. GYVA.LT: an initiative to promote environmentally friendly living and sustainability in Lithuania

- **Paula Downey**. CultureWork for a world in transition

This chapter brings together three stories of graduates who are working nationally and internationally to promote sustainability at community, society and international levels. They are independent, and certainly 'self-appointed' change agents given the scope of their visions, although this designation applies to all MSc graduates in effect. In these accounts we see: explorations of values, purposes and faith as people inquire into their bases for taking leadership; how paths of development unfold through a combination of agency, opportunities and patience; reflections on what leadership means from a radically systemic appreciation; working through connection; the values of publicising ideas and activities to inspire others, make connections and exchange practical advice; how ideas and practices feed each other; and the emotional challenges and vulnerabilities of being activists for sustainability. In these accounts the social and global nature of sustainability issues is especially overt, and the stories explore what it means to act with integrity in this space. Also there are reflections, as we see in other chapters, on effectiveness, potential impacts and the elusiveness of knowing what one has contributed.

The journey to CONVERGE

Ian Roderick MSc4, 2000–2002

I received the email request to write this contribution in a hotel bedroom in Buda-pest halfway through the 'kick-off' meeting for a four year, international research project to 'Rethink globalisation in the light of contraction and convergence'—we call it CONVERGE for short. I'm leading that project. How on Earth did I get here?

Let's start far enough back to make sense. In 1999, at the age of 48, I was at a loss what to do. It could have been easy and I know that many friends remain puzzled as to why I didn't retire early and sail off around the world. The software company that I had co-founded in 1982 was bought out by Sage plc for £12.5 million. Not all of that came to me and my wife but enough to maintain us well indefinitely. We could be out there now, chasing the sun.

During my career, leadership had not been a major preoccupation. I had run departments for business planning for an American multinational and then, in our own company, I was the technical leadership. My team were the guys who made things and then fixed them when they broke. I was fortunate that my business part-ner was commercial, the front man who led the company. We developed a wonder-ful bond of unconditional trust.

All that was over and now I was at a turning point with some knowledge of leadership—a mix of propositional and experiential—but no great desire to lead anything. But something happened: by chance I saw an advertisement in *The Economist* for an MSc course in Responsibility and Business Practice. This was an indulgence I could afford, it might also be good for my wavering Christian beliefs; it might strengthen my search for meaning. While I can see myself in the Christian community, and take part in ritual and gain from that, what I'm signed up to is not what I believe. I'm not the only one who feels this way: there is a conspiracy among churchgoers, which speaks a belief, lives without it, searches for meaning through it, yet is destined to never find that meaning—it is unknowable. My 'Chris-tian belief' is anything but the anchor I seek!

I may have thought it was a route to meaning but little did I anticipate the con-sequences of RBP.

One strand started with the thesis. I picked up on an earlier career in operational research and I linked this to corporate social responsibility. I got involved with the UK Systems Society (UKSS), not just joining but active and I ended up as president from 2005 to 2008. I didn't plan to do this job but I am extremely pleased that it hap-pened and that UKSS is firmly a part of my life. I was just trying to be useful and to pursue an interest but I ended up in leadership, or did I just let others unburden it onto me because I wanted to be the leader?

The two most formative strands of consequences started next. I am sure that for the majority of participants the week spent at the Schumacher College transformed them. All the ingredients for deep personal change are there: retreat from the real world, renewal of personal relationships, communal living, self-examination, enchanting habitat, exposure to deep ecological principles and Gaia . . . organic and wonderful food, alcohol, meditation, poetry, books and ideas—everything needed for environmental and social orgasm. This was my reintroduction to Fritz Schumacher, although at the time I didn't take much notice.

It was about two years later that, entirely by chance, I looked at the Schumacher Society website. I found a page that described future plans and there it was—a proposal for the Schumacher Institute for Sustainable Systems. It could have been written for me: to research into what makes our systems viable in the long term. And it was happening just up the road in Bristol.

I phoned up to find out how far the plans had got. Richard St George, then director, in his wonderfully expansive and inclusive way, invited me in for lunch. I discovered that nothing more than the website page had happened and this was based on a four-year-old proposal. But I agreed to come in maybe once a week and see if we could build on the idea. Well, blending an interest in systems thinking, Schumacher's philosophy and the whole sustainability agenda proved irresistible. A 'thoughts' document led to a 'vision' document that led to a 20-page proposal and the Institute started. We ran seminars and workshops, built up a list of interested people, appealed for some money, and started writing. Thursdays became our madhouse days—brainstorming with large sheets of paper and coloured pens. Volunteers turned up, mostly young people, some stayed and some didn't.

The Schumacher Society is a membership organisation and its main purpose is public education in environmental and social justice. Most people know of it because of the annual Bristol Schumacher Lectures. It is run by a Council, the president is Satish Kumar and the vice-president is John Pontin. John has supported many initiatives in sustainability over the years. His company, JT Group, were pioneers in sustainable design and building. John has supported the Institute from the beginning. However, John and I were destined to get involved in other ventures as well; this was mostly due to the coincidence that we both live in Chew Magna, a rich little village that lies eight miles south of Bristol.

John was keen on an initiative of the Royal Society of Arts (RSA) to move towards a zero-waste society. What would this mean to a community such as Chew Magna? What might happen if people picked up the idea and changed their lifestyles? The format that the RSA proposed was to organise coffee house conversations—so John invited me to join other people from the village. I remember well sitting in a cafe with one of these discussion groups when the topic arose of finding someone to become the leader. It was the smallest hand gesture from John that suggested me and the group pounced on it. It was impossible to say no—so I didn't. But then maybe I had put myself in the right place for that hand gesture?

Go Zero, a community action group for a zero-waste society, was born. The enthusiasm in the village to tackle the idea of zero waste was palpable. It was like breaking a dam; people appeared out of the woodwork with knowledge, ideas and skills. My role was to hold this lot together somehow—it was a rollercoaster ride. As a community group it was strong on talk but it did do things as well. We developed four groups: waste and recycling, energy and transport, people and consumption, and converging world. These are fairly self-explanatory, we worked at many of ideas to reduce, re-use, recycle, repair; we insulated, installed and substituted; we went local. You name it, we had a go to be green and the uptake was quite remarkable, but let's not get too carried away; it was still a relatively small proportion of the village that got involved. The hype exceeded the reality by far but so what? The news spread and the news came, local papers and then the nationals, local TV and then the BBC News. We did our bit to raise awareness.

The converging world group was special for me. It came from the concept that the community had a responsibility to other communities and a dependence on them, particularly those in the developing world. We formed links with an organisation in India and this group led to John and me co-founding a charity called The Converging World, based on the concept of Contraction & Convergence™[1]—a principle of equal per capita right to emit greenhouse gases within a global cap. This lies at the heart of the Kyoto Protocol.

Go Zero has finished its job and passed the baton to Target 80, a community interest company that serves the Chew Valley, which has a population of nearly 15,000. Small was beautiful for a while but we now operate at the appropriate scale for carbon reduction and community energy supplies. Meanwhile The Converging World (TCW) migrated away from the village and into Bristol—its focus is on building a wind farm in India—pretty big machines.

I had written up the TCW story in a Schumacher Briefing (Pontin and Roderick 2007); this allowed me to explore the theoretical ideas of convergence (with contraction implied) and to place it in a systems thinking framework. Vala Ragnarsdottir, then Professor of Earth Sciences at Bristol University, suggested that we put in a bid for an EU grant to research and develop the concepts further—could I refuse? Two young people, Alice-Marie Archer and Matt Fortnam, put in a huge effort to produce the CONVERGE proposal and, to my surprise, it was accepted and now I am leading a team of eight partners from the universities of Bristol, Lund (Sweden), St Istvan (Hungary) and Iceland with the Natural Step, GreenDependent and SCAD in India. Four years and €1.4 million to get through—am I mad? Are we capable of extending the concept of convergence into the systemic nature of all human activity? Watch this space.

At the time of writing, I feel that, despite financial uncertainties, the Schumacher Institute for Sustainable Systems is thriving. Since 2009 we have run a programme called Open Platform which recognises what we do well. Ever since we started we have seen a steady stream of people, mostly young graduates, come through the

---

1 Contraction & Convergence™ is a trademark of the Global Commons Institute.

door, get involved and then move on enriched and vitalised having shared experiences and ideas. Open Platform gives structure to this through mentoring and coaching, through education (Schumacher, sustainability and systems thinking, of course) and through many different projects. Daphne Kourkounaki runs this programme. I don't know how she does it but she is looking after 70 young people, giving them a great sense of belonging in this time of employment uncertainty.

This story has explored my freedom to act and the vagaries of chance. The various strands of consequences of RBP have woven together to arrive at the CONVERGE project. I have chosen to do things because they take me towards what I want to be and my perception of what I should be: this ideal 'good' person maintains his goodness through an inner dialogue with a reified unknowable entity called Christ. Yet I have not deliberately manufactured a future for myself. It's as if people have jumped on me, as if I'm the person they have been waiting for—someone to do something for them. It's an internal tension between meeting their expectations and me being a charlatan, a dilettante, blown by the wind while wanting to be whatever it is they and I think we want. But something emerges, unplanned and ill-defined: is it the result of not being able to say no? Or is it really ambition?

I feel that what I do is like steering on that edge. Yes, it is about serving others but also about being served to achieve a purpose. It means applying an active reinforcing feedback (chaos) while also maintaining a diminishing one (order), I have to stay at this edge playing two (or more) conflicting/complementary roles at the same time (or at least alternating between them).

Working with volunteers in a sustainability organisation that was created from the largesse of donors, one in particular, is a far different beast to ride than running a high-tech software company where the boundaries are clear and fixed. I think it requires a determination to make a difference, but you achieve that by allowing great freedom to those working with you. However, it is a freedom governed by a common purpose and a set of principles for how to work.

Over these years, since the MSc, I have changed greatly. Once I would have baulked at standing in front of a large audience; now I enjoy it. I take the time to see myself doing things, to note mentally those missed opportunities to do better or occasionally to congratulate myself on handling a question well, or getting the mood just right. I know how the 'buzz' feels and it is good. This ability to reflect was awoken in those two years of the degree course; it was not a sudden revelation, just a slow opening that has had a profound effect: everything is learning and the most important thing to learn about is you doing that learning. My change is due to conscious attempts at living systems thinking so that they may become unconscious, while realising the paradox of objective observation of oneself as subject.

I have suffered procrastination and burn out, times of frozen inactivity while there was too much to do. I have not played the game as well as I could, failing often to follow through, to glad-hand and make connections. I have a conceit that I don't need help. But I put these failings against the successes I see through the loyalty and enthusiasm of those around me. Would I do anything different if I had the chance to start again? I don't think I actually did anything—anything just did me.

Postscript

I'm finishing this chapter in a hotel bedroom near Edinburgh the day before a seminar on Community Resilience run by my good friend Tony Hodgson of the International Futures Forum—my God, whatever unknowable purposeful system that is, I'm having fun.

Reference

Pontin, J., and I. Roderick (2007) *Converging World* (Totnes, UK: Green Books).

GYVA.LT: an initiative to promote environmentally friendly living and sustainability in Lithuania

Indrė Kleinaitė MSc7, 2003–2005

I graduated from the MSc in Responsibility and Business Practice in 2005, so it has been five years since the time I stepped out into 'reality' to try out MSc ideas in practice. There are things that I have done I would not have done without undertaking the MSc course. It was a life-changing experience, a whole-person transformation, which stimulated inner strength, courage and creativity. It was a real challenge to sustain and nourish it, and I have to admit I was not always good at doing that. At the time it was my intention to find ways to make a positive contribution to mainstreaming sustainability in Lithuania. The MSc course gave me a lot of progressive ideas and I felt an urge to share these ideas with a wider audience. I had to communicate what I got from the course in my own authentic way.

I have taken seriously the ideas of systems thinking, that small 'disturbances' in a complex system can make a significant difference to the whole. One of my strategies was to make my voice heard, and to try to put an alternative viewpoint into the mainstream. Since 2003 I have been cooperating with the media (newspapers, magazines, radio and less often TV) in promoting sustainable development, corporate social responsibility (CSR), ethical consumption and environmentally friendly lifestyle ideas in Lithuania. From October 2005 until the end of 2006 I was intensively cooperating with a newspaper *Atgimimas* by contributing weekly articles related to sustainability, responsibility and environmentally friendly living. I wrote about responsible consumption, climate change, ethical business, new economics, politics, natural health, GMOs (genetically modified organisms), education and culture. It has been a very creative time for me and I am particularly proud about my articles on economics, climate change and GMOs. At the same time I also collaborated with journalists from different media by sharing information, giving interviews or writing articles and, in 2007, the magazine *Stories* called me an 'Importer of Ideas'.

My action-inquiry process during the MSc led me initially into connection with UNDP Lithuania and from January 2007 until September 2008 I worked there on a regional CSR project financed by the EU. The main objective of this project was to accelerate the implementation of CSR practices in the new EU Member States and candidate countries, namely Bulgaria, Croatia, Hungary, Lithuania, Macedonia, Poland, Slovak Republic and Turkey, because despite tremendous achievements in adaptation to a market economy, environmental and social concerns in Central Eastern European and the Baltic States (CEEBS) have received little attention. This project was designed to give a strong impulse in bridging the disparity between the level of CSR practices in old EU countries and new Member States and country candidates. For me, this was the time for learning about what it takes to implement ideas in an institutionalised way. It was a good initiation: it taught me very concrete skills and discipline and made me realise how much time it takes to implement progressive ideas and the importance of being patient, practical and diplomatic. I really learned a lot from my colleagues.

Next I worked at the Nordic Council of Ministers Office in Lithuania on a project for promoting responsible business practices in SMEs (small and medium-sized enterprises). The aim of the project was to promote responsible business practices in Lithuania on the basis of good practices found in the Nordic countries. The project emphasised the need to promote and strengthen the organic and natural products market, more environmentally friendly printing practices and greener architecture: these markets were only just emerging in Lithuania. I found this a very exciting time, working directly with business owners and managers and exposing them to new responsible business practices in Norway, Sweden, Denmark and Finland. I organised study trips for Lithuanian companies to Scandinavia to visit companies and learn about their environmental and social practices. We visited companies dealing with organic products, printing houses that have environmental policies and practices and examples of sustainable architecture. This format allowed participants to learn about responsible business practices by interacting with colleagues in Nordic countries and through direct experience. This project was less bureaucratic than working at UNDP and involved more direct contact with people. The project was wrapped up with a conference for participants to share experiences and to discuss the integration of lessons learned into their practice.

In 2007 I participated in an essay competition 'Visions for Lithuania' organised by a national newspaper. I called my vision 'Gyva Lietuva' because *gyva* in the Lithuanian language means 'alive, living, full of vitality' and *Lietuva* is a Lithuanian name for Lithuania. I wrote my essay in a fairy-tale style, outlining a vision of how people might live in Lithuania in the future if sustainable development principles were endorsed and implemented practically. It covered such areas of life as agriculture, energy, housing, industry, business, science, education and arts. It was awarded the accolade of greenest vision for Lithuania by the European Commission Office in Lithuania and earned me a nomination for the national 'Woman of the Year 2008' competition, in the category 'Initiative of the Year'. This nomination was most unexpected and in my opinion marked an important milestone in the process of mainstreaming sustainability ideas in our country. Although I did not win in that category, the concept of a 'green' and sustainable Lithuania got a lot of publicity, and I felt very honoured to be acknowledged for the work I have done in communicating ideas of sustainability for Lithuanian society.

Encouraged by these events, in the summer of 2009 I launched a website GYVA.LT: a platform to promote environmentally friendly living and sustainability in Lithuania in a more coordinated manner than I had been doing before. I put there articles I have written since 2003, and related articles by other authors. They are grouped into such subjects as health, organic farming, responsible consumption, climate change, energy, politics, business, economics, education, culture and architecture. In addition, my colleagues and I have created an e-gallery[2] of the very first organic farmers, who started the organic farming movement in Lithuania 20 years ago. GYVA.LT is also a platform to announce news and various initiatives. In addition, we collaborate with the most popular news portal in Lithuania by providing them with articles that we write ourselves. Our intention is to focus on sustainability communication and education, to provide inspiration and support for those who wish to undertake a path towards sustainability, and provide advice and consulting as well as green marketing services.

The economic crises created a whole new set of circumstances for promoting sustainability in Lithuania. It suddenly made sense to a lot of people that our economic model is not sustainable, because we saw it crashing with our own eyes. People are much more informed and educated than they were five years ago; the media is publishing more information and analysis about sustainability-related issues; there are more businesses dealing with natural products and greener energy; and politicians are following the pulses of society more sensitively than before. In 2010 Lithuania celebrated the 20th anniversary of the Declaration of Independence from the Soviet Union and it is very inspiring to remember how courageous our country was in daring to confront the power of the Soviet Union. I see a connection between events 20 years ago and the current resurgence in searching for a truly sustainable path.

In all of this, I have been working with other people both locally and internationally, and have felt part of a larger community, especially through the RBP network and Association of Sustainability Practitioners. But what I often missed were opportunities to meet face to face, to learn directly from other people's experiences and to get inspiration. Therefore, at times I have felt dispirited. But it did not make me doubt the importance of 'changing course' and about making my modest contribution by being a sustainability communicator. When I wonder what difference I am making, I try not to think about it, because when you put out information, you no longer 'own' it and it is complicated to track the impacts it creates, unless you get direct feedback, or accidently track the connections 'between the dots'. In addition, you are never making the difference alone, but together with others. But I do know for sure that there are people I informed and inspired, who are now doing their bit in the emerging 'sustainability' community in Lithuania. I have added value to making a change in Lithuania, I just can't say exactly what this value is. Whatever it is, it is not yet enough and there is a long way to go. It is still just the beginning.

2   www.gyva.lt/../articles/view/124, accessed 1 January 2011.

CultureWork for a world in transition

Paula Downey MSc5, 2001–2003

I want to write about a very big thing, which is Ireland, my home . . . and a tiny, tiny thing, which is me and my life, and to describe how these two levels of reality have intersected in the modest opportunities I've had to pursue an audacious ambition: to challenge my culture to change.

Cultural hypnosis

The madness of the so-called Celtic Tiger has been the impetus behind my work for more than ten years. In that time Ireland graduated from winding *bohreens* and secondary roads to confidently cruise into the economic fast lane, indulge in victory-laps for a decade, and finally slam into a wall when catastrophic bust followed meteoric boom.

In the early days I watched, disoriented, as a nation casually trampled its deeper values, proclaimed economic progress an unambiguously good thing, squashed dissent, jeered at those who questioned what we might be losing, and dismissed as a sideshow the social and ecological consequences of turning life into cash. An envious world looked on, rubbing its hands and licking its lips.

The MSc was a way to make sense of what I experienced as a country 'out of its mind' and I used my research to explore the relationship between business, politics and the media, the systems of power that construct and hold in place the cultural 'story' or myth within which we live. Through my inquiry with leaders in these institutions I came to appreciate the subtle processes by which their worldviews have quietly aligned behind the 'story' of economic growth as the defining human project, and how the abstract money-world overwhelmed the flesh-and-blood human, cultural and ecological realms. And I finally understood how an entire nation can be seduced down a path signposted 'self-interest', even when it leads to disaster.

I saw how people in powerful positions largely operate within flawed assumptions of cause-and-effect linearity, predictability and control, and choose not to see their fingerprints on events that unfold. With little appreciation of the non-linear, interdependent, systemic nature of life they can easily sidestep responsibility when things go wrong. They can watch the context decline and yet stand by and behave as if they are powerless to change it. In fact, those who protect the status quo get rewarded for the inaction that slows down change, while disturbers-of-the-peace who send warning signals are disparaged, demoted or dismissed.

I've come to believe that the real problem is the *mind-set* at the heart of our culture and I don't think it will be possible to animate a significant cultural shift without the will and leadership of our dominant institutions—the corporate bards and storytellers who mediate our lives and whose decisions structure the space in which life is lived—shaping the 'story' of who we are, where we're going, what's important and so much more.

Right now, they aren't telling the truth about the urgency of our predicament because for the most part they just don't get it. We've broken up the world in order to explain and manage it, but lost the intelligence that makes it whole again.

We have to 'join the dots' and I believe my role is to challenge my culture by reweaving narrative threads that are always presented as if they are separate. But it's not enough to present a radical critique or pose a challenge that simply pulls the rug from under people. You have to help them respond, and support the task of cultural renewal. For me, culture challenge and cultural renewal are two sides of the same coin, and with my partner David Youell, that's what I've been exploring these past few years.

Seeing systems

Deepening my understanding of life and the principles of living systems has become the lens through which I live and work and the ground on which I stand. The MSc opened my eyes to this way of seeing and transformed my life. As Gregory Bateson said, our most intractable problems are a clash between the way we think and the way the *real* world works.

The *real* real world is not a stove-piped, hierarchical, tidy place but an interdependent, webby, messy place in which things nest inside each other like Russian dolls. The *real* real world is not organised to within an inch of its life from the top-down, but self-organises from the bottom-up. Despite appearances, the *real* real world is not fixed and solid but comes to life moment by moment, as the parts of the system enter into relationship with each other. The *real* real world is not homogeneous and undifferentiated but relentlessly diverse. And much as we'd like it to be, the *real* real world is not controllable and predictable; chaos and uncertainty are part of life.

Seeing people, organisations and nations as living systems and understanding myself as part of an interdependent web of relationship in which everything affects everything else, has transformed my understanding of how things work, how things change, and how to be more effective. Liberating myself from the mechanistic, managerialist, hierarchical 'story' that dominates modern life and experiencing myself instead as a participant in a self-organising living system that is shifting, moving and always on the edge of possibility, has transformed my understanding of how change happens in organisational systems that previously seemed so unyielding.

However, experience has also taught me that while these principles can be easily understood they pose a practical challenge to long-cherished but unhelpful concepts of organising and organisation, power and participation, leading and leadership, and ideas of what 'change' and 'success' look like—including my own. Almost everything we do is the wrong way up. There's so much to unlearn.

Developing an emergent practice

After the MSc I began to use a systems lens to write and speak out about the institutional and cultural dilemmas around me, in essays and articles intentionally aimed at a mainstream audience. I was just telling the truth as I saw it, developing my point of view, finding my voice and 'sending up flares' to anyone who, like me, might feel trapped by the mechanistic assumptions of modern life and be willing to approach culture and change differently.

With the Celtic Tiger in overdrive there wasn't a peep from the conventional corporate world. The people who responded and became clients for our emerging cultural work were of a different quality from our previous commercial and state clients. I'd describe them as curious insiders and change agents from different parts of the 'machine': local government, education, social projects, citizens groups and, curiously, quite a few religious congregations. Some had formal leadership roles; others didn't. Some felt disillusioned within their organisations; some were explicitly challenging conventions and routines. Some were victims of the establishment; others marginalised within it. They came to us because their system was broken, and they knew it. They were searching for a better way.

As well as developing a systemic lens and language we were working with these people to find ways to access the deeper dimensions of culture—values, behaviour, relationships, purpose, story—based on the simple principles of changing the conversation, exploring subjective experience and surfacing complex realities.

By doing the work that needed to be done—often with limited resources, sometimes with none at all—living frugally and funding our own choices, we were free to work on our own terms, deepen our understanding of these ideas and develop our practice in practice. I was also deliberately stepping out from behind my professional fig-leaf and bringing more of myself to the work: my certainties and uncertainties, my strengths and vulnerabilities, my serious-mindedness and my sense of humour. And I was explicitly positioning myself as co-learner and co-creator rather than 'expert' or 'knower', moving towards a participative way of working that privileges a kind of grasping for answers and feeling our way forward together *with* people rather than *for* them.

Evolution happens as nature plays, experiments and learns its way forward, mirroring the simple instruction at the heart of action inquiry: take action about something you care about, and learn from it. By deliberately working the way nature works I've evolved a practice without ever planning to. By standing my ground and refusing to do work that compromises what's important I've come to an internal clarity that helps me navigate uncertainty (just) a little more skilfully than I might have in the past.

As I write this, I realise I've been engaged in a significant action research project, and the project is me! I've been holding on to my convictions, learning to let go, finding my voice, developing my practice, deepening my worldview *in experience*. By experimenting and taking risks, leaving behind what was comfortable and familiar and trusting that I could discover something new, this 'knowing' is propositional (informed by theories and ideas), practical (expressed in my professional practice), experiential (grounded in experience as I witness and live with the consequences of working this way) and presentational (embodied in the way I speak, write and engage with others). That is what I understand to be action research (Reason and Bradbury 2008).

CultureWork for a world in transition

Combining a radical critique with a hopeful perspective describes what I want to do in the world: to say in an unequivocal way that human culture is on the rocks, to name the source of our problem, and to call forth the will and courage we need to refound our civilisation based on a very different understanding of the world and our place in it.

The experience of the last ten years has now culminated in a living-systems approach to organisation and change that we've branded **CultureWork for a world in transition**.[3] It's an approach to cultural renewal that offers five 'ways in' to the subtle territory of culture, and the metaphor we use is gardening: it's not about *making* change happen but *helping* change happen by cultivating the conditions in which change becomes possible.

We've framed this as a service for leaders and change agents in the context of a deep cultural crisis, a cultural crossroads and a choice-point for society and the institutions that shape it. Standing in front of people in different public settings and challenging them with this perspective, I've discovered that simply telling the truth about the enormity of our problems, without couching it in politically correct ways, seems to release human energy. Deep down, people already know the system is done for—they are just relieved when someone says it! With the truth on the table, CultureWork seems to provide a clarifying lens: a way of framing what's happening; a way to see it anew. It shifts people's perception, knocking on the head the idea that we're tiny cogs in a machine that operates of its own accord. No, we're active participants in a complex system that's evolving *through us*. We are *not* too small, and there is *no* small act. Either way, we shape what happens. We have a role. And we have a choice.

---

3   www.dya.ie/culturework.html, accessed 31 December 2010.

Walking naked into the land of uncertainty

> Deep change means surrendering control. Most of us build our identity around our knowledge and competence in employing certain known techniques or abilities. Making a deep change involves abandoning both and 'walking naked into the land of uncertainty' (Quinn 1996: 3).

I use this passage to invoke a sense of what the experience has been like. Sustained by each other, by the strength of our conviction, and by knowing that in the light of all that's wrong there's nothing else to be done but what you believe is right, the past decade has been about letting go. There's nothing left of our previous life, materially or metaphysically.

If I'd been writing this essay even a couple of months ago, it would be ending differently. Up to then, we were not certain that what we were engaged in had any value. But synthesising what we've learned into the CultureWork philosophy seems to have struck a chord, and being able to speak coherently about what we believe—not merely the nature of the problem, but offering a different way of thinking about it and working with it—has prompted very positive feedback from people in institutions of all kinds. The *Irish Times* columnist John Gibbons included our work in an end-of-year salute to people making a difference 'at the frontline of the ecological crunch' and said our work was 'among an Irish vanguard of thinkers preparing in the broadest sense for the unfolding new realities' (Gibbons 2009).

Despite (or perhaps because of?) my strong views, I've just been appointed by the government to the board of the Broadcasting Authority of Ireland, the body responsible for regulation and oversight of the broadcast environment. It's a forum where the powerful interests of business, politics and the media collide, where important decisions are made, in meetings that look commonplace, through processes that seem benign, by ordinary people just like me. Here (as on 'the outside') I am watching the patterns of power play out in real time, working with the moving, shifting nature of it all, spinning plates, dancing between macro intentions and micro openings, trying to do something meaningful between the lines.

After years of living in what seemed like a parallel universe, the recent positive response to our ideas and our work is an embarrassment of riches. At the same time, writing those words feels like an overstatement, like making a claim for something I don't feel. Truth is, like everyone else I feel small, a David figure squaring up to the Goliath-like forces of conventional thinking with nothing more than a sling. Unlike others, I haven't been engaged in A Great Big Project. I've just been trying . . . trying my best to work with what's in front of me while holding inside me what I believe.

And yet, in writing this essay, I realise that without really knowing it, without consciously trying to, we've been creating a platform on which to stand, and from which we may be able to really do . . . something. It feels as if we're only just beginning, like we've been breaking ground for something else.

References

Gibbons, J. (2009) 'Seasonal Salute to Those Making a Difference', *Irish Times*, 24 December 2009.

Quinn, R. (1996) *Deep Change* (San Francisco: Jossey-Bass).

Reason, P., and H. Bradbury (eds.) (2008) *Sage Handbook of Action Research: Participative inquiry and practice* (London: Sage Publications, 2nd edn).

11
Working with young people

- **Jane Riddiford**. Growing food—growing people
- **Joanne Bailey**. Learning for sustainability: living a new worldview
- **Lalith Gunaratne** and **Mihirini De Zoysa**. A journey of dialoguing: peace and inner peace

This chapter brings together three accounts from four graduates working with young people on issues of social justice and sustainability. Their approaches have strong similarities in wanting to listen to young voices, work collaboratively, and foster participants' sense of agency and potential for action. In the stories we see how the graduates have formulated what they are doing in terms of ideas and practices, and how their work is developing. The emotional challenges of engagement are explicit. In Lalith Gunaratne and Mihirini De Zoysa's story the political challenges of the Sri Lanka context are also highly apparent. Given intergenerational issues in notions of sustainability, working with young people means engaging at a political edge. (Working with the younger generation is also an explicit theme in Charles Ainger's story; see Chapter 9.)

Growing food—growing people

Jane Riddiford MSc11, 2007–2009

Three consistent strands of my life over the last 20 years or more have been: exploring the inner terrain of consciousness through meditation and self-inquiry, a love of the outdoors (which began as a child growing up on a farm in New Zealand) and working with children and young people. Thanks in large part to the MSc, I have been able to integrate these three strands of interest into my work with Global Generation (GG), which is a London-based charity dedicated to supporting young people to take a lead in generating positive environmental and social change in urban communities, particularly in and around King's Cross in London. I am a co-founder and the executive director of GG.

The inquiry I carried out while on the MSc encouraged me to think more deeply about what the word 'consciousness' actually means for me. It is a word I use with some reluctance as it can be interpreted in different ways, and is one that I continue to grapple with. However, I chose to use it here because it not only points to that which animates my own inquiry but perhaps more significantly to what I bring to the work I am doing with GG. I experience consciousness as the ground of being and as a creative impulse to make a positive difference in the world. This heightens awareness of a profound and expanded sense of self, where the Me merges with the We. In this depth of self, I recognise myself as the positive life force which is in complete contrast to the sense of being separate and limited. This recognition carries a sense of awe and raw responsibility for the whole of life.

My recognition and understanding of the 'Being and Becoming' dimensions of consciousness has been developed by participating over many years in retreats led by the spiritual teacher Andrew Cohen. I am also grateful to my tutor Tim Malnick and the interest of fellow students that the role of consciousness in young people's education for sustainability became central to my MSc inquiry. This presented the challenge of finding relevant and meaningful ways to introduce the interior dimension of self. I discovered that the words associated with producing local food offered a way of encouraging awareness of consciousness as self without needing to use language which I felt would be alienating. I am writing about this inquiry into 'growing people' as the fire of it is still burning . . . in fact it won't leave me alone.

Over the last couple of years GG has involved children and young people together with local businesses, such as Guardian News and Media, Wolff Olins and a number of construction companies, in the creation of a living web of bio-diverse food growing sites in the bustling heart of King's Cross. Together we have 'greened' the top of office buildings, school grounds, housing estates and developers' land. This process is transforming the challenges of a changing and highly urban area into opportunities so that high-quality produce is now being grown and sold to local restaurants by local young people.

GG has been particularly successful at bringing people from different sectors, with different worldviews, together. For example, on one of our projects you might see an asylum seeker or young carpentry apprentice with a 'traditional' worldview working alongside a 'modern' land-developer and a 'postmodern' liberal newspaper employee. A few of us involved with GG have been particularly interested in the juice that generates a shared sense of purpose among these participants. As exciting as creating a vegetable garden on the roof of an office building can be, the success of the work is due to the fact that it is not just about exterior transformation. 'What's different about what we do at Global Generation is, not only do we change the outside—but we change the inside too' (Ciara, GG Generator, 17 years old, November 2008).

Ken Wilber speaks strongly to this point. 'Those focussing only on exterior solutions are contributing to the problem. Self, culture and nature must be liberated together or not at all' (Wilber 2007: 101). I would say that pivotal to GG's approach is the attention given to developing awareness of the territory inside ourselves. This creates a space in which a shared sense of vision towards the future can grow and where different values connect.

> We achieved something only a team could do. We created a living atmosphere and a welcoming place. Working with strangers from all sorts of places and backgrounds helped us achieve this, as it brings everybody together with the common cause (Zac Nur, GG Generator and youth leader, 16 years old).

I was introduced to the concept of collaborative inquiry while on the MSc programme, which inspired me to ask participants of all ages to reflect on their experience in silent, written and verbal ways. Their description of their 'felt experience' alongside my own observations of their behaviour has deepened my belief that awareness of consciousness is a powerful resource in helping us begin to address environmental challenges. I also learned from the times I provoked a sense of fear by overemphasising the consequences of climate change and the practical steps we might take to curb it. On these occasions I was met by eyes glazing over and the hollow sound of my own words. A significant step in my inquiry was discovering that, when I encouraged participants to take a few minutes to stop and let everything go, so they could experience the 'ground of being' inside themselves, the sense of having a problem was dispelled. Consequently there was a more active engagement in discussions about our world and its future. 'It was a unique moment (a silent walk) . . . it felt good and peaceful, it was like I could start afresh, everything bad just went . . . like now I want to do more good stuff' (V, a 15-year-old who was in trouble at school).

In order to create a structure for the work of engaging people in meaningful ways, GG has drawn on the principles of integral theory (Wilber 2007). We have developed a potentially all-encompassing methodology which we call 'I, We and the Planet'. Integral theory is a multi-levelled, inner and outer approach to change which points to the 'big three' issues of **consciousness**, **culture** and **nature** (Wilber 1996: 248). GG uses 'I, We and the Planet' in two distinct ways:

1. Inner and outer (unseen and seen)

   - **I.** A deeper sense of self (as consciousness) which carries a sense of meaning, purpose and connection, is without problem and is the foundation for creativity and positive values

   - **We.** The collective field and emerging potential between individuals, a recognition of the interdependence of all of life and our part in the evolving and dynamic life process

   - **The Planet.** Tangible things that support the future of the planet

2. Broadening of perspective

   - **I** only care about myself (self-centric)

   - **We.** I am interested in meaningful engagement with others

   - **The Planet.** I recognise that we are all part of and responsible for the planet (global-centric)

I have noticed that once a deeper and more healthy sense of 'I' is developed, an awareness of 'We' naturally emerges. This in turn can awaken an impulse towards acting in ways that are more responsible for the planet.

One of our regular GG events involves schoolchildren and local business employees in workshops at the Skip Garden. This is one of the visible 'Planet' parts of GG's work: a productive vegetable garden in a series of skips in the middle of the King's Cross development site. Considering what will be built over the next ten years has been a potent starting place to begin discussions about growing a new kind of community; who will live and work in those buildings? What kinds of value do we need to build a more generative 'we'?

Andrew Cohen says; 'in order to go forward you have to go back to the very beginning' (Wombacher 2008: 54). Working on a development site helps bring the concept of the future down to a human scale. Cohen's statement came to mind when I observed that people were more willing to engage in discussions about the future if they had (even to a small degree) experienced the dimension of life that is out of the stream of time, in other words the place inside themselves before anything ever happened.

One of the ways I regularly do this is by taking time within a practical garden session for the participants to sit together. Amid the background sound of trains and cranes, I ask them to go back . . . right back to the very beginning, which can be found in the stillness inside themselves. I ask them to commit to being really still and completely silent for a few minutes; to relax by letting everything go and at the same time to be totally aware. Once they have all committed there is a change in atmosphere and a tangible 'We' space opens up. Sometimes it helps to provide simple guidance and encouragement during the exercise; however the main thing is that I am still in myself and that the stillness and silence is held among the group.

I have found it helpful to follow up 'sitting still' with a values card exercise. Identifying and discussing the value of particular human attributes, strengthens the ability of individuals to make positive choices and to approach challenges as opportunities. The participants are asked to silently select a card, from a range of cards with positive values printed on them such as respect or integrity, and to speak about why the word they chose is important. Another powerful 'We' exercise is to get participants to speak about their experience of the day as a no hands up conversation. This encourages them to really listen for the thread of the conversation which is carried in the collective atmosphere of the group. 'How can an adult be apathetic, when a young person is speaking about their vision for the future? Being involved with Global Generation's young people has already motivated many of our staff in this way' (Hannah Judge Brown, Sustainability Manager, Guardian News and Media, September 2009).

David Bohm provides a compelling description of why developing awareness of a deeper sense of self is so pertinent to sustainability:

> The entire past is in each one of us in a very subtle way. If you reach deeply into yourself, you are reaching into the very essence of mankind. When you do this, you will be led into the generating depth of consciousness that is common to the whole of mankind and that has the whole of mankind enfolded in it. The individual ability to be sensitive to that becomes the key to the change in mankind. We are all connected. If this could be taught, and if people could understand it, we would have a different consciousness (Jaworski 1996: 80).

GG is finding ways to make the theory real and practical. The Planet part of our workshops helps ground the more intangible work and I think this gives confidence to people that something real is actually happening. Paul Richens is a passionate and knowledgeable gardener who leads the GG's food-growing workshops. Over the last couple of years he has successfully helped our participants to grow a cornucopia of vegetables in relatively harsh environments. A visitor to the garden once commented on the verdant explosion coming out of disused builders skips as 'the signature of consciousness' (Christopher Cooke, September 2009).

We are continually learning about the ways we can apply the 'I, We and the Planet' approach into our projects and into how we run Global Generation. I experience this as a process of letting go of known ways of surviving in order to adopt a less secure and more inclusive way of being. I am grateful to my colleagues for their commitment to this journey in which the future is calling . . . me to we, inner to outer, lower to higher.

References

Jaworski, J. (1996) *Synchronicity: The inner path of leadership* (San Francisco: Berrett-Koehler).

Wilber, K. (1996) *A Brief History of Everything* (Boston, MA: Shambhala).

—— (2007) *The Integral Vision* (Boston, MA: Shambhala).

Wombacher, M. (2008) *11 Days at the Edge: One man's spiritual journey into evolutionary enlightenment* (Forres, UK: Findhorn Press).

Learning for sustainability: living a new worldview

Joanne Bailey MSc12, 2008–2010

I think back to March 2008 after attending my first workshop of the MSc and remember being overwhelmed with the feelings of shock and despair when confronted with the notions of peak oil, peak water, overpopulation and the impending tipping point of climate change. There began a reality check, as I suddenly realised that I had been living within a worldview common in New Zealand: idyllic, isolated, detached and cushioned from the outside world's issues. This was also the time when I began to fully comprehend the concept of systems and interconnectedness. I also had a strong desire to act but a deep sense of feeling isolated within my familiar surroundings, a sense of doom that something was very wrong with the world, together with not knowing how to articulate this in order to share with the others around me. On my return to New Zealand I attempted many discussions and conversations with my family, friends and peers about these issues. I was confronted aggressively by people of the baby boomer generation. They seemed to have a different view of the world and my notions and ideas challenged and questioned their financially well-planned and materialistic worlds. These discussions began to frame the action of the need in me to *do* something and the words of the poet Drew Dellinger (Plotkin 2008: 2) seemed to bring meaning to my feelings: 'what did you do, once you knew?'

It was during this period of trying to make sense of what I was learning on the MSc towards articulating what I was going to *do* that I participated in a number of different discussions that made me reflect on what exactly my actions would be. This inquiry process (Reason and Bradbury 2001) provided me with a framework to create an educational programme for young people, which I called Learning for Sustainability (LFS). Through my professional role as the general manager of a private training establishment I had been engaging in observations and discussions with young people, and I had began to notice a general demonstration of 'sustainability illiteracy': a gap in awareness, deep understanding and holistic actions towards sustainability. This notion of 'sustainability illiteracy' was exemplified by young people as they would 'do' recycling, 'green' or environmental projects at primary school but would often only see these as school projects and not integrate their learnings back into their personal actions of living. I wanted the LFS programme to engage young people and shift them towards a more systematic rather than linear approach with their actions around sustainability. I also wanted them to own and demonstrate leadership through their actions. Paulo Freire (1970) once wrote that 'the purpose of education is human liberation' and I firmly believe that, if individuals are given opportunities to use education for their own 'in-powerment' (McArdle 2004), then they will be more responsive to their own learning outcomes.

I also began to realise that, as an adult living in New Zealand, I did not understand the true meaning or reality of what it meant to live within a system. As odd as this now sounds, I had never considered New Zealand as being part of a larger system linked to the actions of all countries on Earth, nor the notion that the planet's resources were limited. I became curious about whether or not other New Zealanders also saw the world like this, or was it just me? Using action research practices of discussion and reflection, it became evident that others around me did think the same, so this notion was also integrated into the LFS programme. There is a focus within the programme on the concept of one-planet living and consumption, with the intention of shifting the students' thinking from a linear model within the materials economy (Leonard 2006) of extraction, production, distribution, consumption and disposal, to a systems approach where disposal is taken out of the model. The aim is to encourage students to critically think about how they might see their world as a linear system and then unravel this and explore ways in which to move to a more sustainable systems approach. The programme's content is delivered through a variety of different and interactive ways using stories, DVD clips, reports, science, technology, music, movies, documentaries and guest presenters. The material provides students with different points of views using global and local examples to bring meaning to the issues.

During 2009, together with a co-facilitator, I delivered the LFS programme in ten schools to 243 students within the Waikato region of New Zealand. During this time we experienced the heights of excitement and jubilation to the depths of despair and frustration from the varying reactions and responses by the students to the programme's content. The students expressed feelings of guilt, sadness, disbelief, anger, disengagement and flippancy at the thought of how we are trashing our planet and the need for multiple planets to service our needs. They were really annoyed that the planet is in this state and they are confused as to why the 'adults' or the government aren't doing more to conserve our resources. They question why it should be left up to them to clean up the adults' mess; why isn't more being done to fix the problems; isn't it somebody else's problem, like China's or India's? They struggle to understand that climate change has no borders and they are just as much a part of the problem as everyone else is in the world.

I noticed a number of interesting observations during the delivery of the programme. First, the girls were generally the most motivated into taking action. They seem to genuinely understand that there is a need for urgency around what is happening to the planet. In contrast, boys didn't seem to have the same depth of feeling and distanced themselves somewhat or lost interest in the LFS programme once they were called to action; this was evidenced through absenteeism. This observation of the girls supports Ray's (1997) work on 'Cultural Creatives' and that most 'core' and 'green' creatives are female. Second and surprisingly, I have also observed that there seemed to be no difference in relation to the level of student voice offered around these issues between indigenous (Maori) and non-indigenous students.

This is particularly interesting as Maori culture is traditionally entrenched and blended in the experience of a living Earth. Current literature also identifies this disconnection from the environment by Maori and is also being expressed as a concern by Kaumatua (elders) as lifestyle trends shift their people towards more urban and Western-style living.

The young people who did demonstrate their leadership within the programme were amazing in spreading the word about sustainability. They took actions and demonstrated their leadership by using their voice, in their own ways, to their own communities. They planned and implemented activities and events across the whole of their schools that addressed issues of resource over-use, consumption, pollution, waste, energy, climate change, marine and environment conservation. They have done this with day- and week-long Expos on activities including information/static display boards, plays, competitions, raps, quizzes, posters, story boards, PowerPoint presentations, electronic collection days, trash2fashion competitions, live video footage, theatre productions, poster competitions, music presentations, rubbish audits, interactive displays and sustainability obstacle courses. Within their communities they have raised the awareness of ethical consumption, carbon and water footprints, fair trade, water conservation, the harmful effects of plastics, landfills, advertising and marketing drivers. But more importantly they have offered their communities practical ways and suggestions on how to move towards a more sustainable approach to one-planet living.

Since 2008 my need to 'do' has led, transformed and involved young New Zealanders through a sustainability programme that has given them the opportunity to 'connect' with their world on global and local levels. For me personally this concept of 'interconnectedness' means more than just a systems approach where humans interact; it now means to be part of a circle. I have been fortunate to have been within the MSc 'interconnected' circle over this journey and so I now understand how such circles, which hold family, friends, communities and nations together, are more than just words. They are actions of strength that bind and grow individuals who can influence and make a difference within them. While being held by the MSc group I developed the confidence in my own ways of knowing to create and deliver the LFS programme, and these learnings are now woven through my daily practice of living. During many times over this period I have had to stand alone within my New Zealand space as my view of the world has become different from those around me, but I have been fortunate to have been supported by the MSc group through this process of discovery and learning. I now feel stronger in my actions around raising the awareness of sustainability within these communities; I no longer feel alone within this emerging worldview. My passage of walking between two worldviews of New Zealand and the global community has merged into one space. What that is exactly, I am still inquiring about, but I know that it isn't the dominant, mechanistic, postmodern view that I started with in March 2008, nor is it quite at the 'Earth community' view. This remains an ongoing inquiry for me.

In reflection I see a leader as one that holds, leads and guides but also one that needs to be held within a circle to sustain the strength needed for leading change.

References

Freire, P. (1970) *Pedagogy of the Oppressed* (New York: Herder & Herder).

Leonard, A. (2006) *The Story of Stuff* (DVD; Washington, DC: Free Range Studios, Tides Foundation & Funders Workgroup for Sustainable Production and Consumption).

McArdle, K.L. (2004) *In-powering Spaces: A co-operative inquiry with young women in management* (PhD thesis; Bath, UK: University of Bath).

Plotkin, B. (2008) *Nature and the Human Soul: Cultivating wholeness and community in a fragmented world* (Novato, CA: New World Library).

Ray, P.H. (1997) 'The Emerging Culture', *American Demographics* 19.2: 29-35.

Reason, P., and H. Bradbury (eds.) (2001) *Handbook of Action Research: Participatory inquiry and practice* (London: Sage Publications).

A journey of dialoguing: peace and inner peace

Lalith Gunaratne MSc8, 2004–2006
Mihirini De Zoysa MSc11, 2007–2009

As we walked into the training for the intercultural dialogue (ICD) orientation and team-centred leadership programme, we noticed a sense of anticipation, excitement and trepidation in the young people. The 'hopes and fears session' communicated this; many wrote 'we hope they will not brainwash us'. We were bewildered, having worked with many organisations over the years, and never encountered such a statement. We soon realised they viewed the world differently.

Background

Early in 2009, Sri Lanka was mired in the 30-year ethnic conflict between the Sinhala majority-led government and the rebel group Liberation Thamil Tigers of Eelam (LTTE), claiming to represent the Thamil people. (The Sri Lanka population of 20 million is 70% Sinhala, 11% Thamil, 19% Muslim and Burgher or European descent.) The army was relentlessly pushing ahead to destroy the rebels. LTTE, supposedly using Thamil civilians as human shields, led the international community to urge both sides to stop fighting, to save lives. The war subsequently ended in May 2009, but everyone knew real peace in this ethnically fractured society would come only through a post-war reconciliation and rebuilding process.

The British Council-sponsored ICD programme was timely, initiated with university students to facilitate the rebuilding of post-conflict societies, generate trust, understanding and create positive social change.

Students were chosen as a social group as historically they initiated political and social action. Sri Lankan university education is free and the quota system ensures that the rural poor have access to a good education. Yet Sri Lanka is dominated by an urban English-educated minority who work through the 'old boy network'. The first resistance to the elite was the 1971 Che Guevara-inspired rural youth uprising in universities. Many young lives were lost and resistance reared its violent head again in 1988, to be brutally quelled by the government. This movement, Janatha Vimukthi Peramuna, was de-proscribed in the early 1990s and allowed to participate in mainstream politics, enabling rural people to enter the urban elite bastion.

The ICD participants consisted of three communities, Thamil, Muslim and Sinhala. Among them were students with a strong sense of Sinhala-Buddhist nationalism. Government propaganda to garner public support for its war reinforced this.

ICD design

Students were invited by the British Council to form a core group and were trained in communication, dialoguing, leadership and team-building skills. The aim of the project was to inspire the core group to engage in a cultural dialogue with a wider audience of students. We facilitated a five-day training for this multi-ethnic core group to share their backgrounds and ideology, using dialoguing sessions, creative arts and team games along with aspects of balancing IQ with emotional intelligence (Goleman 1995) and spiritual intelligence (Zohar and Marshall 1999). IQ is a traditional, left-brained, rational approach. Emotional intelligence includes self-awareness, esteem, social skills, managing emotions and relationships; and spiritual intelligence the search for deeper meaning in life through the practice of self-awareness and values based on integrity. These are not alien to our culture and this helped in connecting with our participants at a deeper level.

The ethnic divide and conflict is rooted in a creation story that tells of a Sinhala ownership of this island, so we exposed the group to speakers illustrating the history of Sri Lanka based on anthropological evidence and DNA studies, comparing this evidence with the mythology of the creation of the Sinhala race. This information challenged the creation story. Exploring these myths was crucial to the notion of the pure Sinhala race's right and superiority.

After the training, the core group created the SiThEn Project to design and develop programmes for fellow university students (SiThEn is coined from the first two letters of the three main spoken languages of Sri Lanka—Sinhala, Thamil, English; it is also the Sinhala word for 'from the mind').[1] The purpose was to explore and hold a dialogue on identity and culture and learn about each other in the current Sri Lankan conflict context with a view to creating a peaceful future.

Us and them

Paulo Freire, in his *Pedagogy of the Oppressed* (1970), writes of 'Conscientisation', learning to perceive social, political and economic contradictions to take action against oppressive elements. Our aim was to explore how the participants saw the world and its contradictions, and enable them to act in a skilful manner, without violence or coercion. We wanted to 'liberate' them from their worldviews of ethnic and social divides to embrace a wider view acknowledging the compassionate humanness in us by understanding and respecting each community to develop a unified Sri Lankan identity. We helped them acknowledge their fears that drove anger, hatred and separatist ideologies in order to become free of them.

Our background was probably different from most in the core group. We were from an economically privileged urban English-speaking, Western-educated background, without experience in Sri Lankan universities. If our world was what they

---

1 Information about the SiThEn project can be found at www.britishcouncil.org/srilanka-projects-and-networking-intercultural-dialogue.htm, accessed 1 January 2011.

were rebelling against, it was ironic we were their trainers. Not wanting to be brain-washed is based in fear—a fear of the world outside their system and a challenge to their current worldview. They acted on the fears of losing their identity through conscientisation.

We acknowledged that the content of the training was close to our hearts. This challenged us to authentically present ourselves (our ideology, where we were from) while facilitating the dialogue and learning with participants without push-ing our agenda.

On the other hand, we are idealists. We have hope for humanity, believing that love, compassion and the inbuilt moral compass will liberate us from our inner fears. We want to be open-minded, to continue to dialogue in order to understand each other and the world better from different perspectives, without which self-awareness is incomplete.

The MSc's impact

Our Buddhist background made us feel at home with the inquiring nature of the MSc. Yet it challenged us to become focused and logical in our critical analysis as our education and upbringing was of non-judgement and acceptance. Being open, focused and simultaneously questioning and analysing in our inquiry was an important learning.

The MSc gave us confidence to inquire and question the status quo. To see, for example, the contradiction of economic value of resources when converted into consumable form: a tree has value only when chopped for firewood. We learned how the world works; the establishment of the World Bank and IMF twins, US hegemony and the reasons why the world is lopsided towards the West.

The MSc also provoked our right brains through haiku, freefall writing, art and self-awareness through meditation and tai chi to become inquiring and mindful. We were moved by rituals such as Joanna Macy's 'Council of all Beings' (Macy and Brown 1998), the deep ecology walks on Dartmoor, exploring our relationship with the more-than-human world. These opened us to the creative possibilities of learn-ing in different ways, resonating with our own heritage of esoteric and spiritual rituals.

Action research calls for holding a reflective mirror to self, to know through doing, being aware of the subjective participation of the doer/inquirer; this contrasts with the Cartesian worldview, where the knower is separate from the known, and is bet-ter aligned with our Buddhist worldview of interdependency.

Action research was new to us but its focus on deliberative democratic dia-logue in working together, gathering information, reflecting and taking action was aligned with our practice. Western science and management continue to dominate over Eastern philosophy in post-colonial Sri Lanka, and this gave us a legitimate Western accepted model to work with.

The MSc in a Western school of management, teaching us to question the very philosophies and sciences on which the economic success of the West is based, gave us courage and confidence that the IQ-based approach and learning can be questioned and challenged. It enabled us to realise and deal with the contradictions in life, while engaging our emotions and spirituality to be mindful about the impact we have on people and nature around us.

Using MSc learning

The MSc helped us to frame the ICD programme through a collaborative inquiry process. We shared with each other our emotions and experiences and inquired on how we managed ourselves, our openness to learning, authenticity and how we worked as a team. This was a difficult process, as in contrast to our experience of corporate training, raw emotion emerged and at times one of us would lose our composure. We helped each other to centre ourselves and provided feedback on how we could respond more skilfully, in use of language or non-response to an inflammatory statement made by a team member.

Norman Uphoff (1992) makes a case that people move from aggressive to generous and altruistic behaviour through positive interventions. We saw members of the core group, especially the few extreme thinkers, make such a move. Dean (not his real name) said, referring to Lalith, 'When I first met this old man, I wondered what the f . . . he could teach me.' Later he said, 'Over the days watching both of you, I realised that you walk the talk, like when I saw you running and exercising early morning', referring to our philosophy and practice of balancing mind and body.

We helped the core group develop a third-person influence as they developed SiThEn programmes with other university students around the country. They organised a three-day programme, with 70 students from 11 universities, at the height of the war (one month before it ended) in the east about 60 km from the war zone. It was an emotionally charged time with many civilian deaths as the armed forces pushed to destroy the LTTE. The core group was empowered to own the event, and we worked only as facilitators to help them develop the agenda.

The 70 students came together unsure of what the three days had in store for them: some Thamil and Muslim students were meeting Sinhala peers for the first time in their lives. The first session had the three communities exploring a 'time line' to inquire how they saw history shaping Sri Lanka to where it is today. When the Sinhala team presented historical turning points—populist Prime Minister Bandaranaike's Sinhala language policy in 1956 and Black July in 1983 where innocent Thamils were killed in Colombo—it struck a chord with the Thamil team who said, 'We never realised Sinhala people looked at our history in this way'. The Thamil team had the same events in their presentation and immediately found common ground. Ironically, the Muslim team felt marginalised when they said, 'See, neither the Thamil nor Sinhala team mentioned us and this is what is happening to us, we are caught between both sides and ignored by all.'

The programme used dialoguing techniques (based on David Bohm's principles) and tools such as 'fish bowl' to discuss difficult emotional issues to create better understanding. One young Thamil student studying film-making at the Eastern

University lamented that his parents did not let him go to Colombo to continue his studies. A Sinhala student responded, 'Your parents are right in discouraging you coming to Colombo. These are difficult times with all the security. When I see a young Thamil in the bus, I too wonder whether he is a terrorist. But this will change.'

As facilitators it was difficult to stay in the background and at times we wanted to intervene. When we did make suggestions for a session, the core group deliberated and declined. This was humbling to our own role as trainers, as our sense of power eroded as they developed.

How can we turn this into a national movement? Universities have always been instigators of social change in Sri Lanka, with tragic consequences at times, but here was an opportunity to bring the nation together. The core group conducted two such programmes, and other universities have shown interest in conducting similar events. We are hoping this will take a life of its own as a ripple of transformation takes place.

Diana Francis, in her chapter, 'Stages and Processes of Conflict Transformation' (in Francis 2002), states that 'dialogue is crucial to get to the process of reconciliation and resolution towards peace'. The government propaganda has equated defeating the LTTE to peace and the majority is convinced. We inform people differently. The conflict is over, but peace is a long way off, requiring Francis's path of preparing for dialogue, mediated or non-mediated negotiation, settlement and reconciliation towards a durable peace. Yet Sri Lanka does not have a defined Thamil community body for such a process. As they are fragmented the process can be more organic. The university initiative has promise as the younger generation looks at the future differently—more inclusive, global and open.

We continue our own journey, paying attention to our inner dialogues of tensions and paradoxes, exploring ways to bring these inner dialogues to external spaces with others, exploring ways to express and act our espoused beliefs in the real world and trying to find authenticity in the way we act and live.

References

Francis, D. (2002) *People, Peace and Power: Conflict transformation in action* (London: Pluto Press).

Freire, P. (1970) *Pedagogy of the Oppressed* (New York: Herder & Herder).

Goleman, D. (1995) *Emotional Intelligence* (New York: Bantam Books).

Macy, J.R., and M.Y. Brown (1998) *Coming Back to Life: Practices to reconnect our lives, our world* (Gabriola Island, Canada: New Society Publishers).

Uphoff, N. (1992) *Learning from Gal Oya: Possibilities for participatory development and post-Newtonian social science* (Ithaca, NY: Cornell University Press).

Zohar, D., and I. Marshall (1999) *Spiritual Intelligence: The ultimate intelligence* (London: Bloomsbury Publishing).

12
Reflections

In the spirit of inquiry, what have we collectively learned about taking leadership for sustainability through the life of the MSc and the development of the RBP community? You will have drawn your own conclusions from the narratives in Chapters 4 to 11. Here we point tentatively to eight themes that we take as important.

In doing this, we are seeking to speak out from a community with its own languages and practices, to connect up with people with similar concerns and join in current conversations about what change and leadership for sustainability requires. This speaking out is one form of third-person action research, and so contains all the dilemmas about what makes for effective action that our graduates explore in their stories, and more. In particular it includes choices about framing, purposes and therefore voice: who are we addressing and what exactly *are* we trying to say here?

There are developing debates about leadership for sustainability in both practitioner and academic communities. For practitioners one example is Business in the Community's recent report in the UK entitled *Leadership Skills for a Sustainable Economy* (Business in the Community 2010). We appreciate that 'classical leadership skills are more relevant than ever' (p. 12) to foster transformational change, and yet, as this volume shows, think that we need to go well beyond these to envision new forms for organisations and societies. Academically, there is the recent, much welcome, volume edited by Redekop (2010), asking why mainstream leadership theorising pays so very little attention to sustainability issues, asserting that these are urgent and incontrovertible, and bringing together scholars who explore what ideas might help us understand leadership for sustainability. We share many of their interests in systemic thinking (Satterwhite 2010), leadership as an emergent process (Wielkiewicz and Stelzner 2010), attention to storytelling (Melaver 2010), the importance of citizen leadership (Birmingham and LeQuire 2010) and more.

But in this closing chapter we are not situating our community's work academically or in relation to other reports. We want instead to speak fully and clearly from the RBP community—respecting the importance of practice, the vitality of inquiry, our many ways of knowing—offering some paths that RBP members have found useful; posing dilemmas that cannot be avoided but have to be lived with some form of integrity; seeking to do justice to the plethora of choices that taking leadership for sustainability involves. Just as challenges of sustainability and social justice call for us to reconceive society, so we also need to reconceive, and diversify, notions of leadership.

There are messages we see threaded through the book:

- Connect inner and outer purposes

- Systemic understanding and relational practice are critical

- Act from inquiry

- Seek to move beyond the limitations of conventional action logics

- Complement strategic awareness with skilful attention to the detail of practice

- 'Success' is inevitably difficult to identify

- The work is difficult and challenging—leadership for sustainability requires that you take care of yourself physically, emotionally and spiritually

- Nothing can be taken for granted, nothing is without paradox and dilemma

Connect inner and outer purposes

Many stories tell how people's choices of positioning and action are informed by their values and senses of purpose, or by their ongoing quests to identify and express these. They want to *imbue* (Helen Goulden's word) their working and community lives with attention to sustainability and social justice. Kené Umeasiegbu is surprised that so many people in corporations 'who long for a better world . . . respond to this only in their private life because their job offers little platform for action'. An evolving understanding of their passions, motivations and purposes underpins the issues people seek to work on and the ways they take leadership for sustainability. And, lest we romanticise such choices, we see in several stories the emotional challenges of doing this, and the potential sometimes to experience something close to despair.

Many people take Masters' degrees in schools of management as an investment of money and time in search of career enhancement and later financial reward. In contrast, MSc participants were often stretched by the course experience in ways that challenged the foundations of their current careers, leaving them uncertain about their next steps. And while many people now may pay lip service to questions of social justice and sustainability, the commitment shown by those on the MSc, the nature of the personal challenges and experiments they undertook, and the transformations they experienced, threatened to disrupt their alignments with current organisational purposes, practices and cultures. Having encountered highly confronting and disturbing issues on the MSc also led many graduates to re-evaluate their work/life choices and question much that is taken as everyday practice in corporate and private life, for example a routine acceptance of air travel (Sewill 2005). Seeing the world differently can then seem an act of significant courage, and to require an activist orientation to change.

Motivations for participants' commitment to influencing change for sustainability varied and are expressed in many different ways. Not everyone was able to clearly articulate their purposes when they came to the MSc, as if the course was something they had been seeking without really knowing what they were looking for. For some it was a development of a previous commitment. Chris Preist writes of his 'desire to fundamentally question the direction of my professional life and the contributions I was making, with a view to reorienting it towards the sustainability crisis'. James Barlow and Prishani Satyapal want to see what contributions can be made from within business organisations. Prishani articulates her 'central belief that to influence the behaviour of business so that it was positive and responsible was a noble and honourable goal'. For others, joining the course was part of a search for meaning: Ian Roderick writes about finding this and strengthening his 'wavering Christian beliefs'; and Jon Alexander sought to address his underlying doubts, as a successful young man, about the 'very rules by which I played'.

Many people have told in their stories how more broadly based motivations become focused on particular projects: Vidhura Ralapanawe to design, build and commission the world's first apparel eco-factory; Nick Pyatt to create a company that will benefit a community in Orissa, India; Paul Dickinson and Jen Morgan to influence the finance system to better reflect ecological and human realities; Jo Confino to engage with the community of Katine, Uganda, in a participatory form of development and to tell the story through new media.

Others expressed their purposes in terms of their identity. Kené Umeasiegbu brought his sense of self as an African man working in Western business and his direct experience of social and environmental injustice impacts on his extended family, which renders the costs in 'stark human terms'. In contrast, Helen Sieroda's work explored the 'rootlessness of modern life' in the UK and 'What might it mean to have one's identity and behaviour shaped and nourished through participation in a specific place'.

Some participants came to the MSc programme with strong concerns about ecological sustainability; others developed these through the course. Simon Hicks had already dedicated his working life to be 'in the service of wildlife conservation' and was stimulated by his discovery of Gaia theory and inquiry to enhance his approach to doing this. Helen Goulden writes of her 'responsibility to bring sustainability to the heart of any work I undertake . . . believing that we humans should live lightly upon the Earth and respect and honour her rhythms and complexity'. For Charles Ainger his 'motivation is a deep belief, based on science and intellect, plus a love of wild nature, that we must live within the limits of the planet, and that every individual deserves empowerment and quality of life'. Other participants brought a stronger concern for the interweaving of human justice with ecological issues, notably Kené Umeasiegbu, Lalith Gunaratne, Mihirini De Zoysa and Helena Kettleborough.

For other people, the realisation of disconnection between their lives and the reality of environmental challenges grew on their journey through the MSc programme. After workshop one, Joanne Bailey felt that the New Zealand lifestyle is 'idyllic, isolated, detached and cushioned from the outside world's issues'. Mark Gater's 'uncomfortable realisation was that, as an employee of a retail financial institution, I was part of a system that is driving unsustainable growth'.

In all the stories, we see a strong belief that there should be a direct connection between the inner self and sense of values, and outer action. This is one of the founding ideas in Torbert's (2004) approach to action inquiry, as it strives to make the possible disconnection between these more conscious and the subject of active experimentation.

For some people commitment was expressed in spiritual terms. It was unusual for these to be publicly espoused early on in the MSc programme, but participants increasingly discovered and shared their own particular ways of articulating them. They also recognised the challenges of sustaining such connections in the everyday work of organisations. Christel Scholten writes that as a change agent for sustainability within a large corporation, 'constant awareness of your values and identity is needed so that you do not lose yourself in the process', so as not be subsumed by the 'drive by business to grow and create shareholder value'. She writes about the personal practices she draws on to re-establish her sense of purpose, including the Sacred Passage ritual in the wilderness. Jane Riddiford bases her work on spiritual practice connecting inner and outer, working with young people to link a deeper sense of 'I' with the collective 'We' and the wider 'Planet'.

For others, maybe for most, motivation borders on outrage, at least at times, and the sense that our culture and planet is on its way to 'hell in a handcart' and no one is doing anything significant about it. Paula Downey expresses this through an attempt to grapple on a large scale with what she saw 'as a country "out of its mind"' so that she:

> came to appreciate the subtle processes by which their worldviews have quietly aligned behind the 'story' of economic growth as the defining human project, and how the abstract money-world overwhelmed the flesh-and-blood human, cultural and ecological realms. And I finally understood how an entire nation can be seduced down a path signposted 'self interest' even when it leads to disaster.

Purposes changed, grew more complex and better articulated, initially helped by the MSc process and continuing after the course. David Bent's commitment to environmental accounting in the first years after graduating changed as he saw the flaws in this approach, and he describes how he found a 'new place to stand' in linking the environmental crisis to business strategy. Vidhura Ralapanawe tells how his purposes became quite fiercely focused as he led the eco-factory project. Charles Ainger, nearly ten years after completing the course, reflects on the different demands and opportunities of moving into formal retirement.

Our sense, from the stories presented here and our broader understanding of people's learning journeys, is that finding their base in purposes and values was an important contribution to participants' sense of insight into what is needed and what they specifically and uniquely can contribute. It also grounds the courage they need to find how to take action, even when it is uncomfortable and places them beyond previously known ways of operating. There are echoes here of the systems intelligence that Senge *et al.* (2005) suggest leaders need to be able to see patterns of connection and into possible, generative, futures. Graduates' stories show that this is helped by adopting an attitude of inquiry and by engaging collaboratively with others, for support and challenge.

For many graduates of the MSc, their capacity to discern opportunities and engage in experimental action is supported by membership of the RBP community, which has become a significant reference group. There is a highly active virtual forum open to all graduates, and many are members. Questions are asked, information exchanged, debates engaged. There are some face-to-face meetings too, and some graduates work together or provide expertise to each other's projects.

We notice how often people use the notion in their stories of 'making a contribution', as we do ourselves, to refer to what they are seeking to do, recognising that they are 'one source of influence in a complex changing reality' (Dunphy *et al.* 2007: 322). Finding out how to put purposes into action involves placing oneself in relation to organisations and society, as we explore in the following section. Some talked overtly about this process as *discovering a place to stand*, as does David Bent. No one can do everything, and so it is important to develop clarity about one's abilities and the context in which one is living and working, to inform one's sense of engagement. From a sense of alignment, even if this is only temporary, may come satisfaction, even joy, that one is making a contribution in these extraordinary times.

Graduates' stories show that, while they are committed to organisations, their thinking and action is not bounded by organisational horizons. Leadership for sustainability is not just about converting more companies to corporate social responsibility as an end in itself, although this may be a valuable effect, if interpreted sufficiently radically. The MSc graduates are acting in, through and with organisations, but their canvas is wider society and its capacity, or lack thereof, to become more environmentally sustainable and socially just. They therefore continually need to orient themselves in constantly shifting landscapes, as they seek to pursue 'responsible careers' (Tams and Marshall 2011). Their ways of thinking about this are supported by the notion of tempered radicalism. And so we see finding a place to stand as a lifelong process, always provisional, always open to review. As the graduates' stories show, they are very willing to move on to new organisations, lives and challenges.

Kené Umeasiegbu articulates especially well the dilemma of whether to protest or engage, which echoes other people's choices. His account shows him doing both in some ways, and reflecting on the consequences. Both he and Charles Ainger exhort us to appreciate how contributions from actors in different positions in society can be congruent and mutually reinforcing, especially how activists and campaigners can provide impetus that supports those working for change within organisations.

Reflecting on the range of purposes outlined above, we are reminded of Joanna Macy's advice and elaboration of choices. The primary purpose, she asserts in a chapter title, is 'To Choose Life' (a motif James Barlow adopts from another source for his story). She then identifies three core tasks to address issues of sustainability now, describing them as:

> . . . three areas or dimensions that are mutually reinforcing. These are: 1) actions to slow the damage to Earth and its beings; 2) analysis of structural causes and creation of structural alternatives; and 3) a fundamental shift in worldview and values. Many of us are engaged in all three, each of which is necessary to the creation of a sustainable civilisation (Macy and Brown 1998: 17).

Above all, Macy and Brown argue the importance of countering apathy, 'that numbing of mind and heart' (Macy and Brown 1998: 24) that is the legacy of the 'Industrial Growth Society'. The narratives of graduates show they are not apathetic!

What we think distinguishes some change agents for sustainability is their understanding of the need for a fundamental shift in worldview and values. While this is mostly tacit, assumed, in MSc graduates' stories, we know that it is there. It perhaps shows itself in the wider realm of knowing and action they are paying attention to, their willingness to play and experiment with inquiry and systemic practice, their willingness to act from the margins, in hooks' terms (hooks 1990). And it means that power is always an issue, especially in the third and fourth dimensions discussed in Chapter 3, since what we can 'reasonably' think and our potential scope of action is framed by current discourses and structures.

Systemic understanding and relational practice are critical

All the graduates in their different ways are seeking to contribute to systemic change. They find their varied ways to do this, using the locations, strategies and tactics available to them. Finding a place from which to inquire, influence and act, involves locating ourselves within a systemic appreciation of some kind, and from that position identifying opportunities. Taking a long view is essential; while the challenges are urgent, little can be achieved unless change does become radical and systemic. For many, as for Helen Sieroda, understanding one's place in broader systemic patterns is a way of combating powerlessness. For others, working system-ically means seeing the wider potential consequences of specific actions and pro-jects and seeking to influence patterns and rules beyond one's immediate domain, appreciating that these are subject to multiple influences. The graduates hope to contribute to an ecology of possibilities which can become self-reinforcing, in which new initiatives can emerge and flourish, working with the vitally significant human, organisational and social dimensions of change. For Vidhura Ralapanawe the Thurulie eco-factory is of course important in its own right, but the story of its conception and development has wider implications for apparel manufacture in South Asia, for his company, and for Sri Lanka. Roland Widmer recognises that specific actions may fail but their potential systemic impact makes them worth undertaking.

Relational practice is critical to working systemically, which is seldom, if ever, about unilateral control. Relational practice involves: building strong relationships with immediate colleagues and potential external partners; connecting across dif-ferences; gaining a voice and respect with those with influence in one's organisa-tion; finding a place in wider networks of like-minded people in which one can both give and receive support. This involves, too, working over the long term to stay in relationships, even when signs are not good, and treading the path between radicalism and pragmatism. These are the micro-practices of leadership to com-plement more strategic approaches (see the section on complementing strategic awareness, below).

Graduates found notions of systemic thinking useful in different ways. Some, like Charles Ainger, argue overtly the need to go beyond reductionist and cause-effect approaches. Others write about the insights that thinking systemically has brought them, and how these have opened up their choices of practice, as they think widely and longer term, assess potential impacts within a bigger picture of potential change, and look beyond their own egos. These messages are overt: for example, in the stories of Charles Ainger, Charles O'Malley, Ian Roderick, Nick Pyatt, Pris-hani Satyapal, Roland Widmer and Simon Hicks. If people are seeking to influence significant change from relatively lower hierarchical positions (for example Chris Preist and Christel Scholten), systemic notions give them a rationale for thinking about how their actions might have amplified impacts.

Systemic thinking helped people choose critical intervention points with poten-tial to influence wider systemic patterns. Roland Widmer selects emblematic cases to work on. Ian Roderick uses his developed systemic awareness to find his way through potential projects and connections. Charles O'Malley explores different initiatives to stimulate environmental innovation, building on a notion of living system. Indrė Kleinaitė publishes articles to promote awareness of sustainability and corporate social responsibility in Eastern Europe and the Balkan States. Sys-temic thinking suggests working at multiple points, spreading information into new places, connecting up feedback loops, so that change and action are dispersed and multifaceted rather than reliant on one person or organisation's deliberate action. These are the crafts of contextual intelligence.

Several graduates seek to influence finance and money systems as key dynamics in current global society with far-reaching consequences which help maintain unsustainable, growth-oriented patterns in a materialist form of capitalism— Christel Scholten, Jen Morgan, Mark Gater, Paul Dickinson and Roland Widmer. They thus confront the power of taken-for-granted discourses. Doing so provokes resistance, so finding an effective approach within this self-justifying system is remarkably challenging.

Jen Morgan reports a careful orchestration of bringing potentially influential people together in the Finance Innovation Lab to reconceive money systems, in ideas and potential practices, working through a long-term developmental process. This is an example of opening up a communicative space for inquiry and discussion (see Chapter 3). That the conversations have happened is itself a systemic intervention. Any potential outcomes may well be distanced in time and space and not easily attributable. Mark Gater's approach, working from his mainstream credibility, was to ask questions of fellow senior managers in his financial organisation. This, too, was as much process as outcome directed, seeking to influence his colleagues' awareness. His practice was partly about maintaining the relationships in which challenging discussions could happen.

Another chosen area for systemic intervention was cultural practices that connect to values, assumptions and patterns of behaviour. We see this in Paula Downey's attempts to contribute to cultural renewal in Ireland, Lalith Gunaratne and Mihirini De Zoysa's work with youth in Sri Lanka creating dialogue across cultural differences, Jane Riddiford's and Joanne Bailey's work with young people to foster sustainability awareness and practices, and Indrė Kleinaitė's project promoting responsible business in Lithuania based on Nordic countries' practices.

Adopting processes that contradict current patterns of power has the potential to encourage alternative ways of working and thus different sorts of outcome. Some graduates deliberately operated from equal notions of power in situations where dominance, overtly or tacitly, has been more the norm. This was the approach in the story of Katine told by Jo Confino. It is also the underlying dynamic in the accounts from Nick Pyatt and Simon Hicks. Their stories demonstrate in detail the relational nature of systemic work, and the patience this requires. People articulate varied practices for building networks that can foster change. Both Simon and Nick are independent change agents, affording them certain kinds of opportunity and a chance to think beyond current system constraints, while not attributing formal power. They cannot therefore short-circuit systemic change by being more directive.

Simon connects up people he thinks may be able to contribute to species survival across previous boundaries or lack of acquaintance. He visits, and visits again. He finds text formats for convening dialogues between different groups in ongoing email chains. Both he and Nick articulate notions of systemic thinking to guide their approach, overtly work through inquiry and dialogue, and show their commitment to the potential wisdom of process and participants. They want to promote systemically valuable outcomes. This apparently non-partisan approach—or aligning with the black-maned lions in Simon's case—can seem puzzling to others involved.

Those in mainstream organisations can use their convening power to work across boundaries and connect up potential energies for change. Alison Kennedy and Kené Umeasiegbu give successful examples, contributing to a grading system and database for sustainable paper supplies and the Cadbury Cocoa Partnership, respectively.

Meeting resistance and power is commonplace in systemic work. Current patterns are often held in place by entrenched power, in one form or another (see Chapter 3). In several stories we see contradictory forces in play, the espoused interest in change or new practices, but the enactment of established ways of operating which will make these impossible to achieve. Karen Karp and Nick Pyatt speak from apparently different worlds, but both encounter an incumbent power-holder who effectively blocks potential change. Karen has been given significant organisational remit to source local foods. Nick's legitimacy is more diffuse. But similar dynamics occur. We see the systemic practitioner's vulnerability. Formally espoused change is not enough. Only change that permeates practices, assumptions and organisational priorities has the potential to be systemic. And the change agent can be repelled by various forms of blocking, often disguised, until they run out of energy, time or money. Systemic awareness needs to appreciate multiple dimensions of power lest it become over-optimistic, and unawarely vulnerable.

In systemic terms, setting oneself against something, especially a person with formal power and credibility, is likely to pull dynamics of confrontation and competition, and is unlikely to achieve wider systemic benefits. We see graduates therefore intentionally developing more inclusive approaches, as Nick did, appreciating this at a macro level and demonstrating the micro processes of enacting this in practice. And the line between this and collusion is a fine one, needing to be held with discernment.

Systemic thinking raises issues of how close to be to other parties and their agendas, judging whether to fit in or challenge prevailing patterns. Paula Downey's analysis and intuition are to keep faith with alternative spaces from which challenging questioning and radically different views of society can be nurtured. And in time, as she holds this space reflectively, people move towards her, wanting to engage. Helena Kettleborough's story has a contrasting dynamic. She is convinced that action research will help local government both achieve its core tasks and learn for a more sustainable future. To enable people to engage, she is willing to align with other languages that are more readily appealing, those of coaching, for example. And in time the practices she is offering become recognisable to others, whatever they are called. In both stories, however, after long, persistent, patient work, with limited recognition or appreciative feedback, a shift seems to happen, a movement in which others become more eager to engage, and themselves take initiatives, generating momentum. These might be the stirrings of systemic change. And they might not. How to maintain a sense of radical edge when what was novel and 'alternative' appears to be gaining acceptance is a challenge. Is the next step co-option, becoming watered down in the dominant image? These are pointed dilemmas of this sort of practice. David Bent explores them in relation to places to stand and in the ways that he searches for a framing, and detailed wording, that will encourage companies to place sustainability at the heart of their strategy.

Working with notions of systemic thinking and complexity, we appreciate what might otherwise appear small-scale action as a significant way to introduce difference and seed new behaviours and patterns to contribute to change. Attention to the details of action appears in many stories; see the section on complementing strategic awareness, below. It is explicit, for example, in those of Helen Goulden (as she places sustainability awareness at the heart of all she does), Helen Sieroda (paying attention in daily life and to relationships), James Barlow (introducing walking and talking as a form into meetings) and Jon Alexander (in his awareness and articulation of being animal first, influencing sport through his Eco-Ironman activities). Developing new practices in these ways has the potential to go beyond change that is 'more of the same'.

Working systemically means being open and continually reflective about outcomes; see the section '"Success" is inevitably difficult to identify', below.

A consistent, systemic message in the stories is that alone people cannot influence change, that taking leadership for sustainability is not, generally, the work of the solo hero. James Barlow, for example, says: 'Alone, I cannot honestly claim to have been the cause of much change, if any.' And Chris Preist: 'The nature of such work is collective, rather than based on individual heroics, and so I cannot claim unique responsibility for the changes that have taken place—merely that I made some contribution to it.' Mark Gater suggests that the best any of us can contribute is to live our values.

Act from inquiry

Taking leadership for sustainability through inquiry, with associated experimentation and connection, is a key advocacy of graduates' and our accounts. It will be obvious that this is a language of the RBP community, fostered by the action research approach of programme and tutors. We think we need to live the dilemmas of seeking sustainability, such as how to reconcile urgency with patience and determination, and that inquiry in its different forms gives us some foundational resources to do so. Examples of what this means in practice are threaded through this book. We will not elaborate this theme further here.

Seek to move beyond the limitations of conventional action logics

While we appreciate that good and important work can be done from Achiever and Expert action logics (as explored in Chapter 3, pages 60-65)—the design, execution and everyday management of an innovative project will often require these—we believe that systemic leadership for sustainability requires being able to draw on the capacities of Strategist and more post-conventional frames of mind, at least at times. These open up the potential to work from alternative worldviews and question established logics. Our experience of running the programme lends some support to the leadership development framework's suggestions that late-stage action logics are associated with triple-loop learning, and with the capacity to examine and review purposes both strategically and moment-to-moment (Bateson 1972).

Many of the accounts in this volume demonstrate this capacity. Vidhura Rala-panawe is able both to attend to the immediate goal of building an eco-factory within a tight deadline *and* see that the venture is about creating and then telling a new and inspiring story that could influence the future. James Barlow shows how being successful means negotiating both the immediate goals of his organisation and the wider purposes of sustainability. In his behaviour he engages with the complexity of maintaining an identity which is organisationally credible enough and at the same time modelling openness, inquiry, and hence vulnerability. Lalith Gunaratne and Mihirini De Zoysa describe how they created and held a forum in which representatives of the many sides of the conflicts in Sri Lankan society could come together in dialogue. Mark Gater shows how he can draw on his membership of the financial services industry and at the same time see this in its wider context and find ways of exploring the significant contradictions posed, recognising that he is therefore living in 'two worlds'. Openness to multiple ways of knowing also characterises these accounts. None of these people would immodestly claim they work consistently from a Strategist action logic, but their narratives point to the 'both/and' qualities that this framework invites us to embrace.

As we say in Chapter 3, while many people move towards or into an Individualist action logic, seeing through and relativising conventional mind-sets, it is much harder to support moves fully into the Strategist action logic. It is incredibly difficult to maintain a successful identity within current organisations while at the same time questioning the very basis of their existence. It is personally challenging and stressful, as several of the stories show. As we look at our colleagues and associates in the broad sustainability movement we might interpret many who are making important contributions in specific fields and communities as acting from Expert and Achiever roles. And the sense of urgency many people now, appropriately, have about sustainability issues favours pragmatic action and doing what is possible. But far fewer people seem to be engaged in working between communities and worldviews, and stimulating the questioning of purposes and the qualities of inquiry we see as important if we are to learn our way into a more sustainable future. It is these complex, demanding, elusive, paradoxical ways of operating that we think need developing. When we see them in action they have a generative, opening and integrative potential.

We suggest that there is hugely important educational work to be undertaken: to create communities of inquiry in which people can explore and develop post-conventional capacities of knowing, acting and being, and also to understand better the educational and developmental processes required.

Complement strategic awareness with skilful attention to the detail of practice

While systemic and strategic awareness are essential, at the same time, as Charles Ainger puts it, 'the devil is in the detail . . . of asking the right questions, of the right people, at the right time'. The disciplines of action research enable people to move between systemic/third-person level and micro/first-person strategies. The social constructionist perspective tells us that our reality is created in the minutiae of our interaction, so the link between the strategic and the specific is both conceptual and practical.

Attending to the detail of one's actions—micro-practice in our terms—means being constantly alert to the ways we do or do not enact our purposes and intentions in the world. In an action-inquiry approach, this means keeping alert to the relationships between our purposes, strategies, moment-to-moment behaviour, and the response of the outside world. Skilful micro-practice enables us to be 'crafty' in our behaviour (Torbert 1981), seize the opportunity of the moment (Shepard 1975) and sustain delicate but fruitful dialogue. Simon Cooper writes about the importance of being in the 'right place (in terms of skills, knowledge and contacts) at the right time'. On the other hand, with an unfortunate choice of words, gesture or tone of voice we can slip away in an instant into misunderstanding and conflict. (Although in such circumstances an in-the-moment attitude and practice of inquiry may well be more valuable than concern about getting things 'right' or 'wrong'.)

We can see in the stories how people are alert to these possibilities—in themselves and in others—and are using reflective processes and frameworks to help them notice the detail of what they do. Jen Morgan frames her whole story within the Art of Hosting approach, which offers an overall design for successful dialogue, and talks about the detailed attention she pays to the qualities and flows of relationship. Chris Preist suggests that stories can bridge different worlds. Simon Cooper emphasises the significance of asking good questions. Christel Scholten, Helen Sieroda and others refer to the importance of opening and holding spaces where new conversations can happen. Helen Goulden tries 'to effect subtle, small changes or what might be called gentle action' looking for 'a chink or an opportunity to drop something into a conversation and . . . when the best action was to say or do nothing'.

This emphasis on micro-practices points to the subtlety of the best of action research: while pragmatic, it is not necessarily about 'doing things', setting objectives and achieving them. For some, this action-orientation is part of the (sustainability) problem. It may be more about *being* differently as well as doing differently; it may mean doing less and striving for less. As Simon Hicks writes, one sometimes has 'to visit often, to wait, watch, and talk to everyone, with the occasional reminder' that more help is on offer.

'Success' is inevitably difficult to identify

Given the complex and challenging context of leadership for sustainability, what is success, and how do we measure it? It can involve both achievement of identifiable steps towards justice and sustainability and more subtle contributions to changes in mind-set and system properties. But both are fragile: one's work can easily be eradicated, for example, by a company takeover, or be dissipated in the inertia of the wider culture.

People who are concerned with contributing to fundamental changes in the way society works are probably destined never to see the full fruition of their endeavours. They will have 'small wins', maybe many of them; but there will also be times when all endeavours appear to be seriously set back, as must have occurred for many who worked valiantly to achieve agreement and action at the 2009 international climate negotiations in Copenhagen. Maybe most challenging is the grinding sense of working against the prevailing winds, waiting for the sea-change that never seems quite to happen. The psychotherapist James Hillman titled his book *We've Had 100 Years of Psychotherapy: And the World's Getting Worse* (Hillman and Ventura 1992); and many in our field feel we've had nearly 50 years of environmentalism (since the publication of *Silent Spring*, Carson 1962), and even more of campaigns for human rights, and the world is getting very seriously worse.

David Bent points to an important theme in this regard, suggesting there is a pitfall in focusing on 'deliverables', on seeing the report, or the policy, or the new marketing strategy as what is important. Mark Gater reflects similarly that he was unsuccessful in his ambition to help create a new kind of financial institution, but was able to facilitate radical conversations among senior managers and preserve a quality of inquiry in his work. Others, too, balance process and capacity development with goal-oriented action.

Of course, some of the stories in this book do point to significant and specific outcomes. Alison Kennedy developed a supply network and grading framework which moved the publishing industry towards sustainable sourcing of paper. Vidhura Ralapanawe and his colleagues did build an effectively zero-carbon factory, which is now used as an exemplar for others in the industry. Paul Dickinson and his colleagues in the Carbon Disclosure Project have helped place carbon on the agenda of the financial system by creating an index that is cited at the highest levels. Kené Umeasiegbu helped establish the Cadbury Cocoa Partnership, contributing to Cadbury's Fairtrade accreditation for its milk chocolate. Karen Karp influenced food procurement in New York schools so that more fresh and local products were offered to children. And there are many more significant achievements in the stories. But for many, 'success' is diffuse, slippery, difficult to define clearly and difficult to maintain. And even when we can point to a 'success' such as the Thurulie eco-factory or the Carbon Disclosure Project, the significance is not only in the immediate achievement but in its wider influence.

So what is success, and how do we measure it both qualitatively and quantitatively? Contributors ask questions such as, 'What is enough?'; 'How do I get feedback?'; 'How do I work with disappointments and setbacks?'

One could argue that success lies not in the achievement so much as in the process of learning. The argument might be expressed as follows: as a society we do not know how to respond to the challenges of justice and sustainability; single- and double-loop learning will tend to reproduce the current state of affairs so that 'success' within the current worldview may not be successful in helping shift it. So what is required is work to create triple-loop learning in ourselves and others through which we can transform our sense of identity and purposes as well as our ideas, behaviours and capacities for further learning. This means, we suggest, developing the approaches and practices of inquiry and experimentation. Certainly as tutors, while we encouraged participants to celebrate the small wins advocated by the tempered radical perspective, we also emphasised that maintaining an 'attitude of inquiry' and creating learning processes was as important. But if we focus on learning processes and see goal-directed behaviour and 'end-gaming' (as Inner Game practitioners call it; Gallwey 1986), as unproductive, that pushes even further away any sense of knowing where to place our energies and what is worthwhile in our endeavours. Charles Ainger expresses well the challenges of judging success or failure:

> There is some feedback on immediate outputs, but not on longer-term *outcomes*. I can sometimes judge successes from unsolicited comments. My MWH retirement plaque says: 'in gratitude . . . for providing us with challenge and inspiration' . . . However, I am cautious about such responses, as over-flattering. Because when I try to push boundaries and raise harder questions, some feel embarrassed about not doing enough, or fast enough; and they can compensate by being over-enthusiastic about my own, not so effective, role.

For Charles, the failures are 'more like disappointments', because change always takes longer than you think and may not show where you expect it to, and lack of effect is not only caused by resistance to change but by what he describes as the 'everyday incompetence' of organisations.

Charles also points out that personal success is difficult to measure because one is always working through others; and other contributors write about influencing others, building networks, creating space for new forms of discussion. So Christel Scholten describes how, in her early work with ABN AMRO, she built a network of like-minded others, particularly young people, and drew on many different approaches and on informal power to 'put sustainability on the agenda whenever and wherever I could to begin shifting the system', an approach very like that adopted by Chris Preist. Alison Kennedy, Helen Sieroda, Helena Kettleborough and others all see success, at least in part, in terms of building formal and informal networks based on mutual interest and influence. Understanding the nature of success also means understanding how broader systemic and power patterns work and seeking points of influence within them.

For example, systemic thinking informs Roland Widmer's assessment of the impacts of his work. His reflection shows some of the complications of judging effectiveness, given complex interacting patterns of power. Might 'losing' a specific court battle about destruction of the rainforest perhaps lead to more public awareness and resistance to damage in the future, and therefore be a valuable outcome in some ways? Or might 'winning' a battle encourage financiers and companies to mask their activities, becoming covert and elusive to avoid being monitored, allowing them increased freedom to do harm? Acting with a systemic sense means working with these dilemmas, seeking to act for the good of wider patterns. But discerning what these are and how to attune behaviour is complex, challenging, paradoxical. And there is no clear answer to questions of what is effective, especially when we track events over time. What appeared a 'good' outcome at one point, can be reinterpreted as 'bad' at a later time because of the unfolding play of forces and powers—and vice versa. We must always reflect on what criteria we use to make such judgements. As Helen Goulden says, we may well never know the importance or inconsequence of our actions.

Herb Shepard, one of the early innovators in organisational change practice, wrote a short piece called 'Rules of Thumb for Change Agents' (Shepard 1975), which many MSc participants read and appreciated. The first 'rule' is Stay Alive, which 'counsels against self-sacrifice on behalf of a cause that you do not wish to be your last'. The second rule, 'Never work uphill' is difficult to follow when one is seeking radical change, but the first corollary to this rule, 'Don't build hills as you go', is often relevant. Helen Goulden, for example, seeks to laugh it off when she is called 'the resident greenie', to avoid boxing herself into a narrow identity. A further corollary is 'Never do alone what two can do' which directs us away from individual heroism towards networking and collaboration. Maybe the most useful rule is 'Light many fires', which chimes with the tempered radical proposition of 'small wins': don't put your heart solely into one grand, world-changing scheme which might leave you bereft when it fails to measure up to your hopes and plans. Scale and ambition are important to match the challenges ahead, but they must be tempered by addressing what is immediate, engages others, and gradually builds a basis for further change that may take us by surprise when it emerges.

So understanding success means widening what one attends to, going beyond the immediate and the deliverable. It means maintaining and building one's potential positions of influence, attending to and developing relationships. It means understanding what one is trying to accomplish within a systemic context, and being open to and working with unfolding processes, and appreciating that outcomes may not be as expected. And it means living from a spirit of inquiry, singly and collectively, in the midst of whatever arises.

The work is emotionally and spiritually difficult and challenging

For many of us (tutors as well as students) the MSc experience was an emotional (and spiritual) rollercoaster: we had moments of sublime recognition of the planet and its inhabitants as an interconnected whole; we had moments of despair at the degeneration of complex ecosystems and the foolishness and destructiveness of our species. And we struggled with how to cope with a 'normal' world that, for the most part, acts as if none of this is happening.

As early cohorts progressed through the programme, we began to see a pattern that gives some indication of the emotional demands of taking leadership for sustainability. The excitement would build as applicants came in, were accepted, and began to meet each other. As the group gathered for the first residential week with all the usual qualities of early group interaction (Who am I to be here? Will I be included? Will people like me? See e.g. Srivastva *et al.* 1977) there was intense delight in meeting fellow travellers, others sharing similar concerns, and many felt they came with some relevant expertise, understood the issues and had something to offer. Then through the first three workshops, as the size, extent and range of the challenges to both justice and sustainability were laid out, as their worldviews and assumptions were challenged, participants would feel overwhelmed, helpless, unskilled, often despairing. Joanne Bailey remembers 'being overwhelmed with the feelings of shock and despair when confronted with the notions of peak oil, peak water, overpopulation and the impending tipping point of climate change' and thus 'feeling isolated within my familiar surroundings'. As David Bent describes it:

> The science tells us that if we continue as we are then the natural world will struggle to support a large, complicated human society. To put it another way, Mother Nature is going to die after a long battle with a mutation from within. We have no time for delay or error, but there is an enormous gap between the required and actual action.

For many these feelings came into focus at the third workshop, spent at Schumacher College in Devon. Working with the resident ecologist, Stephan Harding, groups learned about the challenges to the self-regulating properties of Gaia and the extent of the damage to ecosystems; and through experiential deep ecology exercises (Macy and Brown 1998; Harding 2006) recovered, or even fully experienced for the first time, the wonder of the interconnected biosphere. As Ian Roderick puts it:

> I am sure that for the majority of participants the week spent at the Schumacher College transformed them. All the ingredients for deep personal change are there: retreat from the real world, renewal of personal relationships, communal living, self-examination, enchanting habitat, exposure to deep ecological principles and Gaia . . . organic and wonderful food, alcohol, meditation, poetry, books and ideas . . .

From this sense of profound challenge and disorientation, most participants in their own time found a 'place to stand' over the next year and a half. This was a deeply emotional process.

Helen Sieroda tells how her direct experience of the Cartesian split between mind and matter became 'painfully real' and she responds to this with a quiet re-engagement with the particulars of place where she lives—allotment, garden, moor. In some contrast, Mark Gater describes a full crisis of confidence: he thought he 'understood the problems of sustainability' but discovered 'I was wrong. The whole thing was far scarier and more depressing than I had thought'. So towards the end of the first year of the MSc he goes out on a winter camping trip and has a classic 'peak experience' in the sense that Maslow (1970) described: a direct and fierce experience of transient beauty. This encounter settles him, provides a framing for making his contribution. In another version of peak experience Jon Alexander makes his connection with deep ecology through his sporting engagement with Eco Ironman, learning that he is 'animal first':

> When I saw myself as human first and animal a distant second, many of my benevolent actions were moral. As animal first, my inclination changes, subtly but distinctly. And I believe my actions have gained a new beauty as a result, a beauty which has given me new resources of energy and new bravery in every part of my life, from sport to 'real work' to my relationships with my loved ones.

This emotional dimension of learning challenges again the educational assumptions of a university, and presented faculty with questions of how to respect the former in the assessment process. (Our commitment to multiple forms of knowing and representation provided some means for us to do this.)

The demands continue after the course itself is over, and may become more challenging as the regular contact with supportive peers disappears. It is not all negative: James Barlow writes of 'moments of intense joy, when it feels as if my colleagues and I really are having a positive effect on one of the world's most powerful institutions'. As Charles O'Malley writes of the years following the course,

It is said that you learn more from failure than from success. I have learned a lot! These have been both the best and the worst years of my life. But at least now I know that I am alive!

Nothing can be taken for granted, nothing is without paradox and dilemma

Maybe this is the note to end this book on. While we still hold with Dunphy *et al.* (2007) that 'Change leadership involves owning our own power and using it responsively and responsibly', we hope that we have shown here that this can never be straightforward. We do not, nor can we ever, understand the subtle interconnections of natural and human ecologies. We can never know the immediate, let alone the long-term outcomes of our choices. We do not know whether the current wave of pro-environment behaviour will stabilise the planetary ecology or whether we have passed several tipping points. But we are here participating in the drama and we have found our part in the action, whatever the uncertainty. We hope that we have shown that seeing this action as a process of ongoing inquiry can be a practical form of taking leadership for sustainability.

We have done our best to meet these challenges, with energy over the years that has both surged and flagged at different times. But we consider ourselves privileged to have had the opportunity to meet and work with so many fascinating, committed, honourable people, who have chosen to participate with us in this course. We have enjoyed it hugely and can think of no better use of our time and effort.

Bibliography

Abram, D. (1996) *The Spell of the Sensuous: Perception and language in a more than human world* (New York: Pantheon).

Ainger, C. (2001) *Walking the Tightrope: Learning to be a change agent for sustainability* (Dissertation, MSc in Responsibility and Business Practice; Bath, UK: School of Management, University of Bath).

Ainger, K. (2003) 'Keynote Editorial', *New Internationalist* 360: 9-12.

Alexander Ballard Ltd (2008) *Adaptive Capacity Benchmarking: A handbook and toolkit* (prepared for Hampshire County Council on behalf of European Spatial Planning: Adapting to Climate Events; Winchester, UK: Environmental Futures Group, Hampshire County Council; www.espace-project.org/part2/part2_outputs.htm, accessed 1 January 2011).

Alvesson, M., and S. Deetz (2005) 'Critical Theory and Postmodernism: Approaches to organizational studies', in C. Grey and H. Willmott (eds.), *Critical Management Studies* (Oxford, UK: Oxford University Press).

Argyris, C., and D.A. Schön (1974) *Theory in Practice: Increasing professional effectiveness* (San Francisco: Jossey Bass).

—— and D.A. Schön (1978) *Organizational Learning: A theory of action perspective* (Reading, MA: Addison Wesley).

Ballard, D. (2007) 'Mostly Missing the Point: Business responses to climate change', in D. Cromwell and M. Levene (eds.), *Surviving Climate Change: The struggle to avert global catastrophe* (London: Pluto Press).

Ballard, S. (2005) *Warm Hearts and Cool Heads: The leadership potential for climate change champions* (Swindon, UK: Alexander Ballard Associates).

Barabasi, A.-L. (2002) *Linked: The new science of networks* (Cambridge, MA: Perseus Publishing).

Barfield, O. (1957) *Saving the Appearances: A study in idolatry* (London: Faber & Faber).

Bateson, G. (1972) *Steps to an Ecology of Mind* (San Francisco: Chandler).

Beck, D.E., and C.C. Cowan (1996) *Spiral Dynamics: Mastering values, leadership and change* (Malden, MA: Blackwell).

Beinhocker, E. (2006) *The Origin of Wealth: Evolution, complexity and the radical remaking of economics* (London: Random House).

Belenky, M., B.M. Clinchy, N. Goldberger and J. Tarule (1986) *Women's Ways of Knowing: The development of self, voice, and mind* (New York: Basic Books).

Bent, D., and S. Draper (2008) 'Leader Business Strategies', Forum for the Future; www.forumforthefuture.org/library/leader-business-strategies, accessed 31 December 2010.

—— and J. Richardson (2003) 'SIGMA Guidelines—Toolkit: Sustainability accounting guide'; www.projectsigma.co.uk/Toolkit/SIGMASustainabilityAccounting.pdf, accessed 31 December 2010.

Berle, A., and G. Means (1932) *The Modern Corporation and Private Property* (New York: Transaction Publishers).

Berry, T. (1988) *The Dream of the Earth* (San Francisco: Sierra Club).

—— (1999) *The Great Work: Our way into the future* (New York: Bell Tower).

Berry, W. (1990) *What Are People For?* (New York: North Point Press).

Birmingham, B., and S.L. LeQuire (2010) 'Green Heroes Reexamined: An evaluation of environmental role models', in B. Redekop (ed.), *Leadership for Environmental Sustainability* (New York: Routledge): 107-21.

Boulton, J., and P. Allen (2007) 'Complexity Perspective', in M. Jenkins and V. Ambrosini with N. Collier (eds.), *Advanced Strategic Management: A multi-perspective approach* (Basingstoke, UK: Palgrave Macmillan).

Bouwen, R., and T. Taillieu (2004) 'Multiparty Collaboration as Social Learning for Interdependence: Developing relational knowing for sustainable natural resource management', *Journal of Community and Applied Psychology* 14.3: 137-53.

Bower, J., and C. Gilbert (2005) *From Resource Allocation to Strategy* (Oxford, UK: Oxford University Press).

Boyle, D., and A. Simms (2009) *The New Economics: A bigger picture* (London: Earthscan).

Bradbury, H., and B.M.B. Lichtenstein (2000) 'Relationality in Organizational Research: Exploring the space between', *Organization Science* 11.5: 551-64.

—— and P. Reason (2001) 'Conclusion. Broadening the Bandwidth of Validity: Five issues and seven choice-points for improving the quality of action research', in P. Reason and H. Bradbury (eds.), *Handbook of Action Research: Participative inquiry and practice* (London: Sage Publications): 447-56.

Brockman, J. (ed.) (1977) *About Bateson* (New York: EP Dutton).

Brown, J., and D. Isaacs (2005) *The World Cafe: Shaping our futures through conversations that matter* (San Francisco: Berrett-Koehler).

Bruner, J. (2002) *Making Stories: Law, literature, life* (New York: Farrar, Straus & Giroux).

Bunker, B., and B. Alban (1997) *Large Group Interventions: Engaging the whole system for rapid change* (San Francisco: Jossey-Bass).

Business in the Community (2010) 'Leadership skills for a sustainable economy'; www.bitc.org.uk/resources/publications/leadership_skills.html, accessed 31 December 2010.

Business Week (2006) 'The Best B-Schools of 2006', *Business Week*, 23 October 2006.

Calás, M.B., and L. Smircich (2004) 'Revisiting "Dangerous Liaisons" or Does the "Feminine-in-Management" Still Meet "Globalization"?', in P.J. Frost, W.R. Nord and L.A. Krefting (eds.), *Managerial and Organizational Reality* (Upper Saddle River, NJ: Pearson Prentice Hall): 467-81.

Capewell, E. (2008) 'Action Research as a Means of Mobilising Co-operative Community Recovery', paper presented at the *NATO Science Programme Advanced Research Workshop*, Priština, Kosovo, 18–20 April 2008.

Capra, F. (1982) *The Turning Point* (London: Wildwood House).

—— (1996) *The Web of Life: A new synthesis of mind and matter* (London: HarperCollins).

Carson, R. (1962) *Silent Spring* (Boston, MA: Houghton Mifflin).

Chambers, R. (1997) *Whose Reality Counts? Putting the first last* (London: Intermediate Technology Publications).

Chandler, D., and W.R. Torbert (2003) 'Transforming Inquiry and Action by Interweaving 27 Flavors of Action Research', *Action Research* 1.2: 133-52.

Charlton, N. (2003) *A Sacred World: The ecology of mind, aesthetics and grace in the thought of Gregory Bateson* (Unpublished PhD; Lancaster, UK: Lancaster University).

—— (2008) *Mind, Beauty and the Sacred: An introduction to the thought of Gregory Bateson* (Albany, NY: SUNY Press).

Coghlan, D., and T. Brannick (2009) *Doing Action Research in Your Own Organization* (London: Sage Publications, 3rd edn).

Coleman, G. (2002) 'Gender, Power and Post-structuralism in Corporate Citizenship', *Journal of Corporate Citizenship* 5 (Spring 2002): 17-25.

—— and M. Gearty (2007) 'Making Space for Difference: The CARPP approach to action research', *International Journal of Action Research* 3.1/2: 190-214.

Cook-Greuter, S. (1990) 'Maps for Living: Ego-development stages from symbiosis to conscious universal embeddedness', in M.L. Commons, C. Armon, L. Kohlberg, F.A. Richards, T.A. Grotzer and J.D. Sinnott (eds.), *Adult Development* (Vol. 2, Models and Methods in the Study of Adolescent and Adult Thought; New York: Praeger): 79-104.

Crist, E., and H.B. Rinker (eds.) (2010) *Gaia in Turmoil: Climate change, biodepletion, and earth ethics in an age of crisis* (Cambridge, MA: The MIT Press).

Crompton, T., and T. Kasser (2009) *Meeting Environmental Challenges: The role of human identity* (Godalming, UK: WWF).

Crook, J.H. (2009) *World Crisis and Buddhist Humanism. End Games: Collapse or renewal of civilization* (New Delhi: New Age Books).

Currie, G., and D. Knights (2003) 'Reflecting on a Critical Pedagogy in MBA Education', *Management Learning* 34.1: 27-49.

Dahl, R. A. (1957) 'The concept of power', *Behavioral Science* 2: 201-215.

Deming, W. Edwards (1993) *The New Economics for Industry, Government, Education* (Cambridge, MA: MIT Press, 2nd edn).

Diamond, J. (2004) *Collapse: How societies choose to fail or survive* (London: Allen Lane).

Dickinson, P., and N. Svensen (2000) *Beautiful Corporations* (London: Pearson Education).

Doppelt, B. (2010) *Leading Change toward Sustainability: A change-management guide for business, government and civil society* (Sheffield, UK: Greenleaf Publishing, 2nd rev. edn).

Douthwaite, R. (1997) *The Problem with Growth* (Dublin: The Foundation for the Economics of Sustainability).

—— (2000) *The Ecology of Money* (Totnes, UK: Green Books).

Dryzek, J.S. (2005) *The Politics of the Earth: Environmental discourses* (Oxford, UK: Oxford University Press, 2nd edn).

Dunphy, D.C., A.B. Griffiths and S.H. Benn (2007) *Organizational Change for Corporate Sustainability* (London: Routledge, 2nd edn).

Elkington, J., and J. Hailes (2008) *The Social Intrapreneurs: A field guide for corporate changemakers* (London: SustainAbility; www.sustainability.com/library/the-social-intrapreneurs, accessed 31 December 2010).

Fals Borda, O., and M.A. Rahman (eds.) (1991) *Action and Knowledge: Breaking the monopoly with participatory action research* (New York: Intermediate Technology Publications/Apex Press).

Fenner, R.A., C.A. Ainger, H.J. Cruickshank and P. Guthrie (2006) 'Widening Horizons for Engineers: Addressing the complexity of sustainable development', *Proceedings of the Institution of Civil Engineers, Engineering Sustainability Journal* 159.ES4: 145-54.

Fenwick, T. (2005) 'Ethical Dilemmas of Critical Management Education: Within classrooms and beyond', *Management Learning* 36.1: 31-48.

Ferrer, J.N. (2002) *Revisioning Transpersonal Theory: A participatory vision of human spirituality* (Albany, NY: SUNY Press).

Financial Times (2009) 'The Future of Capitalism', *Financial Times*, April–May 2009; www.ft.com/indepth/capitalism-future, accessed 31 December 2010.

Fisher, D., D. Rooke and W.R. Torbert (2003) *Personal and Organisational Transformations through Action Inquiry* (Boston, MA: Edge/Work Press, 4th edn).

Fletcher, J.K. (1998) 'Relational Practice: A feminist reconstruction of work', *Journal of Management Inquiry* 7.2: 163-86.

—— (1999) *Disappearing Acts: Gender, power and relational practice at work* (Cambridge, MA: IT Press).

—— (2003) 'The Greatly Exaggerated Demise of Heroic Leadership: Gender, power, and the myth of the female advantage', in R.J. Ely, E.G. Foldy, M.A. Scully and The Centre for Gender in Organizations, Simmons School of Management (eds.), *Reader in Gender, Work, and Organization* (Oxford, UK: Blackwell Publishing): 204-10.

Flood, R.L. (1999) *Rethinking the Fifth Discipline: Learning within the unknowable* (London: Routledge).

—— (2001) 'The Relationship of "Systems Thinking" to Action Research', in P. Reason and H. Bradbury (eds.), *Handbook of Action Research: Participative inquiry and practice* (London: Sage Publications): 133-44.

Foucault, M. (1977) *Discipline and Punish: The birth of the prison* (trans. A.S. Smith; New York: Random House).

—— (1980) *Power/Knowledge* (New York: Pantheon).

Francis, D. (2002) *People, Peace and Power: Conflict transformation in action* (London: Pluto Press).

Freire, P. (1970) *Pedagogy of the Oppressed* (New York: Herder & Herder).

French, R., and D. Grey (eds.) (1996) *Rethinking Management Education* (London: Sage Publications).

Gallwey, T.W. (1986) *The Inner Game of Tennis* (London: Pan).

Gaventa, J., and A. Cornwall (2001) 'Power and Knowledge', in P. Reason and H. Bradbury (eds.), *Handbook of Action Research: Participative inquiry and practice* (London: Sage): 70-80.

Gayá Wicks, P., and P. Reason (2009) 'Initiating Action Research: Challenges and paradoxes of opening communicative space', *Action Research* 7.3: 243-62.

Geels, F.W., and J. Schot (2007) 'Typology of Sociotechnical Transition Pathways', *Research Policy* 36: 399-417.

Gergen, K.J. (1999) *An Invitation to Social Construction* (Thousand Oaks, CA: Sage Publications).

Giacalone, R.A., and K.R. Thompson (2006) 'Business Ethics and Social Responsibility Education: Shifting the worldview', *Academy of Management Learning and Education* 5.3: 266-77.

Gibbons, J. (2009) 'Seasonal Salute to Those Making a Difference', *Irish Times*, 24 December 2009.

Goldberg, N. (1986) *Writing Down The Bones: Freeing the writer within* (Boston, MA: Shambhala Publications).

Goldberger, N., J. Tarule, B. Clinchy and M. Belenky (eds.) (1996) *Knowledge, Difference and Power: Essays inspired by women's ways of knowing* (New York: Basic Books).

Goleman, D. (1995) *Emotional Intelligence* (New York: Bantam Books).

Gore, A. (2006) *An Inconvenient Truth: The planetary emergency of global warming and what we can do about it* (Emmaus, PA: Rodale Press).

Gray, R., and M.J. Milne (2004) 'Toward Reporting on the Triple Bottom Line: Mirages, methods and myths', in A. Henriques and J. Richardson (eds.), *The Triple Bottom Line: Does it all add up?* (London: Earthscan): 70-80.

Grey, C. (2004) 'Reinventing Business Schools: The contribution of critical management education', *Academy of Management Learning and Education* 3.2: 178-86.

—— and H. Willmott (eds.) (2005) *Critical Management Studies: A reader* (London: Sage Publications).

——, D. Knights and H. Willmott (1996) 'Is Critical Pedagogy of Management Possible?', in R. French and D. Grey (eds.), *Rethinking Management Education* (London: Sage Publications): 94-110.

Griffin, S. (1984) 'Split Culture', in S. Kumar (ed.), *The Schumacher Lectures Volume II* (London: Abacus): 175-200.

Grint, K. (2005) 'Problems, Problems, Problems: The social construction of "leadership"', *Human Relations* 58.11: 1467-94.

Gustavsen, B. (2001) 'Theory and Practice: The mediating discourse', in P. Reason and H. Bradbury (eds.), *Handbook of Action Research: Participative inquiry and practice* (London: Sage Publications): 17-26.

—— (2003) 'Action Research and the Problem of the Single Case', *Concepts and Transformation* 8.1: 93-99.

——, A. Hansson and T.U. Qvale (2008) 'Action Research and the Challenge of Scope', in P. Reason and H. Bradbury (eds.), *Sage Handbook of Action Research: Participative inquiry and practice* (London: Sage Publications, 2nd edn): 63-76.

Harding, S.P. (2006) *Animate Earth* (Totnes, UK: Green Books).

Hardy, C. (1994) *Power and Politics in Organizations* (London: Sage Publications).

—— and S.R. Clegg (1996) 'Some Dare Call it Power', in S. Clegg, C. Hardy and W.R. Nord (eds.), *Handbook of Organization Studies* (London: Sage Publications): 622-41.

Harman, W. (1988) *Global Mind Change: The promise of the last years of the twentieth century* (Indianapolis, IN: Knowledge Systems).

Harris, G. (2007) *Seeking Sustainability in an Age of Complexity* (Cambridge, UK: Cambridge University Press).

Havel, V. (1985) *The Power of the Powerless: Citizens against the state in Central-Eastern Europe* (New York: Palach Press).

Hawken, P. (1993) *The Ecology of Commerce: A declaration of sustainability* (New York: HarperBusiness).

—— (2007) *Blessed Unrest: How the largest movement in the world came into being and why no one saw it coming* (New York: Viking).

Heron, J. (1996) *Co-operative Inquiry: Research into the human condition* (London: Sage Publications).

—— and P. Reason (1997) 'A Participatory Inquiry Paradigm', *Qualitative Inquiry* 3.3: 274-94.

—— and P. Reason (2001) 'The Practice of Co-operative Inquiry: Research with rather than on people', in P. Reason and H. Bradbury (eds.), *Handbook of Action Research: Participative inquiry and practice* (London: Sage Publications): 179-88.

Hillman, J., and M. Ventura (1992) *We've Had a Hundred Years of Psychotherapy: And the world's getting worse* (New York: HarperCollins).

hooks, b. (1990) *Yearning: Race, gender and cultural politics* (Boston, MA: South End Press).

Howes, R. (2002) *Environmental Cost Accounting: An introduction and practical guide* (Amsterdam: Elsevier).

IPCC (Intergovernmental Panel on Climate Change) (2007) 'IPCC Fourth Assessment Report: Climate Change 2001'; www.ipcc.ch, accessed 1 January 2011.

Jackson, T. (2009) *Prosperity without Growth? The transition to a sustainable economy* (London: Sustainable Development Commission).

Jacobs, M. (2006) 'RSA/Forum for the Future: The economics and politics of climate change'; www.thersa.org/__data/assets/pdf_file/0018/657/The-economics-and-politics-of-climate-change-jacobs-221106.pdf, accessed 31 December 2010.

Jaworski, J. (1996) *Synchronicity: The inner path of leadership* (San Francisco: Berrett-Koehler).

Kanter, R.M. (1977) *Men and Women of the Corporation* (New York: Basic Books).

Kemmis, S. (2001) 'Exploring the Relevance of Critical Theory for Action Research: Emancipatory action research in the footsteps of Jürgen Habermas', in P. Reason and H. Bradbury (eds.), *Handbook of Action Research: Participative inquiry and practice* (London: Sage Publications): 91-102.

Korten, D.C. (1995) *When Corporations Rule the World* (London: Earthscan).

Kuhn, T. (1962) *The Structure of Scientific Revolutions* (Chicago: University of Chicago Press).

Leonard, A. (2006) *The Story of Stuff* (DVD; Washington, DC: Free Range Studios, Tides Foundation & Funders Workgroup for Sustainable Production and Consumption).

Loevinger, J. (1976) *Ego Development* (San Francisco: Jossey Bass).

Lovelock, J.E. (1979) *Gaia: A new look at life on Earth* (London: Oxford University Press).

—— (2006) *The Revenge of Gaia* (London: Allen Lane).

Ludema, J.D., D.L. Cooperrider and F.J. Barrett (2001) 'Appreciative Inquiry: The power of the unconditional positive question', in P. Reason and H. Bradbury (eds.), *Handbook of Action Research: Participative inquiry and practice* (London: Sage Publications): 189-99.

Lukes, S. (2005) *Power: A radical view* (Basingstoke, UK: Palgrave Macmillan, 2nd edn).

Macy, J.R., and M.Y. Brown (1998) *Coming Back to Life: Practices to reconnect our lives, our world* (Gabriola Island, Canada: New Society Publishers).

Marshall, J. (1999) 'Living Life as Inquiry', *Systematic Practice and Action Research* 12.2: 155-71.

—— (2001) 'Self-Reflective Inquiry Practices', in P. Reason and H. Bradbury (eds.), *Handbook of Action Research: Participative inquiry and practice* (London: Sage Publications): 433-39.

—— (2004a) 'Matching Form to Content in Educating for Sustainability: The Masters (MSc) in Responsibility and Business Practice', in C. Galea (ed.), *Teaching Business Sustainability* (Sheffield, UK: Greenleaf Publishing): 196-208.

—— (2004b) 'Living Systemic Thinking: Exploring quality in first person research', *Action Research* 2.3: 309-29.

—— (2007) 'The Gendering of Leadership in Corporate Social Responsibility', *Journal of Organizational Change Management* 20.2: 165-81.

—— and G. Coleman (in preparation) 'Developing Practice in Educating for Sustainability and Social Justice'.

—— and P. Reason (1993) 'Adult Learning in Collaborative Action Research: Reflections on the supervision process', *Studies in Continuing Education: Research and scholarship in adult education* 15.2: 117-32.

—— and P. Reason (2003) *Introduction to Action Research* (CD; Bath, UK: Centre for Action Research in Professional Practice, School of Management, University of Bath).

—— and P. Reason (2007) 'Quality Processes in "Taking an Attitude of Inquiry" ', *Management Research News* 30.5: 368-80.

—— and P. Reason (2008) 'Taking an Attitude of Inquiry', in B. Boog, J. Preece, M. Slagter and J. Zeelen (eds.), *Towards Quality Improvement of Action Research: Developing ethics and standards* (Rotterdam: Sense Publishers): 61-82.

Martin, A.W. (2008) 'Action Research on a Large Scale: Issues and practices', in P. Reason and H. Bradbury (eds.), *Sage Handbook of Action Research: Participative inquiry and practice* (London: Sage Publications, 2nd edn): 394-406.

Maslow, A. (1970) *Religion, Values and Peak Experiences* (New York: Viking).

Mathews, F. (2003) *For Love of Matter: A contemporary panpsychism* (Albany, New York: SUNY Press).

—— (2005) *Reinhabiting Reality* (Albany, NY: SUNY Press).

Maughan, E., and P. Reason (2001) 'A Co-operative Inquiry into Deep Ecology', *ReVision* 23.4: 18-24.

McArdle, K.L. (2004) *In-powering Spaces: A co-operative inquiry with young women in management* (PhD thesis; Bath, UK: University of Bath).

Mead, G. (1997) 'A Winter's Tale: Myth, story and organisations', *Self & Society* 24.6: 19-22.

Meadows, D. (1991) 'Change is not Doom', *ReVision* 14.2: 56-60.

—— (2002) 'Dancing with Systems'; www.sustainabilityinstitute.org/pubs/Dancing.html, accessed 1 January 2011.

——, D.L. Meadows and J. Randers (1992) *Beyond the Limits: Global collapse or a sustainable future* (London: Earthscan).

——, J. Randers and D. Meadows (2004) *Limits to Growth: The 30-year update* (White River Junction, VT: Chelsea Green).

Melaver, M. (2010) 'Leadership for Sustainability in Business: It's all about the stories we tell', in B. Redekop (ed.), *Leadership for Environmental Sustainability* (New York: Routledge): 93-106.

Merchant, C. (1995) *Earthcare: Women and the environment* (New York: Routledge).

Meyerson, D.E. (2001) *Tempered Radicals: How people use difference to inspire change at work* (Boston, MA: Harvard Business School Press).

—— and M.A. Scully (1995) 'Tempered Radicalism and the Politics of Ambivalence and Change', *Organization Science* 6.5: 585-600.

MWH (2008) 'Walking the Walk on Climate Change'; www.mwhglobal.com/MWH/AboutMWH/Climate_Change_Commitment.html, accessed 31 December 2010.

Naess, A. (1989) *Ecology Community and Lifestyle: Outline of an ecosophy* (trans. D. Rotherberg; Cambridge, UK: Cambridge University Press).

Ogilvy, J. (1986) 'Contribution to discussion "Critical Questions about New Paradigm Thinking" ', *ReVision* 9.1: 4.

Olli, E., G. Grendstad and D. Wollebaek (2001) 'Correlates of Environmental Behaviors; Bringing back social context', *Environment and Behaviour* 33.2: 181-208.

Orr, D.W. (1994) *Earth in Mind* (Washington, DC: Island Press).

Ortner, S. (1974) 'Is Female to Male as Nature is to Culture?' in M. Rodaldo and L. Lamphere (eds.), *Women, Culture and Society* (Stanford, CA: University of California Press): 67-87.

Owen, H. (1997) *Open Space Technology: A user's guide* (San Francisco: Berrett-Kohler).

Pascale, R.T., and J. Sternin (2005) 'Your Company's Secret Change Agents', *Harvard Business Review* 83.5: 72-81.

PepsiCo (2008) 'Environmental Sustainability Report 2008'; www.pepsico.co.uk/environment, accessed 31 December 2010.

Pettigrew, A. (1979) 'On Studying Organizational Cultures', *Administrative Science Quarterly* 24: 570-81.

Plant, J. (ed.) (1989) *Healing the Wounds: The promise of eco-feminism* (London: Green print).

Plotkin, B. (2008) *Nature and the Human Soul: Cultivating wholeness and community in a fragmented world* (Novato, CA: New World Library).

Plumwood, V. (1993) *Feminism and the Mastery of Nature* (London: Routledge).

—— (2002) *Environmental Culture: The Ecological Crisis of Reason* (London: Routledge).

Pontin, J., and I. Roderick (2007) *Converging World* (Totnes, UK: Green Books).

Porritt, J. (2007) *Capitalism as if the World Matters* (London: Earthscan, rev. edn).

Pratt, J., P. Gordon and D. Plamping (1999) *Working Whole Systems: Putting theory into practice in organizations* (London: King's Fund).

Quinn, R. (1996) *Deep Change* (San Francisco: Jossey Bass).

Ray, P.H. (1997) 'The Emerging Culture', *American Demographics* 19.2: 29-35.

Reason, P. (2001) 'Earth Community: Interview with Thomas Berry', *Resurgence* 204: 10-14.

—— (2005) 'Living as Part of the Whole', *Journal of Curriculum and Pedagogy* 2.2: 35-41.

—— (2006) 'Choice and Quality in Action Research Practice', *Journal of Management Inquiry* 15.2: 187-203.

—— (2007a) 'Wilderness Experience in Education for Ecology', in M. Reynolds and R. Vince (eds.), *The Handbook of Experiential Learning and Management Education* (Oxford, UK: Oxford University Press): 187-201.

—— (2007b) 'Education for Ecology: Science, aesthetics, spirit and ceremony', *Management Learning* 38.1: 27-44.

—— and H. Bradbury (2001) 'Inquiry and Participation in Search of a World Worthy of Human Aspiration', in P. Reason and H. Bradbury (eds.), *Handbook of Action Research: Participative inquiry and practice* (London: Sage Publications): 1-14.

—— and H. Bradbury (eds.) (2006) *Handbook of Action Research* (London: Sage Publications, concise paperback edn).

——, G. Coleman, D. Ballard, M. Williams, M. Gearty, C. Bond, C. Seeley and E.M. McLachlan (2009) *Insider Voices: Human dimensions of low carbon technology* (Bath, UK: Centre for Action Research in Professional Practice, University of Bath; go.bath.ac.uk/insidervoices, accessed 31 December 2010).

Redekop, B. (2010) *Leadership for Environmental Sustainability* (New York: Routledge).

Reynolds, M. (1998) 'Reflection and Critical Reflection in Management Learning', *Management Learning* 29.2: 183-200.

Richardson, L., and E.A. St Pierre (2005) 'Writing: A Method of Inquiry', in N.K. Denzin and Y.S. Lincoln (eds.), *Handbook of Qualitative Research* (Thousand Oaks, CA: Sage Publications, 3rd edn).

Robertson, J. (1989) *Future Wealth: A new economics for the 21st century* (London: Cassell Publishers).

Rockström, J., W. Steffen, K. Noone, Å. Persson, S. Chapin, E.F. Lambin, T.M. Lenton, M. Scheffer, C. Folke, H. Schellnhuber, B. Nykvist, C.A. De Wit, T. Hughes, S. van der Leeuw, H. Rodhe, S. Sörlin, P.K. Snyder, R. Costanza, U. Svedin, M. Falkenmark, L. Karlberg, R.W. Corell, V.J. Fabry, J. Hansen, B. Walker, D. Liverman, K. Richardson, P. Crutzen and J. Foley (2009) 'A Safe Operating Space for Humanity', *Nature* 461.24: 472-75.

Rooke, D. (1997) 'Organisational Transformation Requires the Presence of Leaders who are Strategists and Alchemists', *Organizations and People* 4.3: 16-23.

—— and W.R. Torbert (1999) 'The CEO's Role in Organizational Transformation', *The Systems Thinker* 10.7: 1-5.

—— and W.R. Torbert (2005) 'Seven Transformations of Leadership', *Harvard Business Review* 83.4: 66-76.

Rowbotham, M. (1998) *The Grip of Death: A study of modern money, debt slavery and destructive economics* (Charlbury, UK: John Carpenter).

Rudolph, J.W., S.S. Taylor and E.G. Foldy (2001) 'Collaborative Off-line Reflection: A way to develop skill in action science and action inquiry', in P. Reason and H. Bradbury (eds.), *Handbook of Action Research: Participative inquiry and practice* (London: Sage Publications): 405-12.

Satterwhite, R. (2010) 'Deep Systems Leadership: A Model for the 21st Century', in B. Redekop (ed.), *Leadership for Environmental Sustainability* (New York: Routledge): 230-42.

Scharmer, O. (2007) *Theory U. Leading from the Future as it Emerges: The social technology of presencing* (Cambridge, MA: The Society for Organisational Learning).

Senge, P.M. (1990) *The Fifth Discipline: The art and practice of the learning organization* (New York: Doubleday).

——, A. Kleiner, C. Roberts, R.B. Ross and B.J. Smith (1994) *The Fifth Discipline Fieldbook: Strategies and tools for building a learning organization* (New York: Doubleday).

——, C.O. Scharmer and B.S. Flowers (2005) *Presence: Exploring profound change in people, organizations, and society* (New York: Doubleday).

Sewill, B. (2005) 'Fly now, grieve later'; www.aef.org.uk/downloads/FlyNowFull.pdf, accessed 1 January 2011.

Shepard, H.A. (1975) 'Rules of Thumb for Change Agents', *OD Practitioner* 7.3 (November 1975): 1-5.

Shotter, J. (1993) *Cultural Politics of Everyday Life: Social construction and knowing of the third kind* (Buckingham, UK: Open University Press).

Sinclair, A. (1998) *Doing Leadership Differently* (extract; Melbourne: Melbourne University Press).

Skolimowski, H. (1994) *The Participatory Mind* (London: Arkana).

Spretnak, C. (1997) *The Resurgence of the Real: Body, nature and place in a hypermodern world* (Reading, MA: Addison-Wesley).

Srivastva, S., S.L. Obert and E. Neilson (1977) 'Organizational Analysis through Group Processes: A theoretical perspective', in C.L. Cooper (ed.), *Organizational Development in the UK and USA* (London: Macmillan): 83-111.

Stern, N. (2006) *Stern Review on the Economics of Climate Change* (London: HM Treasury).

Sukhdev, P. (2010) 'The Economics of Ecosystems and Biodiversity'; www.teebweb.org/Home/tabid/924/Default.aspx, accessed 1 January 2011.

Swimme, B., and T. Berry (1992) *The Universe Story: From the primordial flaring forth to the ecozoic era—A celebration of the unfolding of the cosmos* (New York: HarperCollins).

Tams, S., and J. Marshall (2011) 'Responsible Careers: Systemic reflexivity in shifting landscapes', *Human Relations* 64.1: 109-31.

Tarnas, R. (1991) *The Passion of the Western Mind* (New York: Ballantine).

Taylor, S.S., J.W. Rudolph and E.G. Foldy (2008) 'Teaching Reflective Practice in the Action Science/Action Inquiry Tradition: Key stages, concepts and practices', in P. Reason and H. Bradbury (eds.), *Sage Handbook of Action Research: Participative inquiry and practice* (London: Sage Publications, 2nd edn).

Torbert, W.R. (1976) *Creating a Community of Inquiry: Conflict, collaboration, transformation* (New York: Wiley).

—— (1981) 'Why Educational Research has been so Uneducational: The case for a new model of social science based on collaborative inquiry', in P. Reason and J. Rowan (eds.), *Human Inquiry: A sourcebook of new paradigm research* (Chichester, UK: Wiley): 141-52.

—— (1991) *The Power of Balance: Transforming self, society, and scientific inquiry* (Newbury Park, CA: Sage Publications).

—— (2004) *Action Inquiry: The secret of timely and transforming leadership* (San Francisco: Berrett-Koehler).

Toulmin, S. (1990) *Cosmopolis: The hidden agenda of modernity* (New York: Free Press).

—— and B. Gustavsen (eds.) (1996) *Beyond Theory: Changing organizations through participation* (Amsterdam: John Benjamins).

Turner-Vesselago, B. (1995) *Freefall: Writing without a parachute* (Toronto: The Writing Space).

University of Cambridge (2009) 'Where are they now? Former Engineering for Sustainable Development MPhil students return'; www.eng.cam.ac.uk/news/stories/2009/alumni_presentations, accessed 31 December 2010.

Uphoff, N. (1992) *Learning from Gal Oya: Possibilities for participatory development and post-Newtonian social science* (Ithaca, NY: Cornell University Press).

Watzlawick, P., J.H. Weakland and R. Fisch (1980) *Change: Principles of problem formation and problem resolution* (New York: W.W. Norton).

Weick, K. (1979) *The Social Psychology of Organizing* (New York: McGraw Hill, 2nd edn).

Westley, F., and H. Vredenburg (1996) 'Sustainability and the Corporation: Criteria for aligning economic practice with environmental protection', *Journal of Management Inquiry* 5.2: 104-19.

Whitehead, J. (1989) 'Creating a Living Educational Theory from Questions of the Kind: How can I improve my practice?', *Cambridge Journal of Education* 19.1: 41-52.

Wielkiewicz, R.M., and S.P. Stelzner (2010) 'An Ecological Perspective on Leadership Theory, Research, and Practice', in B. Redekop (ed.), *Leadership for Environmental Sustainability* (New York: Routledge): 17-35.

Wilber, K. (1996) *A Brief History of Everything* (Boston, MA: Shambhala).

—— (2007) *The Integral Vision* (Boston, MA: Shambhala).

Wombacher, M. (2008) *11 Days at the Edge: One man's spiritual journey into evolutionary enlightenment* (Forres, UK: Findhorn Press).

World Bank (2001) *Engendering Development through Gender Equality in Rights, Resources and Voice* (Policy Research Report; Washington, DC: World Bank).

Zohar, D., and I. Marshall (1999) *Spiritual Intelligence: The ultimate intelligence* (London: Bloomsbury Publishing).

List of contributors

Charles Ainger   Visiting Professor, University of Cambridge Engineering Department, Cambridge, UK

Jon Alexander   Sustainability consultant and amateur triathlete, London

Jo Bailey   General Manager, Waikato Institute for Leisure & Sport Studies, Hamilton, New Zealand

James Barlow   European Sustainability Strategy Manager, PepsiCo Inc., Reading, UK

David Bent   Head of Business Strategies, Forum for the Future, London, UK

Jo Confino   Executive Editor, *The Guardian*; Chairman and Editorial Director, Guardian Sustainable Business, London, UK

Simon Cooper   Director, CSR Consultancy Ltd, Bath, UK

Paul Dickinson   Executive Chairman, Carbon Disclosure Project, London, UK

Paula Downey   Partner, downey youell associates, Dublin, Ireland

Mark Gater   Consultant: Project Assurance for Charities and the Third Sector, Leek, Staffordshire

Helen Goulden   Director, Public Services Lab, NESTA, London, UK

Lalith Gunaratne   Director, Sage Training (Pvt) Ltd/LGA Consultants (Pvt) Ltd, Colombo, Sri Lanka

Mihirini De Zoysa   Lead Consultant, Corporate Druids (Pvt) Ltd, Colombo, Sri Lanka

Simon D.J. Hicks	Honorary Director, Conservation Works, International
Karen Karp	President/Founder, Karp Resources, Food and Agriculture Business Consultancy, New York, USA
Alison Kennedy	Production and Distribution Director, Egmont UK Ltd, London, UK
Helena Kettleborough	Director, Neighbourhoods NW & North West Together We Can, Manchester, UK
Indrė Kleinaitė	Founder and Director, GYVA.LT ('Living Lithuania'), Vilnius, Lithuania
Jen Morgan	The Finance Innovation Lab, WWF-UK, London, UK
Charles O'Malley	Sustainability Strategist, Gloucestershire, UK
Chris Preist	Reader in Sustainability and Computer Systems, University of Bristol, UK
Nick Pyatt	Director, 2050 Ventures, Frome, Somerset, UK
Vidhura Ralapanawe	Manager – Sustainability & Communications, MAS Intimates, Sri Lanka
Jane Riddiford	Executive Director, Global Generation, London, UK
Ian Roderick	Director, Schumacher Institute for Sustainable Systems Bristol, UK
Prishani Satyapal	Vice President, Environment and Community Affairs, AngloGold Ashanti Ghana, Accra, Ghana/Johannesburg, South Africa
Christel Scholten	Partner, Reos Partners Brazil and, Founder and Partner, BB Natural Produtos Sustentáveis, São Paulo, Brazil
Helen Sieroda	Independent professional trainer and coach, Devon, UK, and Stockholm, Sweden
Kené Umeasiegbu	Sector Manager (Manufacturing and Industrial), The Carbon Trust, London, UK
Roland Widmer	Eco-Finanças Program Coordinator, Amigos da Terra – Amazônia Brasileira, São Paulo, Brazil

About the authors

Judi Marshall is Professor of Leadership and Learning at Lancaster University Management School, UK, which she joined in 2008. Judi currently works on a range of leadership for sustainability activities, including Lancaster's MA in Leadership for Sustainability. Her interests also include inquiry as life practice, action research, women in management, systemic change, the gendering of corporate responsibility and 'responsible' careers. She always seeks to integrate inquiry, research, practice and life. While at the University of Bath's School of Management, Judi was Director of Studies for the MSc in Responsibility and Business Practice from 1996 to 2008. Working on the programme with colleagues and course participants was a major delight and challenge of her academic career.

Gill Coleman is Co-Director of the Ashridge MSc in Sustainability and Responsibility, and Director of the Centre for Action Research at Ashridge Business School, UK. Since the early 1990s she has been concerned with creating inquiry-based participative learning for sustainability and corporate social responsibility—first at Bristol University, then through Anita Roddick's New Academy of Business. With Judi and Peter she co-founded the MSc in Responsibility and Business Practice in 1996 and has been closely involved with the growing community of inquirers and activists stemming from the course. She continues to work with a wide range of individuals and organisations on questions of sustainability and change.

Peter Reason retired from the University of Bath, UK, where he had been Professor of Action Research, in 2009. His academic work contributed to the theory and practice of action research, and teaching and research about sustainability. His major concern is with the devastating impact of human activities on the biosphere. While he values the 'bright green' work of creating more sustainable institutions, he believes the root of the problem is that too many humans see themselves as separate from, rather than part of, the community of life on earth. Post-retirement he is writing non-fiction narrative, stories of the sea which reflect on our place as participants in the life of the planet.

Index